SOCIAL STRATIFICATION AND OCCUPATIONS

SOCIAL STRATIFICATION AND OCCUPATIONS

A. Stewart, K. Prandy and R. M. Blackburn

Holmes & Meier Publishers, Inc.

New York

© A. Stewart, K. Prandy and R. M. Blackburn 1980

First published in the United States of America 1980 by
HOLMES & MEIER PUBLISHERS, INC.
30 Irving Place
New York, N.Y. 10003

Library of Congress Cataloging in Publication Data

Stewart, Alexander, 1942–
   Social stratification and occupations

   Bibliography: p.
   Includes index.
   1. Social classes—Great Britain.   2. Great Britain
   —Occupations—Social aspects.   3. Social status.
   I. Prandy, Kenneth, joint author.   II. Blackburn,
   Robert Martin, joint author.   III. Title.
   HN400.S6S73   305.5′0941   80–16282

   ISBN 0–8419–0629–7 (cased)
   ISBN 0–8419–0630–0 (paper)

Printed in Hong Kong

Contents

List of Tables

List of Figures

Preface

The data which are original to this book were not gathered on a single project. They are taken from a number of projects within the general research programme of the sociology group in the Department of Applied Economics. Most of the research was funded by the Social Science Research Council without whose help it would not have been possible.

A vast number of people have contributed to the research. We should like to express our thanks to the firms, teaching and research establishments and local and national government departments who allowed us to conduct interviews, and to the staff of these organisations who helped organise and facilitate the interviewing programmes. We are specially grateful to all our interviewees, and we were pleased that almost all found the experience painless and seemed to enjoy it.

The planning and execution of the research involved help from many colleagues. They were involved in a wide variety of stages, from helping to produce the basic intellectual framework to the details of day-to-day work. It would be impossible to disentangle our own ideas from their contributions and we shall not attempt to do so. We can only express our deep gratitude. We should like to thank David Donald, Monty Green, John Scott and Hilda Nichol, who were mainly responsible for the Glasgow interviews in the Social Status project; Joe Banks, Dave Webb, Anne Webb, Anne Cosh, Mary Giles and Cherie Knowles, who took primary responsibility for the Leicester programme; and Keith Dixon, Flo Green and the staff of the Institute of Social and Economic Research at the University of York, who organised the interviews around York and Leeds. For this and for their general help, criticism and guidance we are most grateful.

In Cambridge we were very fortunate to have the help of a large number of very able colleagues. In particular we should like to thank Al Bradshaw, Roy Foster, Dorothy Blackburn, Nigel Gilbert, Steve Nyman, Penny Pollitt and Guy Ryder and Rosalind Volpato, who all made important contributions.

A large number of colleagues, not directly associated with the various research projects, have contributed to our work by making data available, providing computer programs, reading manuscripts, discussing issues and offering constructive criticism. Among those to whom we are indebted are Leonard Broom, Tony Coxon, Paul Duncan-Jones, John Holmwood, Frank Jones, Pat McDonnell, Mick Mann, Joe Smucker and Peter Whalley. At various times pieces of this work were presented to the SSRC stratification seminar. The members of the seminar can take credit for having contributed to a broadening and a sharpening of our ideas.

We should like to thank our teams of very able interviewers, who cheerfully and willingly faced the many and varied demands of large interviewing programmes, and the coders and secretarial staff in the various centres who contributed to the projects.

Finally, we should like to express our appreciation and thanks to the members of the staff of the Department of Applied Economics who have contributed to our work in so many ways. Many colleagues working on other projects have criticised and stimulated us, and we have used all of the facilities of the department: the administration, the library, the data processing and computing provisions, and the typing and machine rooms.

Despite all of the help we have had in preparing this work, we accept responsibility for all of its weaknesses and some of its merits.

1 Introduction

The theme of this book is one which has always been a central concern of sociologists, and indeed of all who have been interested in the social problems of industrial society. It deals with the relationship between occupations and social stratification. However, if the subject is traditional the approach is not. We have chosen to bring to bear a set of different approaches on related issues which are central to our general problem. In content, we hope, it may prove surprising and provoking in its rejection of certain orthodoxies.

There exists in the literature a very extensive discussion of the place of 'occupation' in stratification theory, including the ways in which it relates to other factors such as family background, education and income or, at an apparently more elevated level, to social class and social status. However, almost all of the discussion is conducted as if the meaning of occupation were unproblematic—as if it could enter explanation as a pre-theoretical entity, its major characteristics known, its facticity unchallenged. Thus, conventional occupational categorisations, such as the OPCS Unit Groups, have been adopted uncritically as appropriate bases for very different sorts of undertakings. We wish to show that such practices raise problems of theory and analysis of a very fundamental sort, and that the relationships of occupations and stratification are more complex than has been supposed, while stratification and social experience are correspondingly less incoherent. In particular we shall show how many conventional problems in the area of stratification arise from the unrecognised meanings and constraints implicit in occupational classifications, which are imported unconsciously into the structure of explanations.

At times problems of occupational definition do come to the fore and receive explicit consideration. However, this is invariably within an understanding of occupational structure as a set of occupations with different activities and rewards. Although at first sight this may seem reasonable, we shall go on to show that it is an inappropriately static view, and within such an understanding, problems of occupational definition become narrowly technical matters of formal precision in the specification of job tasks. An important area where this sort of issue has arisen is the use of occupations in reputational approaches to the measurement of stratification, such as prestige scales—a major area employing occupational classification schemes. There are, in any society, conventional notions about jobs, including general conceptions of their nature and attractiveness, which are highly relevant to perceptions of the structure. Yet there is, inevitably, a considerable degree of vagueness resulting from a lack of knowledge of occupations and the variety of jobs actually held within any conventional occupational category. This problem arises even more acutely in international comparisons where conventions of occupational labelling differ from one country to another.

As we have said, responses to this problem have been to provide more and more precise definitions. The clearest example of this approach is to be found in the British CODOT (Classification of Occupations and Directory of Occupational Titles, Department of Employment, 1972), which is an inventory of precisely stated job tasks. This reflects a view of occupational structure as a response to the technical demands of the market. On the face of it, this seems a sound move, but the outcome is in many ways less satisfactory than reliance on conventional common sense categories. The technical demands are for certain types of work to be performed, and do not entail any requirement of how different tasks should be combined in the work of any one person. Precise definitions of job content do not necessarily describe socially meaningful occupations; they may not correspond to the work anyone actually does. Thus precise technical definitions may be ill-related to the conceptions of occupations and the work experience, even of those performing the tasks; and in different societies, or even at different locations within the same society, tasks may be gathered in different ways to form occupations.

We have written so far rather as if job tasks were economically determined by market forces, while their aggregation into actual occupations was determined by non-economic, social factors. As will become apparent, this is not a division we believe in, but it was convenient as a device of presentation. The separation of social and economic factors is, in fact, a familiar feature of stratification theory. The most usual form is to associate 'class' factors with economic forces and 'status' factors with social evaluations. Lockwood (1958, p. 208) puts it thus, 'Class focuses on the divisions which result from the brute facts of economic organisation. Status relates to more subtle distinctions which stem from the values that men set on each other's activities.' We shall discuss the empirical basis of this separation at length in Part

Two. For the moment we shall confine ourselves to the problem of identifying the 'activities' that are being evaluated. Lockwood writes as if class and status factors are both concerned with the same objects (job tasks or aggregates of job tasks) and that the problem is the differing criteria of worth applied to these objects; but in evaluating individuals, or groups of individuals, it is not entirely clear what 'activities' are crucial. Very few individuals do not experience changes in job content throughout their working lives. Sometimes these changes are so predictable and structured that they are incorporated in conventional occupational titles. This would be typical of the professions where progression up a seniority and pay hierarchy occurs 'within' a single occupation. The evaluation of the younger member of the profession is not merely in terms of the rather simple tasks he now performs and his lowly position in terms of authority and income, but upon his future potential.

When careers are not so clearly differentiated problems arise. For example we shall show that people at very different career stages frequently do similar work. Clerks may be young men on the way up, or older men who have recently moved into this type of work and will serve out their time there. The routes to and from clerical work are diverse. If clerical tasks are the 'activities' evaluated, then those on very different careers are being equated because they do similar work at one stage. All occupational classifications confuse whole careers and career stages. We shall show that many of the class/status divisions arise as problems of empirical analysis because of these confusions, imported into the analysis without recognition by the use of conventional classifications.

If careers are largely predictable upon the basis of prior characteristics of the population, some version of another economic/social distinction, made by Parkin (1971, p. 13), seems initially more promising. He divides 'the allocation of rewards attaching to different positions in the social system . . . (from) the process of *recruitment* to the positions'. If we choose one potential influence upon patterns of recruitment—education—we can see that the relationships between positions and recruitment are not simple; the processes of recruitment and reward allocation are not neatly placed one before the other. Dividing the routes to education into full-time and part-time, it is obvious that the former is usually complete at the point of entry to employment, while the latter is acquired largely after entry. We shall see that qualifications gained in part-time education are extensive in the working population and have very considerable influences upon their careers.

Education is not, of course, the sole determinant of advancement. There is also career development in employment which is best understood as success in the job, unsupported by formal qualifications. In terms of both educational and other factors, processes of recruitment are variable through the working population, and for many groups they are not complete until fairly advanced ages. Thus location within the productive system, upon which class identification might be based, or even a clear identification of peer groups in terms of education and occupational experience, may not be stabilised for some considerable time after entry to work.

A more fundamental question, however, is the extent to which reward allocation and recruitment are conceptually distinct, even if linked in practical terms. For the purposes of argument, let us assume that rewards are indeed economically determined by market processes related to the stage of material development. That is, we are supposing that education may determine access but work determines the returns. Yet we soon find that, at least at the higher levels of education in Britain, this is a difficult position to hold. Most education is of a general rather than a vocational sort, and there is no unique allocation to positions in the productive system, by type of qualification. Most qualifications will allow entry to a diversity of jobs with a common feature in a broad equivalence of income. In so far as this is the case, and bearing in mind that many typical careers move individuals and groups across locations in the productive system, strategies to maintain access to highly rewarded positions, in whatever sector of the economy, may sometimes make greater economic sense than strategies based upon influencing the rewards to job tasks. Interests are held in common by those in similar relationships to the processes of recruitment as well as by those with similar relationships to the productive system, and in certain circumstances these may come into opposition.

It is at this point that the distinction becomes problematic. If action by those of similar education affects rewards or if education can be used as the basis of affecting rewards, then the processes of recruitment cannot be distinguished from those of reward allocation. The raising of educational levels, in association with the control of entry, has been a typical strategy of professions to advance their economic interests, and arguments for equivalent incomes are as frequently based upon the similarity of personnel as upon the similarity of job tasks. Though the division of the processes makes apparent good sense *a priori*, it cannot be maintained as theories are elaborated. Starting from an assumption of an economic/non-economic distinction, we find that both the supposedly separate processes have economic consequences. Faced with this contradication the conceptual distinction collapses.

We have raised the problematic nature of the division of class and status, of economic and social factors, not for their direct interest alone, but because we see them as illustrations of fundamental problems not only of stratification theory, but of social theory in general. They are particular manifestations of the fact/value, structure/action distinction so characteristic of modern sociology (and clearly illustrated in the remarks of Lockwood quoted earlier). We believe this to be a false opposition, though extremely difficult to dispense with. We have shown how in particular instances it is difficult to maintain, and we should now like to turn to a more general consideration of the problem with particular reference to stratification.

What we consider to be fundamental problems of social understanding are perhaps best illustrated by an examination of the orthodoxies of the fairly recent past. Theorists who base stability upon the legitimacy of existing arrangements argue that it rests upon agreement on moral values. This is true even of theorists who stress false or forced consensus, who may differ from those espousing true consensus in their general analysis of the production of social forms, but nonetheless share assumptions about the attachment of individuals to social conditions, and ways in which transformations of conditions will be achieved in individual behaviour. On these arguments, when there is general agreement upon the worth of social positions and the distribution of rewards to those positions, societies are stable. Conflict ensues from a breakdown of moral consensus. It is not only or even mainly sociologists who hold this view today. The public debates on present conflicts typically trace their origins to a decline, welcome or unwelcome, in previously accepted moral standards.

The general approach popularly opposed to this type of theory has argued that there are many conflicting needs and objectives within any society and that a stable society is not characterised by general agreement upon the distribution of rewards, but by a balance of power between competing factions within the society. On this view societies are stable unless the competing factions gain or lose in their ability to affect the other factions. When that happens, after a period of uncertainty and conflict, a new balance will be produced. Of course no writer of this school has presented such a stark situation of opposition. In recognising consensual elements in society some have stressed that the conflict view is an orientation to be set alongside the consensus view as a corrective to the worst excesses of the latter, while others have believed that practices established in conflict can in the course of time come to be accepted.

However, it is not in the consensual aspects of their theories that we would wish to associate these apparently opposed theorists, but in a much more fundamental assumption characterising both approaches. This is the assumption that men experience society as action—their own and that of other men. The social system is therefore experienced merely as the sum of inter-personal relationships. In both approaches individuals are seen as being directly involved in producing the social forms which characterise their relationships with other individuals. Society, therefore, always appears as a human product. What is external and perhaps constraining for any particular individual reflects the motives and resources of other individuals or groups of individuals. Residing thus in action, social arrangements are always suitable subjects for moral scrutiny.

We have emphasised the fact that men *experience* society as action within these opposed theories rather than arguing that society is constituted in action in the theories because, of course, there is disagreement about the latter point. Some theorists of structure assert the primacy of the social, while attempting to locate the social in moral categories, i.e. maintained in personal commitments of the actor or of others. The true determination of practices is social, but in its fullest realisation the social is experienced as personal. Writers from positions as diverse as those of Durkheim, Weber, Parsons, Lockwood and Habermas have all, ultimately, identified the 'social' as a 'moral' category. Since moral categories concern values and human action, the distinction between 'social structure' and 'social action' has been precarious. With both concepts constituted in values, social structure often collapses into social action as theories are elaborated and vice versa. Thus on the one hand, there is the fact that value orientations are the primitive concepts of sociologies of action, yet it is difficult not to give them a social life outside their acceptance by individuals. While on the other, if structural categories are truly moral categories they must be maintained in commitment, by which token they are constructed in action. We believe the contradiction lies in the concepts of 'action' and 'society'.

Though a strong emphasis upon society formed in action continues in certain types of social theory (notably certain versions of phenomenology and ethnomethodology which stress society as the skilled production of actors), there has been increasing emphasis (by, for example, Althusserians) upon an analysis of social arrangements which ignores values and perceptions of individuals as significant factors in their determination, attempting an entirely external structural analysis. The presence of the value commitments, central to sociologies of action, is not denied—merely their relevance to social stability and change. While the emphasis on structure is welcome, this form of dichotomy seems to us an arid and unproductive approach to human action.

A more rewarding approach makes, as a point of departure, the observation that, whether or not there is a true level of analysis concerned with the 'social' as a world distinct from the 'individual', the social is experienced as if it occupied a separate realm. For example, Marx believed that the principles of classical economics are accepted by all parties in capitalist society as general principles about the essential nature of economic activity to which all are subject. The determination of social experience is thus seen as a 'natural' rather than a human process. Human action is conceived as efficacious only within the general confines of economic necessity. Though some commentators have argued that this process of reification is peculiar to the capitalist mode of production, others have held that, while it reaches its most pervasive form under capitalism, it is a feature of all social life.

There are important consequences for individual consciousness when society in certain of its aspects is confronted as 'natural', as residing in the operation of general principles external to individuals and therefore descriptively known, rather than in norms or values which are prescriptive and contingent. Attitudes to social arrangements then become questions of knowledge rather than of evaluation. The arrangements belong neither to the actor as reflections of his values and motives, nor to other men as their motives and resources. All parties to relationships are seen as constrained. The relationship belongs to necessary experience rather than to the exercise of choice on the part of either. Moral issues occur within the perceived conditions of social life and not as the substance of society.

However, though this is useful as an initial polemical statement, there are qualifications which need to be made to the rather stark opposition of conditions of action and the nature of action. The first is that conditions and opportunities are never so rigidly divided. The likelihood of changing conditions—of loosening constraints and expanding the potential for competent action—varies considerably, as do the consequences of creating the capacities for change. This is true of 'material' conditions no less than 'social' conditions, and this leads to a further qualification. 'Natural' has been placed in inverted commas when applied to social arrangements because of the deeply held orthodoxy which insists upon a fundamental separation of 'natural' and 'social'. The former is seen as external to man and the object of study in science (a descriptive analytical undertaking), while the latter pertains to the actively created conditions existing among men which must be interpreted to be understood. On this view social principles can only *appear to be* natural. We would suggest that this separation of 'science' and 'society', of 'natural' and 'social', is at the root of the problem of structure and action, and that a view of human activity which dissolves the distinction is necessary. This involves understanding science as actively created as well as understanding society as factually constituted. There can be no simple separation of 'material' and 'social' objects of study at either the practical or the theoretical level. They are continuous aspects of social life inextricably bound together. Social transformation is practical transformation, not merely the transformation of motives and values.

Reflecting the emphasis upon the social as the non-material, there has been too great a stress in sociology upon data descriptive of individuals' states of mind abstracted from actual conditions, rather than upon their own descriptive statements of their practical experience. This has lead to searches for the answers to sociological problems in the wrong places.

The importance of the issues that have been raised may be seen in relation to social change in that the process of change is not that of moral decay, but rather that of factual transformation. The moral problems that arise do so because of the appropriation for moral consideration of things which previously appeared to be beyond human control, where previously existing cognitive categories fail to provide efficient accounts of experience. Regularities associated with these categories may have disappeared in practice, and at the very least will have become contingent rather than necessary; and if they are to be maintained, it must be by injunctions to act in accordance with past behaviour. A more or less confused situation is likely to result which can only be resolved with new explanatory concepts, and these concepts are constrained by circumstances. Thus the most important aspects of social constraint are associated with cognition rather than evaluation. They are concerned with what is known and the means by which things can be known. In the everyday life of the individual, his culture impinges less as a series of moral principles and more as that which is known— perceived facts of existence about which there is no issue of the exercise of will. We are not suggesting, of course, that these perceived facts will form an encompassing, coherent statement in his conscious thoughts, but 'facts' must be mutually compatible when they are brought into conjunction in experience. In this way society exists 'within' individuals, not merely in the sense of internalised norms and values, but more importantly as knowledge towards which the individual has no moral attitude and which is not the subject of direct individual production.

We have already argued that previous theories place considerable emphasis upon the moral judgements made by an individual concerning his social relationships and experience. Where they fail is in specifying the nature and more especially the context of these moral evaluations. In the first place we need to know the extent to which the individual conceives of different aspects of his social experience as being areas within which it is meaningful to make moral statements. The central problem is in deciding the extent to which an individual regards certain matters as so 'natural' that the question of their morality or rightness is virtually meaningless in the context of his present life. Secondly we must know what the area of his experience is. The understandings of experience held by individuals are likely to be heavily influenced by the demands of immediate situations and as such to be variable in character. They are the data which must be explained in theoretical accounts, but are themselves limited and specific. Individual experience does not encompass the totality of social arrangements, but is partial and constrained within the limits defined by structural position. But the existence of a coherent structure does not require that anyone should be able to conceive the whole, merely that—as with the blind men and the elephant—the experience of each individual should be consistent with the whole, however diverse and contradictory the interpretations of the whole may be, based on limited information.

In general, we hope we have made it clear that the context of evaluational statements must be understood if they are to be correctly interpreted. Yet in the literature this is scarcely ever recognised. Though it would seem obvious that the effect of different positions within a stratification system on contexts of evaluation should at least be tested, most previous authors have assumed that everyone asked to evaluate aspects of the system is engaged in the same sort of exercise. Equally seriously there has been an assumption that evaluational statements by individuals about their different positions within the system are essentially similar.

These assumptions give rise to data of a very problematic sort, and the use of such evaluational statements as the bases of social forms, as for example in reputational scales of occupational prestige which we discuss at length in Part One, is conceptually unsound. Most people, if asked to produce an evaluation, will do so even if the result is unrealistic in that it does not bear upon their current experience and evaluational dilemmas. They are quite prepared to speculate about unrealistic circumstances. Such speculations apply not to the present but to abstract, conceivable, future contexts. What is given and not amenable to change by action in the immediate context is not necessarily what is given and fixed for all time. Certainly within our own society most individuals have had direct experience of changes in material and social conditions and thus of the modification of constraints. Knowledge that this occurs ensures that very few current practical constraints are perceived as being so much of the essence of existence as to be beyond any possible, future modification. There are, therefore, conceivable frameworks within which most moral questions can be answered. But the fact that everyone answers evaluational questions must not be taken as indicating that the answers are equivalent. The degree of abstraction from real circumstances and immediate issues of value may vary considerably by location in the system.

Even if the status of the different evaluational accounts is recognised, it is unlikely that the less immediate can be usefully employed in social explanation except as broad indications of desirable developments. Actual developments are unlikely to take the form implicit in the speculations. This is because the process of the transformation of knowledge may involve more than the extension of current basic categories to new areas; in the most important transformations the basic categories are themselves re-created. Speculation about the future is much more likely to consist in unrealistic extensions of the present using current understandings.

For the sociologist both what is 'known' and, so far as they can be identified, the processes by which this knowledge is produced are aspects of structure. Thus social structure in the minds of individuals and social structure in sociological accounts are not identical. The explanation of structure is a sociological problem in that it must be able to account for a potential diversity of conceptions of social experience and yet not be merely descriptive of these diverse conceptions. It must present a coherent statement of diverse 'realities' in the minds of individuals and the conditions of their formation, and attempt to identify, however inadequately, the processes by which they will change.

Theory, in its purest or 'ideal' form, may be seen as intellectual schemes which attempt to explain within a consistent whole the diverse elements of the social world. Though it is not timeless or context free, it seeks to transcend individual cognitive schemes and to understand the social basis of their production. That the 'ideal' is unattainable matters little—the strain towards it is a necessary characteristic of all scientific thought. The point is that a fundamental part of sociological activity is to stand back from the social environment and look at it critically and analytically—to provide explanations of a different order from those of the participants in the every-day situation. Any sociological account of the structuring of social experience must have this character. Of course the sociological account is in no way the property of or only available to the professional sociologist, but we must recognise that this sort of understanding is not easily won.

Moreover, the empirical basis of the understanding must be clearly understood. It is not necessary for the sociologists' concepts to be shared by other people, but they must be relevant to every-day life. These intellectual tools of analysis may be given technical meanings, but they are concerned to explain the cognitive schemes deriving from existence in particular social environments. A large part of sociological endeavour, including much of the present study, is concerned, therefore, with the application of concepts to provide meaningful accounts of social arrangements, and thereby make them more intelligible. This concern with everyday life gives rise to an ever-present tendency for the cognitive schemes of the subjects of enquiry to be incorporated into the explanations. In many cases these are so deeply embedded in our own models of explanation that they are never confronted and so act as a basic constraint upon thought. One example is our earlier illustration of the diverse, implicit distinctions in occupational classifications. Another is the related problem of what constitutes mobility. Some careers are included in one occupation; others, equally predictable, cross occupational boundaries. In previous work those in the first type have been seen as immobile, those in the second as mobile. A great deal of intellectual energy is expended in sociology in producing explanations of data without addressing the theoretical assumptions implicit in their formation. As a rule of thumb we are well advised to be most wary when the nature of our data seems least problematic, when they appear to have a straightforward factual character.

DATA SOURCES

The content, transformations and interpretations of the data original to this study will be discussed at the relevant points in the following chapters. Here we outline the sources from which they are derived. These are three surveys, two major and one subsidiary.

The first is a sample of 1918 non-manual employees,[1] which we refer to as the *White-Collar* sample. Respondents were employed in manufacturing industry, the public sector, building, research laboratories and the insurance industry. They worked in establishments located within 60 miles of Cambridge. The geographical restriction was imposed for practical reasons, but it still allowed an extensive variety in the area covered. It embraced a sizeable part of London, most of East Anglia and Essex, Bedfordshire, Hertfordshire and part of the East Midlands.

The establishments covered were restricted to those with over 500 employees, which is where the great majority of male non-manual workers are employed. Within each establishment a simple random sample of all male non-manual staff (including foremen) was drawn. In order to avoid overweighting the total sample with employees in large establishments, we used a variable sampling fraction to give a sample size proportional to the log of the population. We also used larger fractions in the manufacturing firms to cover the greater occupational variety. Overall the response rate was 82 per cent, which seems quite satisfactory, particularly as much of the non-response was not due to refusals but to absence through illness or holidays during the period of the interviewing (typically about a week).

Clearly there is no way in which the sample can be described as representative of the population of England. On the other hand, it covers most of the range of non-manual employment and relates to a region covering most types of employers. It does, in fact, seem likely that in certain respects it resembles the national population, and this is confirmed by a number of checks we made at various points of the research. These are presented in the text.

This sample was well suited to many of our needs, including the detailed consideration of certain occupations, but at some points the data from a second major source were more appropriate. This source we refer to as the *General* sample. It comprises some 5000 interviews conducted in Yorkshire and regions around Leicester, Cambridge and Glasgow. The sample was drawn to meet several purposes, and will also be the subject of further reports. It was designed to cover a wide range of occupations, manual and non-manual, which were separately sampled. As far as possible, the aim was to work in units of 12 or 24 respondents in an occupation in each region, the 24 being equally divided between those working in urban and rural locations. As usual, though, the

---

[1] For a fuller discussion of this sample and the reasons for its design see Prandy, *et al.* (forthcoming).

achieved sample did not entirely match the plan. This sample has fuller data than that of the White-Collar sample on qualifications and work experience, and has been used as the main basis of general work on these factors presented in Part Three.

A further source was part of the pilot for the General sample. Fifty-one of these respondents took part in a preliminary study on perceptions and evaluations of stratification. In addition to the specific references, both this study and the General sample provided background information to broaden the context of our analysis.

Part One

Measuring Stratification

2 The Measurement of Stratification

We shall begin our examination of the relationship between occupations and stratification with a consideration of the overall nature and coherence of stratification arrangements from a particular standpoint— that of attempts to describe and measure stratification through the creation of scales of occupations. For the most part such scales have been presented as measures of occupational status, which have been assumed to be founded on the prestige of the occupations or their incumbents. In general a single dimension has been assumed, which the scale is intended to represent; but at a more theoretical level it has been widely argued, partly on the basis of difficulties in the scaling exercises, that a multi-dimensional approach is needed. As we have argued elsewhere (Stewart and Blackburn, 1975), we believe the conceptualisation of the scales and their interpretation have been generally mistaken, largely due to a failure to relate methods and theory. There has been a strong emphasis on the development of technique in this area,[1] to the exclusion of theoretical consideration. It is our contention that, on the one hand, an adequate scaling must be firmly located in a theoretical framework, and, on the other, the process of scale construction itself can help to develop our understanding of social stratification.

Part of our purpose in this chapter is to present a scale for grading occupations which we believe will be of value in a wider area of social research. However, in creating the scale we were also exploring the nature of stratification arrangements, and in particular we were testing whether a uni-dimensional conceptualisation is appropriate. The scale, which was developed for use in a number of different projects within the Cambridge research, has had a brief introduction in a previous article (Stewart, Prandy and Blackburn, 1973). It is far from perfect and we shall not pretend that it overcomes all of the difficulties associated with

---

[1] As there has in the study of social mobility where the scales have been much used.

other available scales. Our ideas have developed during, and indeed through, our work in this connection. Most importantly, the more adequate conception of the relationship between occupations and stratification, to which this work is addressed, post-dates the collection of data used in scale construction and to an extent is associated with the process of producing the scale. Accordingly we are well aware that the approach falls short of the ideal.

It will be our argument that our scale lies somewhere between existing scales and a truly sensitive and adequate scale. Yet we suffer no embarrassment in offering it to a wider public. The authors (Goldthorpe and Hope, 1974, p. 1) of another recently published scheme of occupational grading open their introduction thus: 'The diversity of occupational classifications and scales already in use in social research is such that any attempt to add to their number must call for some justification.' This seems an unnecessary sensitivity since no extensive scale of occupations was in existence for this country before they produced their work.[2] Indeed Bechhofer (1969), in a review of available indices in 1969, concludes that the five Social Classes of the *Classification of Occupations*, published by the Office of Population Census and Surveys, remained the best available in a British context. The particular justification that Goldthorpe and Hope (1974, p. 1) give for presenting their scale—that different occupational gradings are needed for different purposes and that theirs was produced 'to meet the specific requirements of a particular research project—a large scale inquiry into occupational mobility in England and Wales'—requires much closer examination and we shall return to it later.

In part then, but only in part, the purpose of this chapter is to present the scale, which we shall also relate to other scales. A more general concern is that which informs the whole of this monograph—an examination of the coherence of the stratification system. We hope to demonstrate both in the discussion of the process by which the scale was established and in the comparisons with other scales that social processes are more consistently ordered than has frequently been apparent.

As we have said, the Cambridge scale arose out of research requirements, in a similar way to the Hope-Goldthope scale, though we

---

[2] The basis of our own scale was published, in the article mentioned above (Stewart *et al.*, 1973), but without the actual scale scores and other details necessary to make it readily usable. In any case Goldthrope and Hope started their scaling research while ours was still in too early a stage to provide any results.

do not believe that it is in any special relationship to our specific requirements. Faced with the lack of a suitable grading scheme, it appeared that if we wished something more extensive than the OPCS five Social Classes, we would have to provide it ourselves. In coming to a decision upon the most efficient way in which this problem might be tackled, we were forced into a consideration of the various methods which had been used to produce occupational scales. Ironically, we shall argue that in certain respects the least sophisticated of previous attempts are in many ways the most defensible. Let us first consider these approaches, which we shall call intuitive measures.

INTUITIVE MEASURES

Conceptions of class are very old indeed, but the first attempts to give systematic measurement of class as a social variable appear at the beginning of this century.[3] The work of major nineteenth century social theorists might have provided a solid base upon which attempts could have been built, but in fact it is doubtful if the authors of these earliest attempts had any knowledge of the works of Marx or of their contemporaries Weber and Durkheim. Their interest in class was much more pragmatic. Stevenson, for example, who introduced social classes into the Census, wished for a measure to use in studies of fertility, and Bowley, another early pioneer, wished to use it in conjuction with demographic data. Neither, from their writings, seems conscious of the conceptual problems of an adequate theory of class. They are measuring what is for them an unproblematic social structure; its arrangements are clear and secure. What marginal difficulties do remain are concerned with the precise placing of minority groups. Bowley (1913), for example, decides that married grocer's assistants are middle class while unmarried assistants are working class.

Intuitive scales are not, however, confined to the history of social research. The Social Classes of the OPCS is just such a scale and is probably the most frequently used measure of stratification in this country. It was first introduced by Stevenson in the report of the 1911 Census. It has been modified several times since, but the modifications have been carried out in the same way as the original scale was

---

[3] At least that was the start of measurement which has developed to the present day. The earliest measures should, perhaps, be attributed to the Romans, who differentiated 'classes' (including the 'proletariat' and 'lumpenproletariat') for tax purposes.

produced, by the considered judgement of the Registrar General's staff. It has survived several attempts, using more complicated techniques, to produce alternative scales.

For many years a similar situation obtained in the USA. Though the first attempts at measurement used the reputational approach, which we shall discuss presently, the first to gain general acceptance was that produced by Edwards for the Bureau of the Census in 1941. Perhaps because of the prestige of the source, this was for a time the most popular measure in the USA, until superceded by the NORC scale, produced by a reputational approach.

The history of the British measure is so long that it has taken on an aspect of self-justification. Edwards, however, produced his scale in a more self-conscious age and was challenged to justify his procedures and give an account of the meaning of his measure. His reply was that it had been constructed from a perception of the likely incomes and educational levels of members of occupations. Several later commentators, (see, for example, Blau and Duncan, 1967, p. 118) accept this as laudable basis, but argue that a more rigorous method in relation to this basis is necessary. Its supercession by later measures was probably due to this lack of rigorous procedures.

These approaches do have a number of advantages, however. They relate directly to their authors' social perceptions and are not mediated through the rather simple processes of supposedly more rigorous techniques. Social stratification is a complex issue, and most approaches to measurement relate to only a few aspects of it. Their apparent rigour frequently excludes the operation of a more sensitive human judgement about the true nature of social arrangements. It is very significant that most sociologists do not find it difficult to point to specific deficiencies in the available measures, and in general, they share perceptions of what these deficiencies are.

In these circumstances one wonders why the superior perceptions necessary to the criticism of the scales are not employed for the construction of improved scales. The rigour of the techniques must not be confused with the relevance of their results as measures of the social phenomena concerned. All research procedures involve a simplification of social issues. In the case of measures of stratification, the simplifications are usually too extensive for the results of the research to be taken as defining the social phenomena to which the research is addressed.

Intuition, of course, should be a point of departure rather than a secure basis for social explanation. But it can be tested and superceded only if sophisticated and sensitive theories inform our research, and are translated into procedural possibilities. In the absence of this, the results of the intuition of a capable social scientist are to be preferred to rigorously devised but irrelevant products.

REPUTATIONAL APPROACH

There is more research using what we call the reputational approach than any other method. It comes in various forms, but we shall consider only a few of the main variants. We want to consider the principal issues involved rather than review all the details of different strategies.

In general terms, the reputational approach attempts to derive a description of the stratification system from evaluations of positions (usually occupations) within that system, made by a set of respondents. In most forms of the approach, each respondent is presented with a list of occupations, chosen for their spread through an assumed hierarchical structure, and then asked to place them in order, or to rate them on a specified scale, say from poor to excellent. The ranking or rating is performed according to some principle which is regarded as a central feature of stratification—usually some variation on the theme of 'occupational prestige' or 'social standing'.

In most early scaling research the method of direct *ranking* was used. Respondents were presented with a complete list and asked to order all the occupations that appeared on it. In the USA in 1925, for example, Counts reports how he asked a sample of high school and college students and teachers to order 45 occupations according to the social standing society accorded to each of them. Davis (1927) used a similar procedure for a cross-national study using school children in the USA and the USSR as his raters. Mapheus Smith (1943) used a rather more fanciful stimulus when he asked a sample of high school and college students to place occupations round a table in terms of their rank at a dinner honouring a celebrity; social position was measured in terms of distance from the celebrity. A limitation of this approach is that it is only possible with relatively small numbers of occupations to be ordered. Respondents find it difficult to handle large numbers of stimuli, and a resulting ordering (even if obtained) may be meaningless.

Part of the process of producing the Hope-Goldthorpe scale was a variation of this ranking procedure. There were several stages to the process, and the ranking by a sample of the population came only after the tasks had been defined by the authors and four 'experts in the fields of labour economics, industrial sociology and industrial relations' (Goldthorpe and Hope, 1974, p. 24). The authors first selected the categorisation of occupations into groups, which appears in Appendix B2 of the *Classification of Occupations 1970* published by OPCS. This gave them 45 rather heterogeneous categories. They then asked each of their four colleagues to disaggregate the groups and reconstitute them as smaller groups 'in terms of *the net extrinsic and intrinsic, material and non-material rewards and deprivations typically associated with the occupations they comprised'* (1974, p. 24, their italics). Where experts disagreed they took the majority vote giving themselves a casting vote. By this procedure the original 45 groups were reformed into 124 categories. Typical occupational titles were then chosen for each category, the number depending on the range of well-known occupations included. In 48 cases ten titles were chosen for each category, and in the other 76 cases five titles each were chosen. It will be seen that this is essentially a use of the intuitive method, except that no formal standing was given to the *ordering* implied in the OPCS groups and the experts' decisions. Final ordering was left entirely to the opinions of a sample of the population.

Obviously presenting every respondent with the task of ranking the 860 occupational titles thus produced was not a practical possibility, and to overcome this difficulty different respondents were asked to rank different sets of occupations. However, every respondent was asked to order, in terms of 'social standing', a set of 20 standard occupational titles as a first step of the ranking procedure. Once this task was completed, he/she was given another 20 occupations to place among the standard occupations. The authors decided that they should have 100 people giving a grading for each occupational category, which would give ten gradings for each title in ten title categories and 20 gradings for each in five title categories. Since each respondent was to order 20 titles, in addition to the standard titles, they required a sample of 620 ($124 \times 100 \div 20$). Their sample was designed to be a random sample of the population, male and female, of England and Wales. The actual scale scores were constructed by first extracting the standard occupational titles and scoring them according to their rank, as if the second part of the ranking task with the other 20 representative titles had not occurred. These scores were then centred about a mean of zero with a standard deviation of one. Representative titles were then given values in terms of their relationship to the standard titles in the respondents' rankings, with the five or ten titles for a category treated as equivalent so as to yield a single score for each category.

We have set out the basis of the Hope-Goldthorpe scale in some detail because we shall be discussing the relationship between it and our Cambridge scale later. The different bases upon which the scales were constructed are important to a discussion of their similarities and differences, particularly in terms of the implications for our understanding of the nature of the relationships between occupations and stratification.

Another popular reputational technique has been to ask each respondent to assess each occupation separately on a short scale of prestige or social standing, ranging, say, from 'excellent' to 'poor'. The answers can then be aggregated in some way to produce an overall scale. By far the best known and most frequently used example of the reputational approach, the NORC study, used this *rating* method. Occupations were rated on a five point scale, with an arbitrary scoring system from one for 'poor' to five for 'excellent'. The first part of this study was carried out in 1947 using a sample of the US population. A replication with a smaller sample was carried out in 1963 and correlated 0.99 with the original. (Hodge *et al.*, 1964). Another important study using this method was that by Hall and Jones (1950) in this country. This was a much smaller undertaking than the NORC study, covering far fewer occupations. However, the particular methods of the Hall-Jones study have proved very popular, and it has been replicated in a very large number of social circumstances in many countries. The main advantage of the rating method is that it can more easily accommodate large numbers of occupations than can the other methods of the reputational approach.

There is a third method which has been frequently discussed but seldom used. Rather than being presented with a complete list, respondents may be given a series of *comparisons* of pairs or other small groups of occupations, and the final ordering constructed from the results of these sets of overlapping comparisons. Again, this method is not really suitable for large numbers of occupations. To cover all comparisons, an interview would take a very long time besides being exceedingly tedious for the respondent. Nevertheless the explicit set of choices is preferable to the less direct judgements of the other two methods, and the method has its strong supporters. It has recently been used by Coxon and Jones (1978) though on a limited number of occupations.

Using mainly reputational scales, Treiman has carried out an extensive series of cross-national comparisons, finding a substantial degree of consistency between the stratification scales for different countries. This has led to his construction of an international scale of occupational prestige (Treiman, 1977).

We have discussed elsewhere the general deficiencies of the reputational method (Stewart and Blackburn, 1975), and we shall confine ourselves here to a summary of the main points. Although it is not an absolute necessity of the method, there has been an implicit assumption that each and every respondent is equally and identically competent in the task of ranking or rating occupations over the whole range of the scale. There has been a failure, for example, to allow for a diversity of individual competence as a consequence of a diversity of social experience. The consequences of this assumption are not, as we have argued (op. cit., 1975), very serious for the nature of the overall scales, but the diversity of individual perceptions which are aggregated to form the scale has frequently been taken as a sign of structural incoherence.

Several authors have discussed the ways in which variation in perception by social experience might be accommodated within the reputational approach (e.g. Moser and Hall, 1954) but to date no extensive study has used these techniques. To a large extent this is due not to perversity, but to an assumption, implicit or explicit, about the nature of stratification and the relationship of reputational scales to it. Let us illustrate this assumption, ironically, by reference to a critic of single scales of social stratification. Hiller, who believes that sociologists have not usually faced up to the diversity of perceptions they have found, sets out the conditions he sees as having to be met before the usual approach to reputational scales and stratification can be justified. He writes (1973, p. 87):

As sociologists, we can say that a single system of social stratification exists: when all members of society independently agree on the number of groups or categories (as the case may be) of people and their relative positions in terms of social evaluations (both of the groups/categories themselves and of the placement of individuals within them); when there is agreement on the criteria determining membership in such groups or categories, on the nature of the relationships existing within and between them, and on the legitimacy of the system (or when, at least on the level of everyday social interaction, there *appears* to those involved to be no major disagreements on the issues contained in these propositions: there must at least be perceived consensus); and when actions, as evidenced by patterns of association, avoidance and deference, are consistent with their subjective definitions of the situation.

On this view 'status' or 'prestige' scales are based purely upon an individuals' subjective definitions, about which we cannot ask whether or not they are correct. Provided the respondent has reported his opinions accurately, his evaluations must be accepted as data. Hiller correctly criticises proponents of this view who, while recognising that different people make different evaluations, have believed nevertheless that these views can be aggregated to arrive at 'the subjective evaluation of the population—the occupational prestige'. In spite of a certain naive plausibility, that approach is theoretical nonsense. The first difficulty is to give any meaning to an aggregate of different subjective views, which aggregate may not represent the evaluations of anyone. This is true irrespective of the nature of the sample used. The use of a random sample, as often advocated, to make the aggregate representative, makes no more theoretical sense and is of no practical help. Let us illustrate this by supposing a random sample which, apart from one man, falls into two equal groups with exactly balanced, opposite views; the contribution from the aggregation of the views of the two groups is to render all stimuli equal, leaving us with the ludicrous conclusion that the views of the one remaining man represent the subjective status structure for the entire population.

Hiller's view, that we may accept a single measure of stratification only if there is a consensus in the population, determining a status structure which can be measured by aggregating subjective judgements, makes more sense theoretically, but is also ultimately incorrect. The coherence of the stratification system does not consist in an identity of experience for all of its members; on the contrary, members are involved in diverse, differentiated relationships. In other words people have different social experience according to their position in the system. Conversely, those sharing a common position in it experience similar social conditions. The images of stratification arrangements will vary with the quality of experience. For the purposes of important day to day activity, distinctions of social position will have varying salience for individuals differently located in the social structure. For example, in most circumstances under which interaction takes place between individuals with very different class positions, fine discriminations are unnecessary. The quality of their interaction would not vary for fairly substantial variations in the class position of either. Put simply, there are few occasions when the distinction in class position between a fitter and a general labourer, for example, would be relevant to the quality of their interaction with a barrister. To him they are both 'working class'; to the workers he is one of 'them'. Similarly the distinction between a

QC and a solicitor may be irrelevant for their interaction with a labourer. The distinctions will, however, have an important effect on the relationships between fitter and labourer, QC and solicitor, and on their relationships with others close to them in class terms.

The images that individuals hold of stratification systems thus vary by social experience. In other words we are here arguing 'typification' on a stratification model. In terms of Schutz' (1972) presentation:

> The farther out we get into the world of contemporaries, the more anonymous its inhabitants become. [p. 181] Anonymity may mean the generality of the typifying scheme . . . the concreteness of the ideal type is inversely proportional to the level of generality of the past experience out of which it is constructed. The deeper basis for this is the fact that, as the interpreter falls back on lower- and lower-level ideal types, he must take more and more for granted. [p. 195]

The integration or coherence of stratification systems does not depend upon either an identity of experience or, what is more commonly assumed, an identity of evaluations, among all of the members. Indeed, for there to be a coherent structure to stratification arrangements does not even require a perception of a totality by members, let alone a complete identity of evaluations; it merely requires that in areas of significant experience there should be no contradiction between individuals in their diverse cognitions, perceptions and evaluations. However, for the most part reputational approaches have been constructed on assumptions of similarities of perception or evaluation. Although many authors have rejected the notion of moral consensus as the basis of social stratification, this has had little impact when it comes to measurement. The moral consensual basis of agreement on ranking or rating occupations has rarely been attacked, though Goldthorpe and Hope (1972, p. 38) provide a notable exception. They argue:

> our interpretation is opposed to the idea that these ratings are evaluative in the sense that they imply moral approval of the occupational hierarchy which they serve to constitute. For example, we would hold that this hierarchy cannot be taken—as it is by structural functional theorists—as indicating how occupations are seen as receiving legitimately differentiated rewards in accordance with their relative importance in meeting social needs.

It should be noted, however, that their results still depend upon a general similarity of perceptions in the population.

CONSTRUCTED INDICES

Before turning to consideration of the approach adopted in our own research, there is one further method which should be mentioned. It is that of constructing indices of stratification from data on characteristics of occupations. What is at present the most frequently used measure of stratification in the USA is an example—the Socio-Economic Index developed by Duncan. Strictly speaking, this method is a means of extending a scale produced by other methods, in Duncan's case the NORC scale. He took the percentage of members of each occupation who were high school graduates and the percentage of members of occupations who were earning over $3500 in 1949 (both variables standardised for age). The data are available from the US Census, but equivalent data are not available for Britain. Weightings were obtained from the regression of the education and income measures on the NORC scale[4] and used in the construction of the Index. The NORC scale covered 90 occupational titles, of which 45 were used in the regression, but Duncan, having derived appropriate weightings, was able to apply them to all occupations used in the US Census Data. The utility of such a measure can not be doubted, but it depends for its validation upon the quality of the reputational scale and the strength of its relationship to that scale. In any case this method is unlikely to be used in most countries, including Britain, as the data on earnings and education needed in its construction are not readily available.

RELATIONAL APPROACH

We now turn to an introduction of the approach we finally decided to use in constructing our scale. In part our decision was governed by the ease with which collection of the data for this approach could be combined with other aspects of our research—questions relevant to the task could be included in the schedule of the White-Collar survey—but

[4] The scale used by Duncan is a little different from the original NORC measure, occupations being scored by the percentage rating them 'good' or 'excellent'.

we were also attracted by several strong advantages of the method, not only for the construction of the scale but also for the light it could throw on the processes of stratification.

At this point we experience a difficulty of presentation. We are about to argue that it may be possible to extract regularities in the stratification system from patterns of association in non-work ·situations of respondents characterised by their occupations. Given the very considerable literature on the relationship between mode of production, market circumstances and life styles in general, we would wish to avoid using terms to describe what we are measuring which would give the wrong impression about our position in that debate. We believe we are measuring material and social advantage and that these are indivisible concepts. We do not believe in the Weberian distinction of classes, which are formed in the rational pursuit of interest in the context of the market, from status groups which rest upon successful claims to special esteem and develop bases for collective identification and action in economically non-rational conventions of consumption and behaviour. Such an opposition is neither useful nor necessary.[5] We have previously used the term 'class structure' for the subject matter of our scale (Stewart, Prandy and Blackburn, 1973), but given the problems of closure and class identity we realise that that term may be misunderstood, and we shall now use the more neutral phrase *stratification arrangements* to describe what we are measuring. We do not want to suggest our measure is a continuous measure of 'class' and that the principal issue is the extent to which the scale can be divided into discrete 'classes'. It is a scale of shared experience which may be cross-cut by class issues. An analysis of social class must be crucially concerned with the production of capacities upon which market relations are founded. For example, it may be that policemen and skilled workers have similar experience and interact with each other as equals, yet their relations to the productive system are different and this can have important behavioural consequences under certain conditions.[6]

---

[5] Perhaps it will help to avoid misunderstanding if we explain that we are not denying that economic resources and social honour can serve as different bases of power. However, that does not mean that market and status are different dimensions of stratification, and in any case the link between prestige and the relational aspect of stratification is not a logically necessary one.

[6] For a discussion of the consequences for police trade-unionism see Reiner (1978).

If we assume that the incumbents of occupations will choose to interact with those of about the same stratification position, then it may be possible to scale occupations in terms of the occupations of persons with whom their incumbents interact. The data for such an approach would involve respondents in very simple tasks. Instead of being asked to rank or rate occupations, they need only be asked for their occupations and those of persons with whom they associate socially.

The relational aspect of stratification has been used on a number of occasions in studies of 'local status systems' where members can be easily identified by name. However, it has been seldom used in a wider context with occupations as the indicators of positions. One reason for this has been the difficulty of analysing the resulting data. The general principles of an approach which would establish an orderly structure from a matrix of dissimilarities have long been vaguely perceived. We are told that Flinders Petrie (1899) had conceived of such an approach to seriation data in archaeology before the turn of the century. However, the techniques for dealing with the problems are of recent origin, and it was not until computers became generally available that the approach became a practical possibility.

There are several types of multi-dimensional scaling which can be used, but the approaches are broadly similar. The basic principle is to take a set of objects, with relative distances defined between each pair of objects, and arrange them in a space. The aim is to place them in just a few dimensions while maintaining as far as possible the original distance criteria. Once the configuration is established, principle dimensions are extracted in a way somewhat analogous to factor analysis, and similarly the dimensions are of declining importance in fitting the data. The inadequacy of the solution in a given number of dimensions is measured by a stress coefficient, representing the extent to which the original criteria have been distorted. Very roughly it may be thought of as analogous to the coefficient of alienation or 'unexplained variance' $(1-R^2)$ measuring the failure of a regression line to represent its data. Thus the method can be used to test the adequacy of a given number of dimensions to represent a set of relations, or to find the least number of dimensions needed for a reasonable representation, and also to locate the objects in the dimensions of any particular solution. Thus, without making any prior assumptions about structuring, the method can be used to extract and evaluate any regularities which are inherent in the data. We should add that the input data need not be actual ratio or interval level distances; all that is needed is differences between objects which can be represented as an ordinal set of distances, though one attraction of the method is that it produces estimates of the actual distances at the ratio scale level.[7]

Some of the advantages of the relational approach are connected with the use of these techniques, but some are of a fairly obvious sort. For example, since it asks questions of respondents which are likely to be meaningful to them (e.g. who are their friends and what are their occupations), their responses are less likely to be constructs of the interview situation than they are with the reputational approach. Then again, there is no assumption of perfect knowledge of stratification arrangements on the part of respondents. All they need know are their own occupations and those of their friends. The distortions which can occur in reputational approaches because of the ignorance of respondents are thus avoided. Since the structural characteristics are established from meaningful *relationships* of individuals, account can be taken of variations in perception and evaluation without having to regard these as in any way indicative of structural irregularities. In this way the approach is rather more sensitive to the complexities of social reality. Finally we may note that while most approaches set out to measure the prestige or 'reputation' of an occupation, when scales are used in research it is not usually as measures of this but of the sort of life assumed to be associated with it, as for example when social background is measured by father's occupation. Thus the relational approach provides a more directly relevant measure for most purposes.

A disadvantage of the approach is that only the occupations which occur directly in the collected data can be assessed. This means that the analysis is limited to the occupations of respondents and/or the occupations of the persons they name (unlike in the reputational approach where the investigators' choice of occupations is independent of respondents). This has implications for project design in that it makes the choice of occupations of respondents, with adequate numbers of each, more important than some sort of representative sample. These disadvantages of the approach seem small in relation to its benefits.

As we have said, the basis of this approach is that people choose to interact with those in about the same stratification position. However, it need hardly be said that not all social interaction, indeed not even all preferred leisure-time interaction, is between equals. It is, therefore, extremely important to identify the particular social relationships which are best associated with stratification. Previous researchers who have used this approach have given considerable thought to this problem,

---

[7] For a basic description of the method see Roskam (1969).

and our thinking was to an extent influenced by that of Lauman and Guttman (1966) who were the first to use advanced techniques on relational data. Their data were gathered from a sample of 422 white male residents of two Census tracts of the city of Boston, Massachusetts. In the course of the interview each respondent was asked, among other things, for his own occupation and the occupations of his father, father-in-law, three closest friends and two next-door neighbours. The information on occupations of both the respondent and those with whom he interacted was coded into 55 occupational categories using a two digit code. A summary 55-by-55 asymmetric matrix was created by cross-tabulating the respondents' code against the codes of the seven others and summing across the seven tables. This was then fed into a form of multi-dimensional scaling developed by Guttman and Lingoes. The results were not as coherent as the authors might have wished. They argued that three dimensions were necessary to represent the underlying structure and a clear interpretation was possible only of the first. That dimension was similar to Duncan's Socio-Economic Index, which, as we have earlier shown, was closely related to the NORC scale. It might, therefore, be considered as approximating to a measure of social stratification. The fact that two other dimensions of some size were needed to describe the structure of their data led them to argue that previous assumptions about the arrangements of classes upon a single hierarchical continuum were too simple. Lauman and Guttman (1966, p. 178) write:

Clearly a more sophisticated theoretical and empirical approach to the study of occupational· interrelationships than that previously assumed in occupational prestige studies is required in future work.

It would seem likely, however, that some of the difficulty lies with their particular choice of data.

The set of social relations they included reflects the influence of Warner on their view of stratification. They (1966, p. 170) write:

Following the Warner tradition, we will define a social class as a subset of the population determined by partitioning of the total population according to such associational relationships as consanguinial and affinal, kinship, friendship, and common residence.

However, in lumping all of the different relationships together, they are not merely acknowledging the importance of the relationships, but are treating all of them as equivalent with respect to stratification. Not only do we think this is theoretically misconceived, but technically and practically it is mistaken. Indeed the authors themselves unwittingly contradict this assumption in practice.

The numbers of neighbours and friends included were the result of their considered judgement of the relative importance of each type of relationship, and the fact that they are different, that more friends than neighbours have been chosen, implies that friends are more important than neighbours in determining respondents' 'statuses'. Neighbours in turn are more important than fathers and fathers-in-law. Even if this ordering of importance is reasonable, it reflects the fundamental point that the meanings of these contracts are not the same in each case. Yet in seeking an underlying structure by the use of multi-dimensional scaling techniques, the items of input should be basically the same with random errors. If they have to be given different weights to reflect their different importance they do not belong together in the same analysis.

Lauman (1973, p. 74) subsequently recognised the deficiency of the procedure. He writes:

> Unfortunately, in order to build up a sufficient number of cases to sustain analysis, we were forced to combine the respondent's reports on the occupations of friends, neighbours, father, and father-in-law—all persons likely to have some kind of relationship with the respondent but, nevertheless, all relationships varying considerably among themselves in their degree of intimacy and modes of formation.

This is at odds with the earlier theoretical justification of the particular social relationships chosen.

In his later work he limits the input to the occupations of friends. Here the occupational categories are limited to 16 and are produced 'to permit explicit identification within various industry groups of those who are self-employed and those who are employees' (1973, p. 75). It will be seen that this is a much more limited exercise in terms of scaling occupations. On this occasion he concludes that two dimensions are sufficient to describe the data. The first is once again assumed to approximate to 'socio-economic status'. The second is taken as corresponding roughly to the size of employing establishment, though the argument in support of this interpretation is rather limited. He does not provide sufficient information on the nature of the different solutions to make any estimate of the relative importance of the dimensions.

For the main task of scale construction we also chose friends, though for certain other purposes we used neighbours and fathers. We believe that friends most closely reflect the stratification positions of respondents. Differentiation within a structural model implies the notion of distance. In the class system, this distance is strongly associated, at the level of subjective feelings, with what Bogardus (1933) has called 'social distance', that is, absence of 'the sympathetic understanding that exists between people'. Feelings of identification and the likelihood of engaging in 'non-instrumental social interaction', in Blau and Duncan's (1967) phrase decline as one moves out from the actor's position. Only friends are freely chosen and engage in non-instrumental social interaction on a basis of equality, and although people might wish to choose friends occupying higher positions, the reciprocal nature of friendship entails a pressure to equality.[8]

We did consider using other relationships, and some have been used by other investigators, but all have significant drawbacks by comparison with friendship. Preliminary analysis in the pilot study pointed to the unsuitability of neighbours. We found that the occupations of neighbours were widely spread and not well related to the occupations of friends. The choice of neighbourhood is largely determined by economic considerations, and one finds younger members of eventually lucrative careers and older members of less lucrative ones living side by side. Friends, however, appeared to be chosen from those following the same or similar careers. The results from the main analysis, which we shall shortly present, confirmed these early findings.

Fathers or fathers-in-law are, next to friends, likely to be closest to respondents in stratification terms. Fathers are generally taken as defining at least their initial positions, and there would appear to be reason for arguing that there is a tendency for men to marry the daughters of status equals.[9] Oldman and Illsley (1966) have argued for an examination of stratification arrangements using occupations of fathers-in-law taken from marriage licences. There are, however, a number of drawbacks to this method, for instance the information is not very precisely or systematically collected and the Registrar General's office does not code it, though it is possible that in certain circumstances they

[8] For a further discussion of friendship and stratification, see Dixon, (1976).

[9] See, e.g. Lauman (1966, pp. 77, 78), Hunt (1940), Centers (1949). Such a pattern is observable in both our White-Collar and General samples.

might be prepared to undertake this work. A general problem with both father's occupation and even more with that of father-in-law, if the information is to be collected in an interview, is the inaccuracy of recall on the part of the respondent (see e.g. Featherman and Hauser, 1973). Also there are problems arising from the tendency for men to marry in a limited range of ages early in their working careers. These are similar to problems involved in using father's occupation, which we shall consider shortly.

Two studies have used data from cross-tabulations of respondents' occupations with their fathers' occupations. Blau and Duncan (1967, pp. 69–75), used the same technique as Lauman and Guttman on a sample of the US population. Rather than Lauman and Guttman's three dimensions they found only two, the first of which is, they argue, a representation of the socio-economic status of occupations. The second is not readily interpretable.

Their results showed not only a smaller dimensionality but also a better fit between their data and the derived solution, which they take as evidence for greater coherence in their data. However, while Lauman and Guttman had 55 occupational categories, they had only 17, and the fact that their results appear better is mainly due to this difference. At the time they were writing there was an assumption that the estimates of the goodness of fit between the derived solutions and the data did not vary with the numbers of points to be placed in the space. Subsequent work showed this not to be true, and a 'better' fit on the statistics available is to be expected merely because fewer points are to be fitted.

MacDonald more recently (Hope, 1972, pp. 211–34) has used Kruskal's MDSCAL programme to examine the regularities contained in data collected by Benjamin for 2600 occupied males who were a systematic sample of the 1951 census schedules for England and Wales. The respondents' occupations were taken from these schedules, and their fathers' occupations were traced from their birth certificates. MacDonald used the resulting data for both inflow and outflow tables in separate analyses. He found that a two dimensional solution is preferable for both his inflow and his outflow data, but the dimensions of the solution are not easily interpretable. By rotating axes he can produce a dimension that might be regarded as a status hierarchy, but the fit is not close and the second dimension is uninterpretable. In these circumstances he argues for extreme caution in the use of the method.

However, there are a number of difficulties in any use of father's occupation, and some of these are particularly acute in MacDonald's approach. In both Blau and Duncan's work and that of MacDonald, respondents are spread through all the ages of the working population. This means that fathers are drawn from a number of different generations who were in the labour force at quite different periods. Furthermore the fathers' occupations relate to specific points in the sons' lives—age 16 for Blau and Duncan and birth for MacDonald. Thus the occupations cover a period of about 40 years and go back, in MacDonald's case, to 1886. It seems unlikely that there have not been changes in the occupational structures during this period which would alter the social significance of holding a particular job.

Probably more important, however, is the way that taking a particular age for sons tends to concentrate the fathers in a narrow age range very different from the age distributions of the sons. (We may also note that a similar, though less extreme, effect occurs in taking father-in-law's occupation at the time of respondent's marriage.) From available demographic data it would appear that the mean age of fathers at the birth of sons over the relevant period of MacDonald's study was about 28 years of age. The distribution of ages around this point for fathers is likely to be highly concentrated with a skew towards the younger ages. We shall see in a later chapter that there is very considerable career development with age and that the distribution of the population by job categories changes very considerably. In these circumstances even if fathers and sons are following the same careers, there will be apparent inconsistencies in the figures. The fathers in Blau and Duncan's study would be in their early forties, and fathers-in-law around 50, different career stages which may not be so far out of line with the majority of respondents' occupations, but will still cause a substantial degree of inconsistency.

Furthermore, fathers' and sons' occupations are commonly used in the study of mobility. Apart from the problems already outlined, the differences between their occupations may be seen as a measure of inter-generational mobility. To this extent they can hardly serve as measures of the same position.[10] If the mobility, in terms of mean distance moved and distribution around the mean, were identical for those starting at each point in the structure, then it would not really matter. But of course this is not possible at the limits of the scale and empirically does not happen elsewhere, so here is another source of inconsistency. Fathers-in-law come out rather better, often being at a point of arrival in a young man's career rather than at the starting point. However, marriage is

[10] Goldthorpe and Hope (1974, p. 10) make the complementary point that a scale so created is contaminated for mobility studies.

usually early in a man's life, before much career mobility has taken place.

It should be clear that shortcomings in the findings are to be expected in studies which use the occupations of fathers or fathers-in-law. Lumping them together with neighbours and friends is only likely to compound the problem. Thus the obvious choice seems to be to take friends on their own.

SCALE CONSTRUCTION

In considering how we constructed the scale it will be as well to start with a brief review of the basic data. They were gathered from our White-Collar respondents—1918 non-manual workers in occupations ranging from foremen and clerk to senior manager and professional, employed in 32 varied establishments within a sixty mile radius of Cambridge. In the course of the interview they were asked to give us their own occupations, their fathers' occupations, the occupations of their nearest neighbours and those of four people with whom they were friendly outside work. They were encouraged to choose occupations other than their own, although friends in their own occupations would be accepted if no others could be given. We did this to ensure a spread of occupations of friends as perfect self choice would have been unsuitable for our analysis, which depends upon differences in the likelihood of interaction with those in other occupations. The procedure has the effect of forcing a diversity upon friendship choices. From our subsequent research it would appear that such a device was unnecessary, and we have not used it in our later research.

Not all respondents could give us either four friends or four neighbours, and in general there was an inverse relationship between stratification position and the failure to name four friends. All of the occupations were initially classified according to the OPCS *Classification of Occupations, 1966*, and then reclassified to the *1970* version when that became available.

There are two separate ways in which we can examine the coherence of interaction inherent in the friendship figures. The first is to approach the problem through the friendship choices made by our respondents. Following this line, we isolated all occupations in which we had ten or more respondents, which amounted to 40, and calculated dissimilarities between them using the index of dissimilarity. This is the measure used by Blau and Duncan in the study mentioned above, and involves in our case summing the positive percentage differences between the distribution of friendship choices for pairs of occupations. Where there is a complete overlap of friendship choices, the index of dissimilarity has a value of zero, and where there are no friendship choices in common it has a value of 100. The resulting symmetric matrix was then fed into the MINISSA program developed by Roskam and Lingoes. This programme uses the basic algorithm developed by Kruskal, and used in his MDSCAL program which we mentioned above when discussing MacDonald's work, but employs somewhat different procedures for making initial and subsequent configurations.

The second way of approaching the problem is through the occupations of the friends ordered by the occupations of respondents who chose them. As mentioned above we encouraged our respondents to choose friends in occupations other than their own. Partly as a consequence of this, the range of occupations chosen was fairly wide and was not restricted to the non-manual area. We were able to choose 85 occupations which contained 20 or more friends, and these occupations were in all areas of the stratification system. A similar procedure to that followed for respondents' occupations produced a symmetric matrix of dissimilarities among those 85, which was fed into a version of the MINISSA program specially modified to cope with a matrix of this size.

We would expect the results of the two methods to be basically similar if they are measuring the same structure, and it will become clear that this is in fact the case. However, before entering into a discussion of the results in any detail, we must examine the problem of the appropriate structures of the solutions in these two analyses.

In some cases users of multi-dimensional scaling techniques have been concerned merely to confirm structures whose characteristics can be obtained from external data. The techniques, however, are most useful when they are the most appropriate methods for examining the structure of data. This is the situation in the present case, which means that although we shall later relate our results to those obtained by other methods, we can not use this strictly as validation. This being so, some internal indication of the quality of results is needed. The available internal measure is S or Stress. As we noted earlier, it is a measure of the deviation of the derived solution from a perfect fit with original data, and is similar to a residual sum of squares. Rough guides for the evaluation of solutions in terms of their Stress values were suggested by Kruskal (1964) and endorsed by Roskam (1968). Unfortunately these rules were created on the assumption that Stress does not vary with the number of points to be placed in the space—an assumption which has proved to be incorrect. Two Monte Carlo studies (Stenson and Knoll, 1969, Klahr, 1969) have examined this problem of the distribution of Stress values, and they show clearly that for randomly generated interpoint distances, Stress values increase with the number of points.

These studies provide a better basis for the interpretation of Stress values. From one of them (Stenson and Knoll, 1969) we have accepted what the authors describe as a rule for the acceptance of the null hypothesis (that dissimilarity data are random and there is no inherent structure). 'Acceptance' must here be understood as conditional—not a positive establishment of randomness, which is not strictly possible, but a failure to reject the null hypothesis, which is the important point statistically. The hypothesis should only be accepted where the obtained Stress value is closer to the mean Stress value for their randomly generated sets of data than twice the width of the range of Stress values in those sets of data.

In other words, where Stress values are below the bottom of this range, the solution is to be regarded as significant, i.e. non-random. The extent to which, in the *respondents'* analysis, our solutions, in from one to six dimensions, fail to meet the condition of randomness can be seen in Table 2.1. The right hand column gives extent to which the observed Stress falls below the random Stress mean, divided by the range of random Stress values. If this is less than two, the solution cannot be distinguished from random, while for greater values the null hypothesis

TABLE 2.1 Comparison of stress values of randomly-generated data and inter-occupation data

	A *Stress value* *of solution* *of occu-* *pation data* *(40 points)*	*B*[a] *Mean stress* *value for* *random inter-* *point data* *(40 points)*	*Range of* *random* *stress* *values*	$\dfrac{B-A}{Range}$
One dimension	.30	.54	<.01	>24
Two dimensions	.19	.36	,,	>17
Three dimensions	.13	.26	,,	>13
Four dimensions	.11	.21	,,	>10
Five dimensions	.09	.16	,,	>7
Six dimensions	.08	.13	,,	>5

[a]SOURCE
Stenson and Knoll (1969)

is rejected. Every one of our solutions meets the criterion for being judged non-random.

It is not clear, however, what status is to be given to the solutions for dimensions above one. Stenson and Knoll did not undertake the task of examining the distribution of stress values in a higher dimensionality for a non-random solution in a lower dimensionality. If in our case, for example, the interpoint distances are an imperfect reflection of a single dimension, i.e. they are accounted for by one dimension plus a large number of errors each affecting only small parts of the data, then an improvement in Stress will still be found with increases in dimensionality despite the 'random' nature of the errors. Kruskal (1964) has suggested that an indication of dimensionality may be gained by examining the Stress values for solutions of increasing dimensionality for an elbow effect—a sudden decline in the improvement of Stress values. Dimensions at and after the elbow would be regarded as non-significant. Unfortunately elbow effects do not always occur and Klahr (1969) has shown that they can occur merely as a consequence of noise, though this is more likely with a small number of points.

More recently a number of writers have proposed techniques to determine the 'true' dimensionality of data, which includes random errors of various levels. Most of these studies deal with small sets of data in a limited range of dimensions (see e.g. Wagenaar and Padmos, 1971), but Spence and Graef (1974) deal with configurations of from 12 to 36 points and spaces of from one to four true dimensions. This is still well below our 85 points in the *Friends'* solution, but comes close to the 40 points of our *Respondents'* solution. Spence and Graef used known configurations to compute dissimilarities which could be fed into a multi-dimensional scaling procedure. The 'distances' so produced were then perturbed by various levels of error. Stress coefficients were then obtained, by level of error and by the recovered dimensionality, for the different 'true' configurations. From this Monte-Carlo procedure two methods of determining the underlying structure of empirically obtained dissimilarities were proposed. Perhaps the more readily interpretable is the procedure suggested by Wagenaar and Padmos (1971). This directly addresses the problem of whether the reduction in stress obtained by adding another dimension is sufficient to indicate that the additional dimension is significant.

First of all the stress for an obtained one dimensional solution is compared with the stress for a true unidimensional configuration with the same number of points and the level of error corresponding to that stress value is noted. The associated 'predicted' stress in a two dimensional solution is then noted. If the actual obtained stress is less than that predicted, it is concluded that the second dimension contains some information and that the appropriate dimensionality is at least two. The obtained two dimensional stress is then compared with the true two dimensional stress and the appropriate error level determined. The 'predicted' stress for three dimensions is then compared with the obtained stress to see if the third dimension contains information. The procedure is repeated until the 'predicted' stress does not deviate from the obtained stress. When this happens the appropriate dimensionality is taken to be the underlying dimensionality associated with the last significant number of dimensions.

We used this method to compare the stress values of *Respondents'* solutions (containing 40 points) with their figures for the various 36 point configurations. The results suggested that there were more than four dimensions (the maximum number about which they have information) in our data. However there are certain weaknesses in the method. There is a subjective element in deciding whether or not the deviation of observed from 'predicted' stress is small enough to be ignored. More importantly, once the level of error is estimated for a given 'true' dimensionality, 'predicted' levels of stress can be obtained for solutions in any number of dimensions and not just for one additional dimension.[11] These can give contradictory results. Thus in our data, when we compare stress levels with those for true two dimensional data, we find not only that the stress in the three dimensional solution suggests more than two dimensions, but also that stress in the one dimensional solution suggests less than two dimensions! Indeed this latter result follows from the fact that the level of stress we obtain for the one dimensional solution is too low to be compatible with any of their figures for two or more 'true' dimensions, even with perfect fit (zero error). In particular our stress level is below their level for one dimension in perfect two dimensional data. This seems to strongly suggest a one dimensional structure.

The contradictory results we have obtained reflect a general inadequacy of the methods but are less of a problem than they may seem.

---

[11] The method devised by Spence and Graef (1974) makes use of this fact for solutions in from one to five dimensions. Essentially it finds the 'true' dimensionality for which there is an error value giving, for obtained solutions in different dimensions, the set of stress values closest to the observed stress values. For our data the result is two dimensions, but the fit is very poor. Indeed, for reasons we will explain, we think a poor fit is inevitable for empirical data such as ours, and we have correspondingly little confidence in the method.

It is essential to consider what it is we are doing in deciding on a number of dimensions. For data of a given dimensionality with *random* distortions it is quite clear, but empirical data is rarely, if ever, like this. 'Error' in empirical data is not truly random but reflects various aspects of reality. We have no doubt there are a large number of dimensions in our data, each of which adds some information, and in this sense the true dimensionality is high. The same would be true of most empirical material. However, the aim is frequently to establish a limited number of more important dimensions, which may then be interpretable. The point is that we are concerned not only with the number of dimensions but also the configuration of points within those dimensions. As Spence and Graef (1974, p. 340) rightly observe, these methods 'may be sensitive to the nature of the error in the data or the distribution of the distances'. Our results so far suggest one major dimension and several 'true' dimensions, but as yet this interpretation can only be very tentative.

Since an examination of stress values is therefore unlikely alone to yield a satisfactory approach to the dimensionality of data, we have chosen, in addition, to look at differences in the proportion of variance due to each dimension in our various solutions. In general one must approach with caution an interpretation of data which takes the proportion of variance due to a dimension of a solution as an indication of the size of a substantive dimension. Monotonic distortion can add dimensions to solutions and also increase the size of dimensions. This problem is particularly acute in a large dimensionality with a small number of points to be fitted. In this case, with such large numbers, the problem is less acute, but we shall return to a discussion of it later. For the moment an examination of the relation between the contribution made by a dimension in higher and lower dimensional solutions will prove instructive. Fig. 2.1 shows that in *Respondents'* solutions, in three to six dimensions only, the first dimension explains a great deal more than succeeding dimensions. The rapid decline from the first to the second dimension and the gradual and regular decline thereafter is clearly illustrated.

The strong elbow effect in this diagram indicates that in all solutions the first dimension is very much larger than all succeeding dimensions. On the other hand the second and subsequent dimensions do not show even a hint of the same relation to succeeding dimensions. In each solution in from three to six dimensions the second dimension has little more of the variance than the third dimension, and so on.[12]

---

[12] Furthermore, only the first accounts for more than the randomly 'expected' proportion of variance.

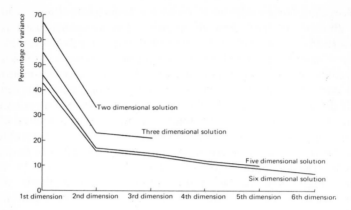

FIG. 2.1 Proportion of variance due to each dimension in respondents' solutions of from two to six dimensions

This strongly suggests a single large dimension in our data. If this interpretation is correct, we would expect that the first dimension would be fairly stable in solutions of increasing dimensionality. This we can test by correlating the first dimensions of the various solutions to examine their consistency, and when we do so we find that they are indeed very well related, and that their relationship becomes increasingly close with increasing dimensionality. Table 2.2 gives the squared correlations—the relative explained variance—between first dimensions in the solutions in one up to six dimensions.

TABLE 2.2 R^2s of the first dimensions in respondents' solutions

	One dimensional solution	Two dimensional solution	Three dimensional solution	Four dimensional solution	Five dimensional solution
Two dimensional solution	.934				
Three dimensional solution	.905	.990			
Four dimensional solution	.891	.994	.996		
Five dimensional solution	.880	.972	.994	.998	
Six dimensional solution	.870	.975	.992	.999	.999

The second and subsequent dimensions should not show the same regularity if they are not important substantive dimensions. There should, of course, be some correlation between the second dimensions in solutions of different dimensionality, and there must be an eventual convergence of values between adjacent solutions as the dimensionality is increased, but there may be considerable initial variation. Table 2.3 shows the R^2s for solutions in from two to six dimensions. This shows the relationships between second dimensions as less strong than those

TABLE 2.3 R^2s of the second dimensions in respondents' solutions

	Three dimensional solution	Three dimensional solution	Four dimensional solution	Five dimensional solution
Three dimensional solution	.791			
Four dimensional solution	.742	.540		
Five dimensional solution	.694	.494	.781	
Six dimensional solution	.639	.412	.647	.324

between first dimensions. In addition the second dimension is defined by a small number of points. If we exclude from the correlations between the second dimensions the two cases at each extreme of the second dimension in the lower dimensional solution, then the correlations decline considerably. Also we see that there is not the same pattern of consistency in the relations between different pairs of the second dimension.

So far, then, we think it can be taken as established that there is one major dimension in the *Respondents'* solution, and dimensions beyond the first make no important interpretable contribution. The same is true of the *Friends'* solution. As we would expect, since substantially more points are involved, the first dimension accounts for slightly less of the variance. Otherwise the results are essentially the same. This finding, of one major dimension, is supported by work done by Coxon and Jones (1978, p. 75) who argue that the structure of their data confirms our results previously reported (Stewart *et al.*, 1973). Using dissimilarities obtained from rating data, they performed an MDS analysis, though for fewer occupations. They conclude, 'the result . . . is both surprising and unexpected: by far the most acceptable fit is for a map of *one*, or possibly two, "true" underlying dimensions.' That their conclusion is based on data which are so different—mean ratings as opposed to friendship choices—is a strong confirmation of the underlying structure.

However, this does not settle the dimensionality of the solution. We may have concluded that only one dimension is of interest, but from the solution in how many dimensions should it be taken? We have used a series of approaches to the question of the nature of underlying structure, but the ideal dimensionality for the representation of that structure is not easy to determine exactly. If data were entirely free from noise of any kind, all that would be necessary would be to find the minimum dimensionality with zero stress. By definition that would represent the most parsimonious resolution of the inequalities in the data. However, though the most parsimonious solution, it would not be the only possible solution of the inequalities. The Kruskal algorithm requires only a monotonically increasing function relating input inequalities to derived distances. It does not further constrain the function, and unfortunately this is not a sufficient requirement to give a unique solution across spaces of different dimensionality. If, for example, a solution is sought in three dimensions for a set of inequalities constructed to be truly one dimensional, then a zero stress solution will be found that resolves all of the inequalities, and which gives non-zero values to the second and third dimensions. A one dimensional input will appear as three dimensional in the outputs. The larger the number of dimensions of the solution, the greater the size of the extra dimensions.

If all data were perfect this would present no problem. The entirely adequate solution in the smallest number of dimensions would be chosen. However, most data to which these techniques are applied are not of this sort. There are likely to be random variations within the inequalities, in which case increasing the dimensions will continue to improve the stress values, but in the process the underlying structure can be distorted. It is possible to specify the type of function which creates these 'ghost' dimensions in perfect data, but in imperfect data the shape may be distorted. From an examination of constructed data we have found that best representation of a known structure which is distorted with random variations is the solution with the dimensionality of the underlying structure.[13] The stress values of this optimum solution may be quite high, and adding dimensions will reduce them, giving a false

---

[13] Other writers have come to similar conclusions. See e.g. Sherman (1972). Spence & Graef (1974); also refer to unpublished works by Spence (1970) and Isaac & Poor (1972).

impression of increasing adequacy. With constructed data the required answers are known, but in real problems we have to make our decisions on the basis of the data themselves.

Returning to our data, if there are indeed dimensions above one, even if they do not extend over a very wide area, they can have distorting effects if not accommodated in the solutions. We have shown that there is no stable second dimension in our data in solutions in up to six dimensions, but that does not necessarily imply that there are no substantive dimensions other than the first. Smaller dimensions after the first can be disturbed by 'random' effects. The method makes the optimum relation of derived distances to dissimilarities in the space provided, and if a second substantive dimension is not large and 'random' errors are considerable, the values on the derived second dimension will reflect a diversity of influences. In these circumstances we do not believe it is fruitful to attempt an interpretation of dimensions other than the first, but the process of deciding the correct number of dimensions, from which to take the representation of the first dimension, involves a decision as to when the addition of further dimensions to the space of the solution leads to a distortion of the first dimension, rather than improving it by extracting the influence of other real dimensions of some size. As it happens, the problem is less acute than might have been feared. We are fortunate in that the first dimension stabilises rapidly, and is virtually unchanged in solutions with six or more dimensions. Clearly there is no need to go beyond six dimensions. The first dimension of six is also very similar to those in four and five dimensions; indeed the difference between four and six dimensions, for respondents, is less than that between four and five. It seems, therefore, that we may conclude that the solution is virtually stable by six dimensions for both friends and respondents. On the other hand, there are progressive changes as the dimensionality is increased, which we would expect to represent small substantive dimension. Such dimensions are to be expected from both situs effects and the effects of differential choice of friends in respondents' own occupations due to different availability. Also, from inspection, the main changes with increased dimensionality were intuitively appropriate. With these considerations in mind, we came to the conclusion that a solution should be chosen in the lowest number of dimensions, which gives a stable solution when compared with solutions in lower and higher dimensions.[14] We

[14] We were also guided, to some extent, by the shapes of the curves plotted as in Fig. 2.2 for different dimensionality, compared with those of known data with random distortions in solutions in too many or too few dimensions.

therefore chose the solutions in six dimensions for both the respondents' data and the friends' data.

The results of the two analyses are given in Tables 2.4 and 2.5. The

TABLE 2.4 Occupations and occupational scores for respondents' solution

	Score
Warehousemen	−130
Guards and related workers	−123
Foremen engineers (so described)	−112
Foremen chemical workers	−111
Foremen rubber workers	−93
Foremen shoe workers and leather workers	−81
Foremen non-skilled engineering workers	−76
Foremen glass workers	−57
Foremen skilled engineering workers	−57
Foremen warehousemen	−46
Technical and engineering assistants	−45
Foremen inspectors in engineering	−43
Supervisory laboratory assistants	−43
Laboratory assistants	−33
Clerks	−26
Draughtsmen	−21
Office managers	−14
Technicians	−6
Supervisory clerks	−3
Supervisory technicians	6
Supervisory draughtsmen	18
Service managers in industry	28
Accountants	30
Civil service executive officers	31
Social workers	34
Managers in engineering	35
Personnel managers	38
Mechanical engineers	39
Architects and surveyors	41
Managers in industries other than engineering	50
Electronic engineers	51
Sales managers	59
Chemists	60
Professional workers N.E.C.	65
Physical and biological scientists	69
Senior officials in national government	70
Technologists	71
Electrical engineers	100
Senior officials in local government	107
Civil engineers	118

TABLE 2.5 Occupations and scores for friends' solution

Rank	OPCS no.	(*Major categories italicised. See text*) Occupations	Score
1.	–	Foremen engineers (so described)	−132
2.	089 090 092	*Foremen: workers in rubber* Workers in plastic Workers in other production process	−108
3.	098	Construction workers	−101
4.	053	Inspectors (metal and electrical Goods)	−88
5.	129 130	*Postmen and mail sorters* Messengers	−87
6.	089 090 092	*Workers in rubber* Workers in plastic Other production process workers	−86
7.	114	*Labourers*, all industries 107−14	−75
8.	030	Electrical engineers (so described)	−75
9.	143	Shop managers, food sales	−70
10.	100 99 101	*Painters and decorators* Aerographers and paint sprayers Coach painters	−70
11.	136	Warehousemen, storekeepers and assistants	−66
12.	172 169	*Service sport and recreation workers n.e.c.* Athletes, sportsmen and related workers	−59
13.	045 046	*Plumbers, gasfitters, lead burners* Pipe fitters, heating engineers	−58
14.	029 039 044 047 054	*Routine engineering* *Assemblers (electrical and electtronic)* Machine tool operators Electro-platers, Dippers etc. Press workers and stampers General assemblers and other engineering process workers	−58
15.	153	Guards and related workers	−56
16.	055 056 058	*Carpenters and joiners* Cabinet makers Pattern makers	−51
17.	040 041	*Foremen, skilled engineering* Toolmakers and tool room fitters Motor mechanics	−48

T ABLE 2.5 (*continued*)

Rank	OPCS no.	(*Major categories italicised. See text*) Occupations	Score
	042	Maintenance fitters and millwrights	
	043	Fitters n.e.c.	
	034	Steel erectors; riggers	
	035	Metal plate workers; riveters	
18.	085	*Compositors*	−47
	087	*Printers (so described)*	
	088	Printing workers n.e.c.	
19.		*Food workers*	−47
	078	Bakers and pastry cooks	
	079	Butchers and meat cutters	
	080	Brewers, winemakers and related workers	
20.	152	Police constables	−46
21.	050	*Precision instrument makers and repairers*	−46
	049	Watch and chronometer makers and repairers	
22.	062	*Cutters, lasters, sewers, footwear and related workers*	−44
	061	Shoemakers and shoe repairers	
	063	Leather workers n.e.c.	
23.		*Transport workers*	−39
	118	Drivers, motormen, secondmen, railway engine	
	119	Railway guards	
	120	Drivers of buses, coaches	
	121	Drivers of other road passenger vehicles	
	122	Drivers of road goods vehicles	
	131	Bus conductors	
	116	Deck and engineroom ratings, barge and boatmen	
	132	Porters, ticket collectors, railway	
	135	Workers in transport and communications n.e.c.	
24.		*Skilled engineering workers*	−37
	033	Sheet metal workers	
	037	Turners	
	038	Machine tool setters	
	040	Tool makers and tool room fitters	
	041	Motor mechanics	
	042	Maintenance fitters and millwrights	
	043	Fitters n.e.c. machine erectors etc.	
	048	Metal workers n.e.c.	
25.	027	*Electricians*	−35
	026	Linesmen and cable jointers	
	024	Electrical and electronic fitters	

TABLE 2.5 (*continued*)

Rank	OPCS no.	(*Major categories italicised. See text*) Occupations	Score
26.	139	Clerks and cashiers	−34
27.	138	Office managers	−34
28.	208	Painters, sculptors and related creative artists	−33
29.		*Foremen: routine engineering*	−32
	029	*Assemblers (electrical and electronic)*	
	039	Machine tool operators	
	044	Electroplaters, dip platers etc.	
	047	Press workers and stampers	
	054	General assemblers and other metal etc. Process workers	
30.	024	Radio and radar mechanics	−32
31.	139	Head clerks	−24
32.	041	Motor mechanic, self-employed	−22
33.	144	Shop assistants	−21
34.	141	Typists and secretaries	−20
35.	–	Engineers (so described)	−18
36.	207	Actors, entertainers, musicians, etc.	−17
37.	012	Chemical workers	−17
38.	143	Shop keepers (food sales)	−15
39.	096	Clerks of works	−13
40.	025	Telephone installers and repair men (P.O. technicians)	−13
41.	139	Civil servants and local authority officials (so described)	−11
42.	154	Publicans and inn keepers	−11
43.	143	Shop managers (non-food sales)	−9
44.	183	Nurses and sisters	−5
45.	143	Shopkeeper, self-employed (non-food sales)	−5
46.	150	Salesmen, services; valuers and auctioneers, self-employed	0
47.	218	Draughtsmen	3
48.	142	Civil service executive officers	7
49.	147	Garage proprietors	7

T ABLE 2.5 (*continued*)

Rank	OPCS no.	(*Major categories italicised. See text*) Occupations	Score
50.	219	Laboratory assistants, technicians	9
51.	215	Social welfare and related workers	14
52.	213	Clergymen	15
53.	096	Builders, self-employed	15
54.	003 004 005 006	*Agricultural workers* Tractor men Gardeners and groundsmen Woodmen and foresters	17
55.	148	Commercial travellers, manufacturers' agents	19
56.	180	Company directors (also 175–7)	19
57.	055 056 058	*Carpenters and joiners, self-employed* Cabinet makers Pattern makers	21
58.	206	Journalists	21
59.	220	Technical and related workers n.e.c.	21
60.	002	Farm managers	22
61.	002	Farmers (self-employed)	22
62.	209 210	*Accountants* Company secretaries	24
63.	150	Salesmen, services; valuers, auctioneers	25
64.	180	Service managers	35
65.	173	Senior government officials	40
66.	177	Managers in mining and production n.e.c.	42
67.	175	Managers in engineering and allied trades	46
68.	149	Finance, insurance bankers and financial agents	47
69.	212 211	*Architects* *Surveyors*	56
70.	193 194	*School teachers* Teachers n.e.c.	58
71.	204	Chemists	60
72.	195	Civil, structural, municipal engineers	61
73.	217	Professional workers n.e.c.	71

TABLE 2.5 (*continued*)

Rank	OPCS no.	(*Major categories italicised. See text*) Occupations	Score
74.	179	Sales managers	72
75.	174	Local government senior officers	84
76.	196	Mechanical engineers	84
77.	178	Personnel managers	85
78.	181	Medical practitioners	86
79.	205	Physical and biological scientists	91
80.	193	Headmasters	93
81.	203 200 201 202	*Technologists n.e.c.* Planning, production engineers Engineers n.e.c. Metallurgists	98
82.	214	Lawyers	101
83.	192	University teachers	119
84.	198	Electronic engineers	144
85.	197	Electrical engineers	159

figures in these tables are the values actually obtained on the first dimensions, but are a little different from those we used in constructing the final scale. As we shall explain, it was necessary to modify the values before combining them, However, the ordering in the separate scales, and hence their interpretation in terms of ordered occupations, is unaffected.

How then are the results to be interpreted? Looking first at the *Respondents'* solution there are a number of striking features. Firstly there is the complete division between the groups of foremen (and guards and warehousemen) and the more traditional white-collar groups. This is in contrast to the findings of Hope and Goldthorpe in both their pilot study and their main study. They speculate that the lack of distinction between manual and lower white-collar groups is a reflection of relatively recent changes in the class structure; but our interpretation, in line with later chapters, is somewhat different, and we shall return to this point when we discuss the relationship between the scales.

Secondly there is the division in the solution between low and intermediate white-collar jobs such as clerks, draughtsmen and technicians and their supervisors on the one hand, and managers on the other. Once again the division is complete. A third feature is the division of managerial jobs from professional jobs. This time the division is less than complete. Though the top eight groups are professionals or senior government officers, five groups of professionals occur below the highest group of managers—sales managers. To some extent this may be due to some ambiguity in the categories. Accountants, for example, do not include only members of the most prestigious professional associations; architects and surveyors have a fair proportion of surveyors; and social workers cover a wide variety of training and seniority. However, it is also true that managerial categories are extremely heterogeneous. The practice of separating managers by size of establishment as does the OPCS and the US Bureau of the Census does not really allow for a meaningful distinction of senior and junior managers. Our respondents all worked in large establishments, but people of very different circumstances were included under the general managerial titles. In research in progress we have established far finer differentiations. With these reservations in mind we would not argue for a clear distinction of managerial and professional jobs. In general the results make good intuitive sense.

On the results of the *Friends'* solution we would place a little less reliance. The two solutions are broadly similar, and the occupations common to both correlate 0.93. However, the non-common occupations are only partially represented in the data in that they are chosen by our sample of respondents who are all in white-collar employment. It is possible that a sample reflecting a wider segment of the population would produce different results. That said, the results once again make fair intuitive sense. The occupational groupings of the friends' solution are rather wider than those for the respondents' solution, and we present all of the titles that fall in each category. In most cases one of the titles is far more important than any of the others in terms of the number of cases occurring, and where this is true that title has been underlined. In general there is a skilled/non-skilled division among manual workers, though in this lower range of the scale there is an important difference from the Hope-Goldthorpe findings. Their respondents place foremen unambiguously above the groups over whom they exercise control, while in our data they are placed very close to the appropriate manual groups. This may be a consequence of using a white-collar sample, but there are good reasons for supposing that it may reflect patterns of social relationships. An examination of our data shows that foremen appear to maintain working-class life styles in terms of the neighbourhoods they live in and the types of leisure time activities they engage in. While it would seem reasonable to rate foremen above manual workers in reputational terms they probably remain members of the groups from which they are recruited. In keeping with this interpretation, since the respondents were white-collar workers, the foremen emerge as slightly below the workers because they tend to be older and more firmly integrated in their section of the stratification hierarchy.

The manual/non-manual distinction is not quite so complete in this solution, though it is still very clear in general, and just above the lowest of the non-manual occupations we have a group of self-employed small businessmen. In among this group are located farmers, farm managers and farm workers. We do not believe that this is an accurate reflection of the patterns of association of the last group. Our speculation is that since our sample is predominantly urban, there will be some positive relationship between income and living in the villages and countryside where farmers and farm workers may be met on a relatively casual basis. An examination of rural patterns of interaction would, we believe, produce different results. Above the small businessmen come the managers and professionals. Once again there is a tendency for professionals to come above managers, but there is even more overlap in this case then there was in the *Respondents'* solution.

The next stage in the construction of our scale was to correct the values on the two solutions for an element of distortion resulting from the method. A feature of the statistic used to calculate stress is that it can minimise the discrepancies between the order of dissimilarities in the original data and distances in the derived solutions by placing points which are involved in reversals of order as far as possible from the centroid of the space. In the case of points close to the centroid, the constraints upon the solution in terms of the ordering of distances are so great that not much variation in the positioning of points is possible. However, the closer points are to the edge of the space, the less they constrained towards the centroid. In these conditions the points most distant from the centroid tend to be forced outwards. In the case of our data we are concerned only with the distances on the first dimension, but the first dimension is so much larger than the other dimension that a similar situation applies. As an illustration of the problem, Fig. 2.2 shows the values on the first dimension of the *Friends'* solution plotted against the ranks of these values, that is, in effect, against an assumption of equal intervals between the points. The

Respondents' solution gives a very similar plot.

We do not wish to suggest that an equal interval solution should be applied, but we do not believe that there is any reason, outside technical features of the method, for supposing that interpoint distances should increase with distance from the mean. It would seem that an assumption of random distribution of interpoint distances would be more reasonable in the absence of further information. This implies that the points should be distributed about a straight line instead of the curve in Fig. 2.2. We decided, therefore, to adopt a prodecure to modify the distances of the solution.

We first identified a regression curve to fit the points in the space of Fig. 2.2, and similarly for the *Respondents'* solution. For this purpose we chose quintics. Then, for each solution, we projected the curve onto a straight line and projected the actual points proportionately. This had the desired effect for the *Respondents'* solution and more or less for the *Friends'* solution, but with the larger number of points there remained a slight tendency to curve at the ends, that is, the interpoint distances at the extremes of the scale still appear rather large. It would seem, therefore, that some more complex exponential function might fit the data better, but the procedure used has the merit of simplicity, while further refinement would have little effect. At this stage we dropped one or two of the occupational categories of the *Friends'* solution, because we considered that they were too vague and their composition was too heterogeneous.

The next step was to combine the two solutions. In order to do this, the solutions had to be expressed in equivalent terms. It will be noted that the occupations at the top ends of the two solutions are common to both, while warehousemen, guards and some groups of foremen are close to the bottom of both. We therefore assumed that the solutions covered the same range, and for each we gave values to produce a mean of zero and a standard deviation of one. Where occupations were common to the two solutions, we took the values as separate estimates of the same position, summed them and divided by two. The remaining occupations which occurred in only one or other of the solutions were given their standardised value on their scale.[15] In the light of our earlier discussion, we then combined manual workers and their foremen,

---

[15] In fact we tested various schemes of differential weighting and different methods of standardisation. This relatively simple method produced results which were very similar to those of more complex methods. Indeed the results varied little by method.

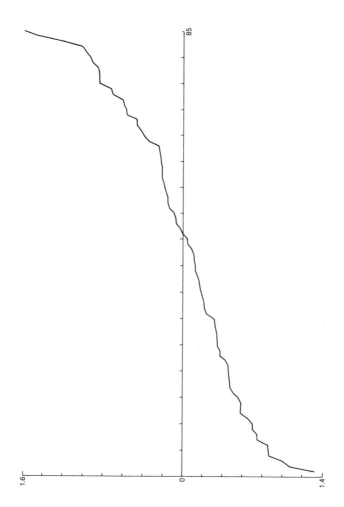

Fig. 2.2 Raw scale distances by rank (unit interval): Friends' solution

giving them the mean score. Also, where more than one of our original categories, based on the 1966 OPCS scheme, are combined in the 1970 scheme, we give the mean value in Table 2.6.

There was one exception to this procedure, and it illustrates our general attitude towards the results. Farm workers were taken from the scale at this point because we did not believe that their scale value was an accurate reflection of their stratification experience. We have already outlined our reservations about allowing the results of research procedures to override strongly held intuitions. Procedures are seldom so well adapted to theoretical considerations as to warrant an automatic assumption that in all respects they are superior to prior intuitions. On this point we agreed strongly with Goldthorpe and Hope (1974, p. 1) on the assessment of results when they write:

> Before, however, we embark on our presentation of this case, it may be useful to make explicit a distinction which authors of social and psychological measures, and even writers on the theory of test construction, sometimes blur or ignore: that is, the distinction between the procedures which one carries out in attempts to produce a valid and reliable measuring instrument, and the evidence one is able to bring forward for the degree of validity and reliability that the instrument actually possesses. Constructional procedures have the sort of bearing on the success of a scale that scaffolding has on a building: the scaffolding may contribute to the erection of a sound and imposing structure, but the final judgement of the critical onlooker will be passed on the building when the scaffolding is no longer in view.

It would seem from their subsequent discussion, however, that they hold a more formal and narrowly conceived notion of these problems than do we. We believe that the validation of scales needs constant recourse to the theory of their use as well as the procedures of their production. Theoretical confusion will be reflected in poor methodology, and mistakes are more likely in the link between theories and appropriate methods than in the operation of methods. One cannot ignore results, but on the other hand they cannot be uncritically accepted.

We take our results to be, first, a strong indication of a structuring, in stratification terms, of patterns of association on the basis of friendship, and only second, a less than entirely adequate scale of stratification arrangements. However, despite its deficiencies, which we will discuss in more detail a little later, we believe it to be an improvement in certain respects on previously available scales.

The next stage in the construction involved our judgement. Like Hope and Goldthorpe we wished our scale to cover all of the occupational categories of the OPCS *Classification of Occupations*, but in certain respects our procedures for making the scale comprehensive are the reverse of theirs. We have outlined how, at the outset of the research procedure, they and their 'expert judges' used their intuition to produce both representative occupational titles and groupings of equivalent occupations. These were never varied thereafter in the process of scale construction. We, on the other hand, chose to analyse the relationships among more or less well defined occupational groups and reserve our judgements to the end of the process, to extend the resulting scale. Either approach seems equally valid, though we have somewhat more information to go on. It will be noticed that there are several cases of extremely similar occupations in our analysis, especially in the respondents' solution. For example we have separately farmer and farm manager, manager in the electrical and engineering industries and manager in other manufacturing industries, two types of shop-keeper, several small business occupations and so on. In the results these very similar occupations end up with very similar scale scores, supporting our intuition of their similarity.

Since intuition plays such an important role in their whole process of scale construction, we cannot understand the decision by Hope and Goldthorpe to maintain what they see as deficiencies of their scale. They argue that the scale that results from their procedures should not be modified even though they have fairly clear conceptions of how it might be improved. We believe most commentators would agree with them about the deficiencies of the scale and, furthermore, would probably agree about the way in which the method created the errors. In these circumstances the decision not to alter the scale seems perverse. Why rely upon intuition so heavily at one point and deny it operation at a later point?

Apart from being able to use the knowledge gained in the research process, leaving the major judgements to the end of the research process has certain other advantages. Results are less affected by prior assumptions, though we would not claim that no judgements were involved in the design of our research. In fact we shall go on to illustrate how certain implicit assumptions built into the method do influence the resulting scale. However, certain extensive, explicit judgements, necess-

ary to the construction of a scale, were introduced only after we had
obtained strong evidence of structuring.

We used the scale positions of the occupations which had appeared in
our analysis as a framework, and placed the other occupations in
relation to them. In so doing, we used our knowledge of general social
arrangements as well as more detailed knowledge of industries and
occupations. Where we were in doubt about the exact nature of
occupations, we consulted both published sources and colleagues. We
cannot be sure that in every case our decisions represent the best
solution, but we performed various tests which suggested that our
procedures were reasonable. In particular we compared correlations
obtained using the full scale of all occupations with those obtained using
a scale limited to occupations featured in one or other of the derived
solutions. We did this for correlations between the several occupation
variables—respondents' first and present occupations, fathers' occupations and so on—and other variables in the data—education and
income measures, for example. In no instance was the product moment
correlation changed by more than 0.01. This would seem to indicate a
very similar construction of the two sets of scale scores.

In creating the scores we felt that it would be inappropriate to attempt
extremely fine distinctions, and for the most part we gave occupations
scores which were the same as, or the means of, the scores of those
occupations in the analysis we believed they most resembled.
Sometimes we had no very similar occupations in the analysis, and in
these cases unique scores which seemed appropriate were given, though
they were, of course, assigned on the basis of comparisons with
occupations between which they were placed.

The complete scale is given in Table 2.6. There are five columns to the
table representing different statuses within occupations. This is in line
with the comparable OPCS Table B.1 of occupations by social class
(and Socioeconomic group) but not with the system of classification in
Table B.2, which was taken up by Hope and Goldthorpe. Where they
divided managers into those in establishments employing less than 25
and those employing 25 or more, we have set out only one category of
manager. As we have said there are very great variations of condition
under the general head of manager, and we do not believe that size of
establishment is the most crucial variable. Finally, where they have two
categories of self-employed with employees, we have only one. In
general those who are self-employed in large establishments should be
included in the managerial categories of our scale. Whether to assign
self-employed people to the category without employees or that with

TABLE 2.6 The Cambridge scale

OPCS unit groups	Employees	Foremen	Managers	Self-employed with employees	Self-employed without employees
Fishermen	−158	−158	−18	−18	−158
Farmers, farm managers, market gardeners			+11	+11	−18
Agricultural workers n.e.c.	−158	−158			−158
Agricultural machinery drivers	−158	−158		−18	−158
Gardeners and groundsmen	−158	−158	−18	−18	−158
Foresters and woodmen	−158	−118	+11	+11	−158
Coal mine—workers underground	−136	−136			
Coal mine—workers above ground	−136	−136			
Workers below ground n.e.c.	−136	−136			
Surface workers n.e.c.—mines and quarries	−136	−136			
Furnacemen, coal gas and coke ovens	−136	−136			
Chemical production process workers n.e.c.	−148	−148			
Ceramic formers	−135	−135		−96	−96
Glass formers, finishers and decorators	−135	−135			
Furnacemen, kilnmen, glass and ceramic	−135	−135			
Ceramics' decorators and finishers	−135	−135			
Glass and ceramics production process workers n.e.c.	−135	−135			
Furnacemen—metal	−135	−135			
Rolling, tube mill operators, metal drawers	−136	−136			
Moulders and coremakers (foundry)	−136	−136			
Smiths, forgemen	−136	−136		−96	−96
Metal making and treating workers n.e.c.	−136	−136			

TABLE 2.6 (*continued*)

OPCS unit groups	Employees	Foremen	Managers	Self-employed with employees	Self-employed without employees
023 Fettlers, metal dressers	−136	−136			
024 Radio and radar mechanics	−104	−104		−96	−96
025 Installers and repairmen, telephone	−44	−44			
026 Linesmen, cable jointers	−118	−118			
027 Electricians	−118	−118		−96	−96
028 Electrical and electronic fitters	−118	−118		−96	−96
029 Assemblers (electrical and electronic)	−136	−136			
030 Electrical engineers (so described)	*	*	*	*	*
031 Foremen (engineering and allied trades)		−118			
032 Trainee craftsmen (engineering and allied trades)	−118				
033 Sheet metal workers	−118	−118		−96	−96
034 Steel erectors; riggers	−118	−118		−96	−96
035 Metal plate workers; riveters	−118	−118		−96	−96
036 Gas, electric welders, cutters; braziers	−118	−118		−96	−96
037 Turners	−118	−118		−96	−96
038 Machine tool setters, setter—operators n.e.c.	−118	−118		−96	−96
039 Machine tool operators	−118	−118			
040 Tool makers, tool room fitters	−136	−136		−96	−96
041 Motor mechanics, auto engineers	−118	−118		−96	−96
042 Maintenance fitters, maintenance engineers, millwrights	−118	−118		−96	−96
043 Fitters n.e.c., machine erectors, etc.	−118	−118		−96	−96
044 Electro-platers, dip platers and related workers	−136	−136			
045 Plumbers, gas fitters, lead burners	−130	−130		−96	−96

* This category is too vague to score.

Occupation				
Pipe fitters, heating engineers	−130	−130	−96	−96
Press workers and stampers	−136	−136	−96	−96
Metal workers n.e.c.	−118	−118	−96	−96
Watch and chronometer makers and repairers	−124	−124	−96	−96
Precision instrument makers and repairers	−124	−124	−96	−96
Goldsmiths, silversmiths, jewellery makers	−124	−124	−96	−96
Coach, carriage, wagon builders and repairers	−118	−118	−96	−96
Inspectors (metal and electrical goods)	−135	−135		
Other metal making, working; jewellery and electrical production process workers	−136	−136		−136
Carpenters and joiners	−123	−123	+8	−96
Cabinet makers	−123	−123	+8	−96
Sawyers and wood working machinists	−158	−158		
Pattern makers	−123	−123		
Woodworkers n.e.c.	−123	−123	+8	−96
Tanners; leather, fur dressers, fellmongers	−161	−161		
Shoemakers and shoe repairers	−117	−117	−96	−96
Cutters, lasters, sewers, footwear and related workers	−161	−161		
Leather products makers n.e.c.	−161	−161	−96	−96
Fibre preparers	−158	−158		
Spinners, doublers, twisters	−158	−158		
Winders, reelers	−158	−158		
Warpers, sizers, drawers-in	−158	−158		
Weavers	−158	−158	−96	−96
Knitters	−158	−158		−158
Bleachers and finishers of textiles	−158	−158		
Dyers of textiles	−158	−158		

TABLE 2.6 (continued)

OPCS unit groups	Employees	Foremen	Managers	Self-employed with employees	Self-employed without employees
Textile fabrics and related products makers and examiners n.e.c.	-158				
Textile fabrics, etc. production process workers n.e.c.	-158	-158			
Tailors, dress, light clothing makers	-117	-117	-106	-96	-96
Upholsterers and related workers	-117	-117		-96	-96
Hand and machine sewers and embroiderers, textile and light leather products	-158	-158			-158
Clothing and related products makers n.e.c.	-158	-158		-96	-96
Bakers and pastry cooks	-115	-115	-66	-66	-96
Butchers and meat cutters	-115	-115	-66	-66	-96
Brewers, wine makers and related workers	-115	-115		-66	-96
Food processors n.e.c.	-158	-158	-66	-66	-96
Tobacco preparers and products makers	-158	-158			
Makers of paper and paperboard	-158	-158			
Paper products makers	-158	-158			
Compositors	-118	-118		-18	-96
Printing press operators	-124	-124		-18	-96
Printers (so described)	-118	-118		-18	-96
Printing workers n.e.c.	-118	-118		-96	-96
Workers in rubber	-181	-182			
Workers in plastics	-181	-182			
Craftsmen n.e.c.	-117	-117		-96	-96
Other production process workers	-182	-182			
Bricklayers, tile setters	-117	-117		-18	-117

Code	Occupation					
094	Masons, stone cutters, slate workers	−117	−117		−18	−117
095	Plasterers, cement finishers, terrazzo workers	−117	−117		−18	−117
096	Builders (so described); clerks of works	−117	−66*	−66	−18	−117
097	Bricklayers, etc., labourers n.e.c.	−157	−157			−157
098	Construction workers n.e.c.	−172	−172		−66	−137
099	Aerographers, paint sprayers	−159	−159			
100	Painters, decorators n.e.c.	−159	−159		−96	−96
101	Coach painters (so described)	−159	−159		−96	−96
102	Boiler firemen	−136	−136			
103	Crane and hoist operators; slingers	−136	−136			
104	Operators of earth moving and other construction machinery n.e.c.	−136	−136			
105	Stationary engine, materials handling plant operations n.e.c.; oilers and greasers	−136	−136			
106	Railway lengthmen	−136	−136			
	Labourers and unskilled workers n.e.c.	−157	−157			
107	Chemical and allied trades	−157	−157			
108	Engineering and allied trades	−157	−157			
109	Foundries in engineering and allied trades	−157	−157			
110	Textiles (not textile goods)	−157	−157			
111	Coke ovens and gas works	−157	−157			
112	Glass and ceramics	−157	−157			
113	Building and contracting	−157	−157			−157
114	Other	−157	−157			
115	Deck, engineering officers and pilots, ship		+22		+22	
116	Deck and engine room ratings, barge and boatmen	−120	−120			

* This is the score for Clerks of Work. For ordinary foremen builders whose trade is unknown −117 is more appropriate.

TABLE 2.6 (*continued*)

OPCS unit groups	Employees	Foremen	Managers	Self-employed with employees	Self-employed without employees
117 Aircraft pilots, navigators and flight engineers			+22	+22	+22
118 Drivers, motormen, second men, railway engine	−120	−120			
119 Railway guards	−120	−120			
120 Drivers of buses, coaches	−120	−120		−111	−96
121 Drivers of other road passenger vehicles	−120	−120		−111	−96
122 Drivers of road goods vehicles	−120	−120		−111	−96
123 Inspectors, supervisors, transport		−111	+22	−111	
124 Shunters, pointsmen	−120	−120			
125 Signalmen and crossing keepers, railways	−120	−120			
126 Traffic controllers and dispatchers, transport	−100	−100	−58		
127 Telephone operators	−78	−58	−58		
128 Telegraph and radio operators	−78	−58	−58		
129 Postmen, mail sorters	−160	−160			
130 Messengers	−160	−160			
131 Bus conductors	−158	−158			
132 Porters, ticket collectors, railway	−158	−158			
133 Stevedores, dock labourers	−158	−158			
134 Lorry drivers' mates, van guards	−158	−158			
135 Workers in transport and communication occupations n.e.c.	−158	−158			
136 Warehousemen, storekeepers and assistants	−176	−111	−111		
137 Packers, labellers and related workers	−176	−176			

Code	Occupation					
138	Office managers n.e.c.	−78				
139	Clerks, cashiers	−78	−58	−58		
140	Office machine operators	−78	−58	−58		
141	Typists, shorthand writers, secretaries	−76	−76			−76
142	Civil service executive officers	+8	+8			−66
143	Proprietors and managers, sales			−58	−42	
144	Shop salesmen and assistants	−69	−69			
145	Roundsmen (bread, milk, laundry, soft drinks)	−158	−158	−158		
146	Street vendors, hawkers	−158	−158	−158		
147	Garage proprietors				−40	
148	Commercial travellers, manufacturers' agents	−5	−5			
149	Finance, insurance brokers, financial agents	+52	+52	+52		
150	Salesmen, services; valuers, auctioneers	−9	−9	+6	−9	−9
151	Fire brigade officers and men	−122	−122	+22		
152	Police officers and men	−122	−122	+22		
153	Guards and related workers n.e.c.	−175	−175	−122		
154	Publicans, innkeepers			−62	−62	−62
155	Barmen, barmaids	−158	−158	−158		
156	Proprietors and managers, boarding houses and hotels			+22	+22	
157	Housekeepers, stewards, matrons and housemothers	−27	+22	+22		
158	Domestic housekeepers	−27	−27			
159	Restaurateurs			+22	+22	−66
160	Waiters and waitresses	−158	−140			
161	Canteen assistants, counter hands	−158	−158			
162	Cooks	−130	−115	−66		
163	Kitchen hands	−158	−158			

T ABLE 2.6 (*continued*)

OPCS unit groups	Employees	Foremen	Managers	Self-employed with employees	Self-employed without employees
164 Maids, valets and related service workers n.e.c.	−158	−158			
165 Caretakers, office keepers	−158	−158			
166 Charwomen, office cleaners; window cleaners, chimney sweeps	−158	−158			
167 Hairdressers, manicurists, beauticians	−69	−69	−51	42	−69
168 Launderers, dry cleaners and pressers	−158	−158	−66	−66	−66
169 Athletes, sportsmen and related workers	−78	−78	−78	+22	−78
170 Hospital or ward orderlies; ambulance men	−158	−158			
171 Proprietors and managers, service, sport and recreations n.e.c.			−51	−51	−51
172 Service, sport and recreation workers n.e.c.	−143	−143			−143
173 Ministers of the Crown; M.Ps. (n.e.c.); senior government officials			+69		+69
174 Local authority senior officers			+114		
175 Managers in engineering and allied trades			+40	+1	
176 Managers in building and contracting			+47	+1	
177 Managers in mining and production n.e.c.			+54	+1	
178 Personnel managers			+64		
179 Sales managers			+69		
180 Managers n.e.c.			+22	+1	
181 Medical practitioners (qualified)	+84	+84	+84	+84	+84

182 Dental practitioners	+84	+84	+84	+84	+84
183 Nurses	−27	−27	+48	+48	−27
184 Pharmacists	+48	+48	+48	+48	+48
185 Radiographers (medical and industrial)	+48	+48	+48	+48	+48
186 Opthalmic and dispensing opticians	+48	+48	+48	+48	+48
187 Chiropodists	+48	+48	+48	+48	+48
188 Physiotherapists	+48	+48	+48	+48	+48
189 Occupational therapists	+48	+48	+48	+48	+48
190 Public health inspectors	+48	+48	+48	+48	+48
191 Medical workers n.e.c.	+48	+48	+48	+48	+48
192 University teachers	+131				+48
193 Primary and secondary school teachers	+58	+58	+95	+95	+95
194 Teachers n.e.c.	+58	+58	+95	+95	+95
195 Civil, structural, municipal engineers	+102	+102	+102	+102	+102
196 Mechanical engineers	+66	+66	+66	+66	+66
197 Electrical engineers	+132	+132	+132	+132	+132
198 Electronic engineers	+100	+100	+100	+100	+100
199 Work study, progress engineers	−7	−7	+22	+22	+22
200 Planning, production engineers	+94	+94	+94	+94	+94
201 Engineers n.e.c.	+94	+94	+94	+94	+94
202 Metallurgists	+94	+94	+94	+94	+94
203 Technologists n.e.c.	+94	+94	+94	+94	+94
204 Chemists	+70	+70	+70	+70	+70
205 Physical and biological scientists	+92	+92	+92	+92	+92
206 Authors, journalists and related workers	+13	+13	+13	+13	+13
207 Stage managers, actors, entertainers, musicians	−78	−78	+22	+22	−78
208 Painters, sculptors and related creative artists*	(−105)	(−105)	(+22)	+13	+13

* This category is too heterogeneous. Our score is for a group comprising mainly technical artists and engravers.

Table 2.6 (*continued*)

OPCS unit groups	Employees	Foremen	Managers	Self-employed with employees	Self-employed without employees
209 Accountants, professional	+21	+21	+21	+55	+21
210 Company secretaries and registrars	+21	+21	+21		
211 Surveyors	+55	+55	+55	+55	+55
212 Architects, town planners	+55	+55	+55	+55	+55
213 Clergy, ministers, members of religious orders	−2	−2	+22		
214 Judges, barristers, advocates, solicitors	+100	+100	+100	+100	+100
215 Social welfare and related workers	+29	+29	+29		
216 Officials of trade or professional associations	+29	+29	+29		
217 Professional workers n.e.c.	+88	+88	+88	+88	+88
218 Draughtsmen	−44	+2	+2	+2	−44
219 Laboratory assistants, technicians	−44	−44			
220 Technical and related workers n.e.c.	−7	−7			

employees may be difficult. Many self-employed tradesmen take on the organisation of fairly large jobs and subcontract work to other tradesmen. Thus, for example, a carpenter may act as building contractor for a house extension and subcontract the bricklaying and roofing to other self-employed craftsmen. He is not then technically an employer though we would code him to the category of self-employed with employees. In general where men merely contract their labour they would be placed in the category without employees.

3 The Scale Assessed

What does the scale measure? Strangely this sort of question has had only limited attention. We do not mean by this that there is not a considerable literature discussing the nature of scales of stratification, but rather that the discussion has occurred within rather narrow bounds. We argued fairly extensively in the last chapter that reputational scales do not measure a consensus on the legitimacy of rewards to occupations based upon their social worth, yet that view is one of the few theoretical statements of what is being measured.

It will be recalled that we came closer to agreement with Hope and Goldthorpe's (1974, p. 133) criticism of the moral consensus view and their conclusion that what is being measured is the general goodness of occupations. Yet their view is hardly a theoretical account of what they are measuring, and they are very loath to extend their treatment to include the relationship of their scale to social conditions in general. They write:

> In other words, while we believe that our scale, understood as one of the 'general desirability' of occupations in popular assessment, can serve in itself as a valuable measuring-rod in studies of occupational achievement and occupational mobility *per se*, it is not, in our interpretation of it, one which entails any assumptions about specific extra-occupational consequences which follow from holding, or moving between, given occupational levels.

But this statement is disingenuous when placed against the process by which the scale was constructed. As they themselves point out, their respondents were asked to assess the 'social worth' of occupations, and the monograph reporting the scale is titled 'The Social Grading of Occupations'. There can be no doubt of the problematic relationship of prestige studies to stratification, but it cannot be solved by such an artificial limitation of concern. It is not sensible to separate the grading of occupations and stratification issues as they wish to do. The relationship cannot be relegated to an empirical question which may be

70

explored after the scale has been constructed. We are sympathetic to the view that a single scale may be unsuitable for all purposes, but close specification of the relation of different scales to theoretical purposes is essential. The problematic relationship of scales to social experience can be seen in such extreme reserve about their meaning and applicability.

For the most part opponents of the moral consensus view of the basis of prestige studies have offered a practical rather than a theoretical critique. They have sought to show that the scales are deficient, in that agreement either is not so extensive as has been claimed or does not have a moral character. While wanting to deny the existence, or at least the degree, of moral consensus, each of these approaches implicitly entails a belief in its relevance for the production of stable social institutions. Such relevance rests on an acceptance of the special status of the data of the social sciences, as opposed to those of the natural sciences, such that society is a direct production of actors whereas nature is externally constituted. As Giddens (1976, p. 15) puts it: 'The difference between society and nature is that nature is not man-made, is not produced *by* man. Human beings, of course, transform nature, and such transformation is both the condition of social existence and a driving force of cultural development. But nature is not a human production: society is.'

One could debate the distinction made here between 'transformation' and 'production', but we have already stated, in the introductory chapter, our opposition to the sort of radical distinction he makes in the first and last sentences.[1] So long as that view is accepted, however, a moral consensus would be an unshakeable basis of social interrelationships, and whether particular institutions or societies are so constituted becomes an empirical question. This explains the search, by apparently radical opponents of moral consensual theory, for unremarked variations in prestige studies or for deficiencies of methodology. For them the force of the findings is undeniable.

As we have indicated, we believe that, despite the form of questions in prestige studies, scales of 'occupational status' reflect practical exigencies of social life. They need not be based upon a consensus, moral or interpretative, and in so far as the basis is practical experience, the underpinning is knowledge rather than commitment. Knowledge may be differentially distributed, but within a coherent system ignorance will be dispelled in predictable ways by any extension of practical experience

---

[1] The point is discussed at greater length by one of the present authors in Holmwood and Stewart (forthcoming).

of the system. In the absence of a need or opportunity to confront practical problems, many forms of prejudice and wish-fulfillment can flourish, but these are unlikely to survive the onslaught of practical knowledge should the individual's experience change so as to render the problems real and immediate.

The sources of variation in studies calling for *evaluation* of social experience are potentially diverse, and though they may be interesting from certain points of view, they are by no means unproblematically related to the structure of experience. That reputational studies in general correlate well does not mean that variations do not occur, but neither do the variations point conclusively to fundamental differences of experience.

We believe that, in general, scales of 'occupational status' measure basic similarities of life-style. Social and material circumstances are closely associated with occupational experience, and the scales may, therefore, also measure market resources or, more accurately, labour market outcomes associated with the system of production. However, it is crucially important to recognise that the scales do not provide measures of the constitution of capacities (of the basic nature of the market), but only of the processes of its operation. The bases of capacities are determined by the nature of the social productive system and are differentiated in ways other than by greater or lesser social and material rewards. The ability to command equivalent salaries, etc., may lead to similar experiences in both work and non-work life, but it does not imply an identity of interest in productive relations. There may be some common interest in the maintenance of the status quo and even common commitment to certain aspects of change, but actual changes are likely to undermine capacities selectively and to highlight common interests among those of different lifestyles.

A great deal of time and energy has been wasted in trying to determine the ways in which scales of 'occupational status' may be divided to offer approximations to 'social classes', but social classes cannot be established upon similarities of life-style. Similarly the debates upon 'social closure', or the extent to which continuous scales of 'occupational status' undermine discontinuous theories of social class, are misplaced. Though clearly related, issues of the constitution of capacities, on the one hand, and of the life-styles associated with the mobilisation of such capacities, on the other, are to a considerable extent distinct.

However, this does not destroy the value of scales of life-style. The transmission of benefit over generations, within the normal processes of reproduction of the society, is likely to be better related to life-style than to the 'relations of production', even to the extent that those of similar levels of privilege will be able to affect placement within a range of differently constituted capacities. This is due partly to friendships established on the basis of similar life-styles, partly to assumptions of common relevant experience, but most directly to the manipulation of education which affords routes to ranges of differently constituted positions.[2]

How well, then, does the Cambridge Scale measure similarities of life-style? We believe our scale lies between those previously existing, including that of Hope and Goldthorpe, and a more or less adequate instrument. Much of the rest of the book is concerned with the relationships between occupations and stratification, illustrating the difficulties of establishing the correct links between them. In particular we emphasise the importance of placing individuals within structured career paths rather than merely identifying them by occupation. People come to similar jobs by very different routes and leave to very different destinations. Yet our scale does not represent an adequate approach to the placement of individuals in their appropriate careers with their typical market circumstances and associated life-styles. In large part this is because, in the beginning, we followed all previous research in seeing the problem of the initial classification into occupational categories as consisting mainly in using a set of sufficiently precise job descriptions. Like most other people conducting research in this area we were aware of the deficiencies, in this respect, of the OPCS *Classification of Occupations*, but, again like other researchers, we felt that these were not so extensive as to offset the value of using an available and established classification. The more serious deficiencies for a study of stratification became apparent to us only when certain decisions had been made about the collection and coding of data.[3]

However, there are advantages contained in our scale, going some way towards resolving the problems of reputational measures, which derive from the method of its construction. While we may agree with Hope and Goldthorpe that reputational studies reflect estimates of 'general desirability', it is not clear that asking about the 'social worth'

---

[2] The limitation of the 'human capital' assumption that education directly creates the capacities that individuals exercise will be discussed in Chapter 10.

[3] In research currently in progress we have attempted to remedy both the deficiencies of information for an accurate assessment of 'career position' and the known deficiencies of existing classifications.

of occupations presents respondents with a clear and unambiguous task. In coming to a general estimate of desirability of occupations, respondents may have to balance somewhat contradictory pieces of knowledge about social relationships. The results of the exercise may be stable, but they may incorporate certain deficiencies.

Occupational categories, as conventionally defined, may contain people with a diversity of statuses. This applies not only where the occupation contains a career ladder with a hierarchy of rewards, but also where the immediate rewards are fairly homogenous, since the meaning of the occupation to incumbents may vary according to where it comes in their overall careers. The latter point applies equally to different occupations where the rewards are similar, but where from any other point of view it would be misleading to regard them as equally placed in a social stratification hierarchy. The lack of distinction in Hope and Goldthorpe's data between lower white-collar groups and manual groups probably reflects a fairly accurate picture of work conditions and rates of income, but not of educational qualifications and career prospects. We have, from the limited data of a small exploratory study,[4] a strong indication that knowledge of all of these features of occupations is fairly widely dispersed. There were few disagreements among the respondents about the relative incomes and working conditions (in terms of interest, variety and control) of a representative sample of occupational titles. The lowest white-collar occupations were placed below the upper manual occupations on all characteristics. Variations by occupation of respondents were slight, though with such small numbers too much should not be made of this. We also asked respondents to rank or rate 38 occupations according to two cues:

   (a) According to their class position
   (b) According to their prestige.

The results from the different approaches were very similar and in general were close to the Hope-Goldthorpe results.

However, our respondents were also aware of differences among incumbents of occupations which would affect their estimates of their positions. In particular, promotion prospects do not inhere directly in occupations; they do not always belong to occupations in the sense that they are equally open to all who hold these occupations, but rather they

---

[4] Based on 50 interviews carried out in conjunction with the pilot survey for our general sample.

belong to those incumbents with advantages of education, trainee status for better occupations (though without formal classification as trainees) and so on. These divisions cannot be represented in occupational distinctions. This being the case, the Hope-Goldthorpe Scale cannot provide such a straightforward measure of 'occupational achievement' or 'occupational mobility' as the authors claim. By using the OPCS *Classification of Occupations* they have imported into their work a confusion of static and dynamic elements of occupational experience. For example, all members of conventional professions, from students and apprentices through those in intermediate positions to those in the highest positions, are coded to the same category so long as they are not self-employed. On the other hand, a vast majority of all managerial employees must start their careers in other conventional occupational categories. We shall show in Chapter 7 how tiny is the proportion of current managers in Great Britain, the USA and Australia who started their working lives as managers or trainees. For the most part, therefore, in studies using their scale, managers must on the whole have experienced unusual occupational mobility and achievement, while professionals must have been relatively immobile. The fact that in both groups there may be equivalent returns to educational levels, for example, in terms of work experience and income cannot be taken into account. It is possible that management has more than its share of personnel over-achieving on the basis of education, but this cannot apply to the whole group who would be counted as mobile.

The reverse situation applies to clerks. People become clerks under diverse circumstances, and many are clearly at early stages of relatively lucrative careers.[5] Yet when people of diverse background hold the same occupation it may be difficult to see prospects as inhering in the occupation. Judgements are then much more likely to reflect the actual conditions of the present occupation.

It could, of course, be argued that what is sought is a scale of occupations only, while the circumstances of the incumbents are of only secondary interest. However, from various points of view it seems unlikely that this was the intention of those who have constructed scales, and it is not achieved by the results. In the first place there is the confusion we have noted of specific jobs and whole careers contained in standard job titles. However, even if sufficiently precise definitions of jobs could be created, such a scale would be best represented by immediate rewards of the jobs, both intrinsic and extrinsic, with income

[5] Just how many can be seen in Chapter 6 below.

providing the best single indicator. That something else is in the minds of the scale producers is testified by their avoidance of the simple procedure of using income, and by their introduction of factors other than direct job rewards into either the processes of producing the scales or their interpretations of the scales' characteristics. It seems obvious that they wish to produce something with more relevance to general social experience.

The relational approach which we have used goes some way towards the solution of these problems. There is a tendency for social relationships to be formed between those of about the same stratification position. In these circumstances the social relationships of men in occupations offering about the same income and general work conditions may be quite different if patterns of recruitment to and movement from the occupations are different. Differences of this sort would be reflected in our scale, and we take this to be the reason for the much clearer division in our results between manual and non-manual occupations than has been found in studies using the reputational approach. We do not hold that the values we have given the occupations represent their 'true' positions. As we have already argued, for many occupations there is no one true stratification position for incumbents; there are a diversity of positions. But if we have to use occupational titles as indicators of stratification, then we think that the relational approach produces better compromise values. It is true that the scale is based on feelings of identity—friendship—but we believe that it also represents a better approximation to mean market circumstances of incumbents of occupations.

In the event, however, the Cambridge scale and the Hope-Goldthorpe scale are fairly well related. For the purposes of comparison we have been able to match 79 occupations which occurred in one or other of our two solutions with occupations in the Hope-Goldthorpe scale. The occupations with their scale values are given in Table 3.1. We have included only once cases where two different occupations have been given the same values in each scale. An example is technician and supervisory technician. Where two occupations have the same scores on one of the scales but different scores on the other scale they have both been included. These practices tend to exaggerate slightly the differences between the scales. Nevertheless the product moment correlation coefficient is 0.88.

Before looking at the relationship between the two British scales in more detail, we should like to introduce, for comparison, two other recently reported scales, one of which is designed to be international,

TABLE 3.1 Hope-Goldthorpe and Cambridge scale scores
(in Cambridge rank order)

Occupations	Scores	
	Cambridge	H.G.
Rubber workers	−182	32.62
Foremen, rubber workers	−182	43.72
Warehousemen	−176	28.35
Guards, etc.	−175	27.10
Construction workers	−172	30.00
Shoe and leather workers	−161	32.62
Foremen, shoe and leather workers	−161	43.72
Postmen	−160	28.35
Painters	−159	35.55
Labourers	−157	18.36
Chemical workers	−148	35.55
Foremen, chemical workers	−148	43.72
Service sport and recreation workers N.E.C.	−143	32.42
Non-skilled engineering workers	−136	35.55
Foremen, non-skilled engineering	−136	46.51
Inspectors in engineering	−135	35.55
Foremen, inspectors in engineering	−135	48.91
Foremen, glassworkers	−135	46.51
Plumbers and gasfitters	−130	37.62
Precision instrument makers	−124	39.87
Carpenters and joiners	−123	37.62
Police constables	−122	68.84
Printers and compositors	−118	39.87
Electrician	−118	50.90
Skilled workers in engineering	−118	45.57
Foremen, skilled engineering	−118	48.91
Foremen, warehousemen	−111	42.08
Radio and radar mechanics	−104	54.12
Self-employed motor mechanics (no employees)	− 96	42.70
Clerks	− 78	39.85
Actors, entertainers etc.	− 78	59.38
Secretaries, typists etc.	− 76	34.62
Shop assistants	− 69	34.62
Clerks of works	− 66	37.62
Publicans	− 62	51.56
Office managers	− 58	56.95
Head clerks	− 58	52.80
Shop managers	− 58	52.80
Laboratory assistants and foremen	− 44	64.05
Draughtsmen	− 44	61.85
P.O. engineer, telephone installer and repairer	− 44	50.90
Shopkeepers (s.e.)	− 42	56.50
Garage proprietors (with employees)	− 40	56.50

TABLE 3.1 (*continued*)

Occupations	Scores Cambridge	H.G.
Nurses and sisters	− 27	61.14
S.E. builders (with employees)	− 18	53.58
S.E. salesmen, valuers, auctioneers	− 9	56.02
Salesmen, valuers, auctioneers	− 9	39.85
Technicians and foremen	− 7	64.05
Representatives and commercial travellers	− 5	39.85
Clergymen	− 2	62.33
Company directors S.D. (small businesses)	+ 1	62.19
Heads of drawing offices	+ 2	56.95
Civil service executive officers	8	61.14
S.E. carpenters and joiners (with employees)	8	53.58
Journalists etc.	13	59.38
Accountants	21	76.29
Service managers	22	68.98
Social workers	29	61.14
Managers in engineering industry	40	66.11
Finance and insurance brokers	52	69.14
Managers in mining and production n.e.s.	54	66.11
Architects and surveyors	55	70.92
School teachers	58	61.14
Personnel managers	64	66.11
Mechanical engineers	66	70.92
Sales managers	69	68.66
Senior Government officials	69	79.53
Graduate chemists	70	70.92
Doctors	84	82.05
Professionals N.E.C.	88	70.92
Physical and biological scientists	92	70.92
Graduate technologists	94	70.92
Headmasters	95	67.62
Electronic engineers	100	70.92
Lawyers	100	76.29
Civil engineers	102	70.92
Local government senior officers	114	69.14
University staff	131	76.29
Electrical engineers	132	70.92

while the other is specific to one country, Australia. We do not wish to argue an identity of occupational and social experience cross-nationally, but we believe that the relationships with these other scales may serve to illuminate some of the discrepancies between the British scales.

The first scale is an amalgam of reputational studies by Treiman (1977). It is presented as a 'Standard International Occupational Prestige Scale', and is constructed from scores taken from 85 occupational prestige studies conducted in 53 different countries. The Scale consists of prestige scores for 509 occupations, though it is a two digit scale and the range is actually 92 points.

The second, Australian, scale called ANU 2 is created by a more complex version of the method described earlier for Duncan's Socio-economic Index. It will be recalled that Duncan regressed income and education measures upon a version of the NORC prestige scores for occupations, and with the weightings of that regression constructed an Index over a wider range of occupations. In the scale presently under discussion the authors, Broom, Duncan-Jones, Lancaster Jones and McDonnell (1977), made similar use of an occupational prestige study (Schleindl, 1975), but the regression procedure was both more complex and covered a much wider range of variables. They used variables derived from age, sex, birthplace, parents' birthplaces, schooling, qualifications, housing and associated facilities, and vehicles. These were chosen as representative of factors thought to be determinants of, or determined by social status. The weightings from the regression were then used to extend the scale to cover 414 occupations or groups of occupations.

The correlation of the British scales was fairly easy to produce as each scale used the OPCS *Classification of Occupations* to establish basic categories, but cross-national comparisons are far more difficult, and to an extent the purpose of the comparison will determine the most efficient method. The central problem is that the scales do not consist of the same occupations or groups of occupations. Variations in coding practice make the scales more or less specific over different areas, and some means of rendering them similar must be found before they can be compared. There is no single best procedure. If the purpose were to compare the scales as research instruments with real data, then the best correlations would be those between the actual scores applied to that data by the different scales. If, on the other hand, the purpose is to examine the similarities of the underlying structures of the different scales, it is best to take account of the differences in occupational identifications by producing matching aggregate categories. For example, if one scale has a single category which in another is divided into several, the best representation of the latter in the former is some single function of the differentiated scores, as it is likely that the composite nature of the former category contributed to its score, whatever the method of scale construction. The easiest function to apply is an unweighted mean, which has the merit of simplicity even if other procedures can be justified. By using this method we were able to establish, from the occupations that appeared in one or other of our two solutions, 67 common categories with the Treiman scale and 63 with the ANU scale.

The product moment correlation with the Treiman scale is 0.93, and with the ANU scale 0.95. Over the same range of occupations the Hope-Goldthorpe Scale correlates 0.90 with Treiman and 0.91 with ANU. Treiman and ANU correlate 0.95 over the 61 occupational groupings they each have in common with the Cambridge Scale. If we restrict all correlations to these 61 common categories, the coefficients do not change. The relationship between Hope-Goldthorpe and the Cambridge Scale is 0.87, just as it was over the 79 occupations. To an extent the correlations of the other scales may be slightly reduced as their categories are determined on the basis of Cambridge ones.

A rather different approach to the selection of occupations is possible in comparing the Hope-Goldthorpe and Cambridge Scale. We may simply take employees in all the occupations of the British OPCS classification, regardless of how scores were derived or whether more than one occupation has the same score in both. This is not particularly instructive for interpreting the implications of the different approaches, but for practical purposes it gives the degree of association between the whole scales as they might be used. In fact the correlation is little different at 0.89.

We have already remarked the differences between the Cambridge Scale and the Hope-Goldthorpe Scale in the placing of foremen. There is something to be said for each depending on the purpose of the scale. Our analysis strengthens other evidence that in terms of life styles and patterns of association they are not far removed from the groups they supervise, but there is no doubt they enjoy somewhat higher incomes and better job conditions. The other two scales do not help much, in that they are incomplete in foremen categories, though to the extent that they do appear, Treiman's Scale puts them closer to our estimates, the ANU scale closer to Hope-Goldthorpe estimates. We decided to omit foremen from the detailed comparisons of the British Scales that follow.

To examine the relationship between values on the two scales, we regressed the Hope-Goldthorpe scores on the Cambridge scores, and plotted the standardised residuals of the regression. The results are given in Figure 3.1. We have done this to illustrate those cases where the Cambridge scale predicts much larger or much smaller values than those

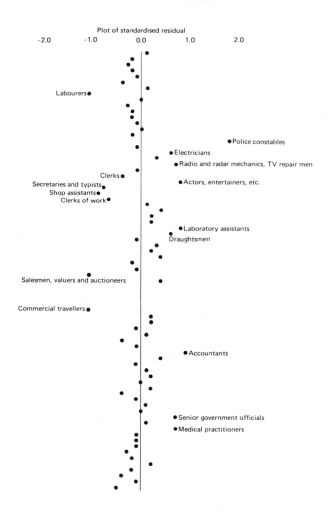

FIG. 3.1 Comparison of Hope-Goldthorpe scale with Cambridge scale

that actually appear on the Hope-Goldthorpe scale. We are concerned only with cases where the residuals are relatively large, so for clarity only these are labelled in Fig. 3.1. The occupations are ordered according to ascending value on the Cambridge scale.

There is no unproblematic way in which we can compare the location of an occupation on all four scales simultaneously. However, because of the general similarity of the scales, it is often possible to make a rough judgement of the placement of occupations in the ANU and Treiman Scales in relation to their positions in the two British Scales. Since we are considering the cases of widest discrepancy, we would expect a tendency for the Treiman and ANU values for an occupation to lie between those in the Cambridge and Hope-Goldthorpe scales, if all reflect generally similar stratification structures. With a few exceptions this is what happens. In most cases (about two out of three) they came closer to Cambridge values, but more importantly their relative positions are generally predictable.

There are two points with very large residuals at the bottom end of the scale. The first is labourers. In our results labourer is not the lowest of the manual occupations. It occurs about the middle of a set of low skill occupations. On the Hope-Goldthorpe scale it is very much the lowest scoring occupation. There is, in fact, some difficulty with this category, which is not simply 'labourers' but includes occupations with a wide variety of titles—indeed the Hope-Goldthorpe category covers five other OPCS codes—and it is not intuitively obvious that it should have the lowest score. Nevertheless, in terms of rank ordering we feel that their positioning of labourer makes better intuitive sense, and this is supported by both the Treiman and ANU scores, but we are not so sure of the scale value it has been given.[6] It is a very long way below the next occupation on the scale, and we think that this is probably due to an aspect of their method rather than an accurate reflection of the position of labourers. Intervals at both ends of their scale are very much larger than those closer to the middle. This is probably a reflection of greater agreement among their respondents on occupations at the top and at the bottom.

The other case of large difference in the bottom part of the Cambridge scale is police constable. Whereas the Cambridge scale places this occupation about the level of skilled manual groups, the Hope-Goldthorpe scale has it above schoolteacher and just below manager in a large enterprise. It is also just above police sergeant. This strange placing would seem to be due to a rather idiosyncratic choice of

---

[6] We think it could be quite misleading in use for some occupations like aircraft cleaner, or where, following the OPCS convention, occupations are coded as labourers for lack of better information. The criticism is given further weight when we realise that, due to the classification system, other 'labourers' are spread above them through over a quarter of the scale range, e.g. warehouse and dock labourers (above them by 15 % of the range), farm labourers (20 %), quarry and clay pit labourers (22 %), textile millhouse labourers (27 %).

equivalent occupations at the outset of the research. Included in the same category are radio operator in a ship, train controller with British Rail and flight controller at an airport. Not surprisingly both Treiman and ANU support the Cambridge score.

Continuing up the Cambridge scale we find that Hope-Goldthorpe has higher values for electricians and radio and radar mechanics, though they do include with electricians, post office engineers, who come higher on the Cambridge scale. Radio and radar mechanic, which includes TV repairman, comes much higher than other skilled groups in their scale. Treiman and ANU support the Cambridge placement of electricians, but are divided for radio and radar mechanics with ANU closer to Hope-Goldthorpe. A little further up there is a lower value on the Cambridge scale for actors and entertainers, but this is a diverse group which might reasonably embrace both values.

At this point we come to some occupations which score much higher on the Cambridge scale, but before considering these we shall deal briefly with the remaining cases where scores are notably lower. Laboratory assistant is one, which is readily explained since the Cambridge scale distinguishes laboratory assistants from technical and engineering assistants and from other technicians, but all of these groups have the same value on Hope-Goldthorpe. Laboratory assistants come below other technicians on the Cambridge scale. This is also true of both Treiman and ANU scores. In fact both are very close to the Cambridge score, Treiman being slightly lower, ANU slightly higher.

Before returning to those occupations which score much higher on the Cambridge scale, we shall deal briefly with the remaining cases where scores are notably lower. Office manager is one, but in the Hope-Goldthorpe scale it is included with service managers and company directors in large establishments. Draughtsman is an obvious problem for Hope and Goldthorpe. It comes above head draughtsman and section leader in a technical drawing office, and as might be expected both Treiman and ANU scores are closer to the Cambridge score. Accountant covers a fairly wide range of particular occupations in our data, whereas in the Hope-Goldthorpe analysis it was included in a group with other high ranking professionals. The Treiman and ANU scores are higher than the Cambridge score, but again closer to it than to the Hope-Goldthorpe score. The senior government officials in our data were all civil servants, mainly senior executive officers, and included none of the rather rare high status jobs in the OPCS category; whereas in addition to manager of a labour exchange and senior civil servant, the

Hope-Goldthorpe grouping included diplomat, member of Parliament and cabinet minister. The nearest equivalents in the Treiman and ANU scales are based on evaluations of rather higher ranking groups than appear in the Cambridge category and the scores are also higher. Finally among occupations relatively undervalued on the Cambridge scale we come to medical practitioner. Since most of our cases were general practitioners, we have chosen the Hope-Goldthorpe value covering GPs and specialists with a private practice, which were included in a group of self-employed, high earning professional occupations. If instead we had chosen their score for employed professionals, including specialists in a hospital without a private practice, who might be expected to come above GPS, the discrepancy would have been greatly reduced. The Treiman and ANU ratings of medical practitioners (undivided) also place them higher than the Cambridge scores.

The group of occupations which are relatively highly valued on the Cambridge scale are all, apart from labourers, low level non-manual jobs. Although the discrepancy is not particularly extreme we have included clerks here because of the general interest. Of these jobs, three—clerks, salesmen valuers and auctioneers, and commercial travellers and manufacturers' agents—were placed in the same group in the initial Hope-Goldthorpe categorisation. That group is extremely heterogeneous and also includes youth employment officer, insurance collector, travel agency employee, library assistant and electric meter reader. The group seems too diverse to be of great value. On the Cambridge scale commercial travellers come well above clerks. In general we believe that the Hope-Goldthorpe value, below the level of most skilled occupations, is too low. As we indicated earlier, because of the diversity of people covered by the occupational category, reputational judgements are likely to reflect the actual conditions of the present job. Clearly no single scale positions can be adequate, but in view of the fact that at any one time the majority of the clerks have prospects of moving to much more rewarding occupations (see Chapter 6), a suitable compromise calls for a rather higher position. Thus we regard the higher values on the Cambridge scale as more satisfactory. In any case the Treiman and ANU scores are both closer to the Cambridge scale, though each is a little below, as we would anticipate since each is, in its different way, based upon reputational studies.

Two of the other groups once again have a single value on Hope-Goldthorpe. These are secretaries and typists and shop assistants. Although our secretaries are mainly female, while they specified males in their research, they come close to clerks on both scales. Once again we believe their scale values are too low, and the Treiman and ANU scores for secretaries back this belief. In each case they are much closer to the Cambridge score and the Treiman score is above it. Their scores for shop assistants are much lower, however, and it may be the aggregation which produces the low Hope-Goldthorpe score. Shop assistant is another example of a category we would expect to be different in reputational and relational scales. It is a young man's employment with very high rates of outflow from first job. Assessed on the job alone, the occupants have very poor returns, but the potential is greater.

Finally among this group is clerk of works, which does not occur in either Treiman or ANU scales. Presumably because it is with 'builders (so described)' in the OPCS grouping, Hope and Goldthorpe include this occupation with skilled occupations in the construction industry. Yet it is quite clear that they are not skilled manual workers, and on the Cambridge scale they come some way above clerks.

We have set out the comparison of the scale at some length because we believe it illustrates some of the problems of constructing measures of stratification. Such scales should never be used uncritically or be shown excessive respect. They all contain compromises which should be known and allowed for.

MEASURING STRATIFICATION

In our approach we have been particularly concerned with the relation between the method of constructing our scale and the theory of stratification. Consequently the scaling process has been instructive for our theoretical understanding. We have seen that there is one predominant dimension in our data, which reflects patterned social relationships and is strongly related to perceptions of occupational 'goodness'. This points firmly to the conclusion that the structure of social stratification is more coherent and consistent than has commonly been supposed.

At the same time the concern with theoretical relevance has led us to be somewhat critical of the result, even though there can be no doubt that it is an improvement on previous scales. But there is a more positive gain here also. Whereas Hope and Goldthorpe (1974, p. 132) feel it necessary to argue 'that no inference should be drawn from the position of individuals or groups on the scale to their social experience and behaviour (in terms, say, of their patterns of intimate association or life-styles) or to their social values and attitudes', we have no need to doubt the relevance of our scale. To be sure there is a need for further research on the relations between different aspects of experience and the structure of social stratification. However, the Cambridge scale has been developed with its relevance for stratification very much in mind. In particular it is directly related to life-styles and social relationships, and associated social experience. These are most often the relevant aspects of experience when a measure of stratification is used in social research. The relevance to market experience needs further analysis, but here again our theoretical approach indicates the nature of appropriate improvements to the scale. However, for such improvements to be adequate, taking account of the various meanings of having a particular occupation for people with different backgrounds (e.g. age, education, sex) and career prospects, would require a substantially more complex structure. Failing this, the present scale provides a useful rough measure.

Finally we may note one important facility for anyone wishing to use the scale. This is the ease with which the scale can be refined to meet particular needs. We have been at pains to explain that the use of occupational titles for stratification positions is far from ideal, but anyone carrying out fieldwork within an occupational area can quite simply create new and more adequate categories. Taking again the category of clerks, for instance, they can be meaningfully subdivided according to public or private employment, according to employment with inbuilt career structures such as banking, according to the clerks' qualifications and their ages and so on. Accountants may be subdivided by qualifications, and medical practitioners by general practice or the various hospital career grades. Indeed there is probably not an OPCS category that could not be usefully subdivided, and some of them very extensively. If such refined definitions are being employed in field research, all that is needed to incorporate them into the scale is to ask the respondents the appropriate question on friends. Estimation of scores is then based on the mean score of friends' occupations for each new occupational category. The logic of the scaling method implies that this mean is the occupation's scale position. In practice, however, there is a slight tendency for respondents to choose to report their higher status friends, and at the extremes of the scale friends tend to be nearer the middle. It is, therefore, advisable to first calculate an adjustment factor by comparing the mean score of friends for the complete OPCS category with the corresponding scale score. The only remaining problem arises from choice of friends within the newly defined occupations. The most sensitive approach is to estimate scores using an iterative procedure, but for most purposes it will be sufficient to give all the score for the overall category, or to exclude them from the calculations.

Part Two

Myths of Stratification

4 Proletarianisation

In this section we begin our analysis of the relationship between occupation and individual work-career experience, as it bears on the problem of stratification. We shall first focus our attention on clerical workers, using an intensive analysis in this area of employment to unravel problems of a more general significance.

An examination of clerical work is particularly apt for a discussion of occupations and stratification. There has always been a difficulty about the appropriate position of clerks in the class structure, and in recent years the debate has intensified as changes in the occupational structure have posed new problems of explanation. The importance accorded to these problems has put them at the heart of 'the great debate', as Goldthorpe *et al.* (1969, p. 1) call it, 'concerned with the evolution of the working class within western industrial society', a debate 'which has been in progress now for more than a century'. We enter this debate not in the hope of final settlement, but to seek to transform it.

In its recent form the debate is concerned with the consequences of the erosion of distinctions between manual and non-manual employees. It is assumed that at some time in the past a division of the working population into manual and non-manual served as a more or less adequate means of distinguishing typical work, economic and status experiences, and that now such a division is more problematic. The form of the argument has varied,[1] but there is a wide consensus that the crucial area of development is around the manual/non-manual boundary, where clerks are seen as a key group.

---

[1] For example Merrill (1961) and Mallet (1963), with reference to the USA and France respectively, have suggested that manual workers have become indistinguishable from non-manual outside work; some writers such as Hamilton (1966), Mills (1956) and Lockwood (1958) have been concerned with the proletarianisation of white-collar workers; Bernard (1956), Mayer (1956) and Zweig (1961) have argued the *embourgeoisement* of manual workers; others, including and more recently Goldthorpe, Lockwood, *et al.* (1969) have claimed a process of normative convergence. Many others have participated in the argument from one standpoint or another.

The development of an industrial system, it is generally agreed, involves a gradual shift of the working population from manual to non-manual jobs. The extent of the shift and the speed with which it is progressing has often been overestimated (see Levison, 1974), but despite a recent claim by Giddens (1973, p. 179) that European experience need not in this respect follow that of the USA, the data for all European countries confirm the trend and suggest that it is continuing (see Bell, 1973). The new non-manual jobs are not, of course, identical to those available at earlier stages of development. The introduction of office machinery, typewriters, copiers, teleprinters, calculators, computers and so on, on the one hand, and the bureaucratisation of office practices, reducing tasks previously calling for judgement and initiative to mere routine, on the other, have transformed the area of lower non-manual employment in such a way as to bring it within the scope of those of lower educational attainment. At the same time the general standard of education within the community has risen, making a larger proportion available for white-collar employment. These crucial changes in the market position of lower non-manual workers have been accompanied by a decline in their previous economic advantage over manual workers. So the argument runs.

Perhaps the simplest and boldest statement of this position is set out by Braverman (1974, Chapter 15). He believes that the distinction between manual and non-manual employees which persists in official statistics and many sociological works bears no relation to current conditions. It continues because it is 'considered serviceable by those who are alarmed by the results of a more realistic terminology—those, for instance, whose 'sociology' pursues apologetic purposes. For them, such terms as "white-collar employees" conveniently lump into a single category the well paid, authoritative, and desirable positions at the top of the hierarchy and the mass of proletarianised inferiors in a way that makes for a rosier picture: higher 'average' pay scales, etc.' (pp. 349–501.) The truth for Braverman is that 'the problem of the white-collar worker which so bothered early generations of Marxists, and which was hailed by anti-Marxists as proof of the falsity of the "proletarianisation" thesis, has thus been unambiguously clarifed by the polarisation of office employment and the growth at one pole of an immense mass of *wage-workers*. The apparent trend to a large non-proletarian 'middle-class' has resolved itself into the creation of a large proletariat in a new form. In its conditions of employment, the working population has lost all former superiorities over workers in industry, and in its scale of pay has sunk almost to the bottom.' (pp. 355–6.) 'At the same time (with the development of office machines in the 20th Century) the labor market for the two chief varieties of workers, factory and office, begins to lose some of its distinctions of social stratification, education, family and the like.' (p. 353.)

To anticipate the conclusions of this chapter the actual situation is not nearly so simple, and Braverman's presentation ignores problems of placing clerks in the class structure which are reflected in studies from many countries. We shall argue that his view is built upon a basic misconception, a misconception that he shares with almost every contributor to the debate, that the significance of occupation in determining class resides in the nature of job, ignoring the relationship of incumbents to jobs. He seeks to explicate the 'class position of clerical labor', but clerical workers do not belong to a single class. Whether or not there has been a 'degradation' of clerical work, clerical workers as a whole have not suffered 'proletarianisation'. To understand the fallacious basis of the general debate, it is essential to maintain a clear distinction between the workers and the work they perform. Such a distinction may seem obvious, but we shall see it has rarely been made and its implications totally ignored.

In this chapter we shall be concerned with male clerks. The debates to which we are addressing ourselves have been primarily concerned with male employment and the data upon which we draw are for men. This does not imply that we are unaware of the importance of the employment of women, especially in routine non-manual jobs. By far the greater increase in numbers in clerical work has occurred among females. Routh (1965) estimates that male clerks in 1951 were 143 per cent of male clerks in 1911, whereas female clerks in 1951 were 787 per cent of the earlier figure. By 1951 women formed a majority of the clerical category with 58.8 per cent of all clerks. Since 1951 the proportion of women has increased to about 70 per cent. Overall employment of men in this category has grown only a little faster than the growth of the male working population. In 1911 male clerks formed 5.1 per cent of all male employees. By 1951 they formed 6.0 per cent and by 1971 they were 6.7 per cent.[2] On the other hand, only 3.3 per cent of female employees fell in this category in 1911, but the proportion had risen to 20.4 per cent in 1951 and 28 per cent in 1971.

It should be remembered that most women employed in the clerical category are not in jobs which place them in direct competition with

[2] The 1911 and 1951 proportions of the population are taken from Bain (1970, pp. 189–91) who revises Routh's figures in such a way that they are more comparable with the 1971 Census figures.

men. A majority of them in 1960 were either secretaries, typists or office machine operators, all occupations in which male employees are rare, and if Routh is correct there was a tendency between 1951 and 1960 for greater concentration of female employees in these female jobs. In 1951 approximately 46 per cent of all women in the clerical category were in such jobs, whereas by 1960 the proportion had increased to 56 per cent. It is also likely that a detailed breakdown of the jobs in other remaining types of clerical employment would reveal further predominantly female occupations. Despite these various modifications to the figures, the growth in the numbers of women in routine clerical positions has been very extensive.

There can be no doubt that the growth of female employment has been part of an important change in clerical work. At the least it has significant consequences for male clerks which we cannot ignore. In the main, even when women have entered the same sort of routine clerical jobs as men, they have not established the same career patterns. They have been located in the most menial clerical tasks with limited opportunities for promotion. Although there are often no formal limits upon their careers, they have in fact occupied the lowest ranges even in those areas of employment, such as banking and insurance or government service, where, as we shall see, male promotion has become almost routine.

ECONOMIC ARGUMENTS

There are few commentators who would disagree with Giddens (1973, p. 190) that 'it is now well established that, in recent years, a series of changes has affected the economic position of the clerical grouping, as compared with the higher levels of the working class.' These economic considerations have been central to arguments about significant changes in the class structure. The simplest argument sees such changes as a direct result of economic changes, but much of the interest in this issue has focused on the apparent inconsistency between economic and other aspects of the stratification position of clerks. For the most part we do not dispute the actual data, but we propose to show that the meaning given to them is largely fallacious and the associated arguments frequently misconceived. To do this we must first review the data and their usual interpretations.

The most extensive review of trends in the distribution of income and occupation in Great Britain in this century is Routh's (1965) work, *Occupation and Pay in Britain 1906–1960*. While it is clear from his analysis that from the mid-1930s to the mid-1950s the trend in incomes was against those in the clerical grouping relative to manual workers, in the period between 1913/14 and 1935/36 male clerks and skilled manual workers maintained parity of earnings. According to Routh both groups averaged £99 per annum in 1913/14, and clerks averaged £192 in 1935/36 while skilled workers averaged £195. Over the same period semi-skilled workers increased their earnings from £69 per annum to £134, and unskilled manual workers from £63 per annum to £129. If we express the average incomes in 1935/36 as percentages of incomes in 1913/14, we obtain the following figures: clerks 193 per cent, skilled manual workers 196 per cent, semi-skilled manual workers 194 per cent, unskilled manual workers 205 per cent. Only unskilled workers improved their position vis-a-vis clerks to any appreciably extent.

Between 1935/6 and 1955/6 the picture is quite different. The average earnings of clerks increased from £192 per annum to £523, which is 272 per cent of the former figure. Over the same period the average for skilled manual workers went from £195 to £622 (319 per cent), for semi-skilled workers from £134 to £469 (350 per cent) and for unskilled workers from £129 to £435 (337 per cent). These figures clearly illustrate the trend summarised by Lockwood (1958, p. 67), who wrote:

> In terms of actual income, we have seen that in the years prior to 1914 the ordinary adult clerk was roughly on a par with the skilled worker. Through the inter-war period the black-coated worker managed to maintain that parity, but during the war and post-war years, differentials between manual and non-manual employment were gradually reduced.

Since the mid-1950s it is difficult to follow just how clerical incomes have changed relative to those of other occupations. Between 1955/56 and 1960 in Routh's figures the trend moves slightly in favour of clerical workers. At least they do not seem to have lost any further ground at that time. Since then, up to 1971, it seems their earnings have not fallen in comparison with skilled workers, but they have fallen substantially in relation to semi-skilled and unskilled workers as the differentials in manual work have narrowed. Clerical earnings have also been falling relative to other non-manual occupations.[3]

---

[3] The figures on which these statements are based come from the Department of Employment Gazette, which includes data of the New Earnings Survey of more recent years. Unfortunately it is not possible to make precise comparisons between comparable categories over the whole period, and conclusions are based on trends in various different sets of figures.

As regards the USA the first extensive figures were presented by Burns (1954). Mayer, in particular, followed this up with the claim that changes in income differentials between occupations were evidence of the disappearance of class stratification. However, his figures were unsatisfactory in several respects, as was subsequently pointed out by Hamilton (1963). Indeed, Hamilton is the one contributor to the debate who has seriously questioned the basic economic assumptions. To be sure, other writers have pointed to advantages other than income which are enjoyed by clerks and not by manual workers, and have insisted that these must be recognised in any calculation of the relative positions of the groups, but the trend to reduced differentials (or increased in the case of skilled as against clerical workers) has not otherwise been disputed. Hamilton pointed out that both men and women had been included in the income data used by Mayer, and as there was a higher proportion of women in clerical occupations than among skilled manual workers, and as women generally earned less, the mean income of the clerical group was thus artificially deflated. In addition foremen had been included with the manual workers, artificially inflating their mean income. Finally Hamilton (1963, p. 369) argued that there was a concentration of clerks in the younger age groups and that these young clerks would not have reached their peak earnings. In comparing clerks and manual workers, the effect of the lower earnings of young clerks had not been recognised. Using data from the National Opinion Research Center, Study No. 367, he attempted to eliminate these errors and concluded that:

Contrary to assertions in contemporary sociology, the findings reported here show neither equality of income nor an inversion of the historical pattern. The white-collar worker typically begins with a higher income than do skilled workers and this difference is maintained through to middle age.

Hamilton's attack on the orthodox view seems to have been all too often ignored, but it has not passed unanswered. In an article entitled 'The Economic Dimensions of Embourgeoisement', Mackenzie (1967) addresses himself to these arguments, using data from the 1960 Census of the Population of the United States. Of this article he (1973, p. 190) later writes,

In the early 1960s Hamilton cast doubts upon the validity of the income data cited by Mayer, charging that the relative affluence of the contemporary blue collar worker was more apparent than real. However, taking into account Hamilton's reservations, I was able to reaffirm that all economic differentials separating clerical workers and skilled craftsmen had disappeared.

In particular his analysis (1967, p. 33) led him to conclude that:

Clerical workers and skilled craftsmen do earn almost identical incomes at every stage of the life cycle. An exception is age group 20–24. Here the median income for clerical workers is $400 higher than that of craftsmen. In all probability, this is because craftsmen are still receiving training in their early twenties.

Parsler (1970, p. 171), writing of data collected in a study in Melbourne, apparently finds that MacKenzie's data are not repeated in Australia. After comparing the incomes of white-collar workers and blue-collar workers over various ages, he writes:

A good deal of MacKenzie's argument is based on his findings of near equality of the income careers of 'Clerical and Kindred' and 'Craftsmen, Foremen and Kindred', and no difference at all in the total yearly median income of these two groups. In this Australian study there is a difference of $1,088.4 between the 'Skilled Workers' (excluding Foremen) and the 'Clerks etc.' on the total yearly median income.

However, the figures are not strictly comparable. Parsler includes with his clerks those in promoted positions within the clerical area. In discussing the question of including or excluding manual foremen he (1970, p. 169) writes:

The view taken here is that the chargehand supervisor, or foreman is a manual worker with a supervisory function and he remains as much a part of the blue-collar group as the clerk promoted to a supervisory position remains part of the white-collar group.

It is integral to the thinking reflected in this quotation that the group of 'Clerks etc.' in his data includes many people in promoted positions. Though he does take Foremen out of the manual grouping for certain purposes, those included in the 'White-Collar' category are never divided by supervisory responsibility. Yet Parsler (1970, p. 176) says,

'The white-collar group had 33.3 per cent who claimed they had supervision of other employees in the capacities of Supervisor, Manager (general policy), and Executive (higher policy).'

Clerks formed 56.7 per cent of the white-collar category, and the other groups were Shop Assistants and Salesmen, Self-employed Shop Proprietors, Storemen and Others. It would seem that those with supervisory experience are at least as likely to be in the clerical as in the other categories. In these circumstances Parsler's figures are for a group quite different from MacKenzie's, and we would expect income differences of the sort he observes. Certainly they do not establish that Australian experience is out of line with that in the United States.

Since the relative income of the different groups is *apparently* a simple empirical question, the data would appear to settle the matter. However, as we shall see, though the data themselves are not in dispute, their interpretation and relevance to theories of stratification is much more problematic. Before passing on, it should be noted at this point that Hamilton made one observation which MacKenzie completely overlooked in this article. That is that those starting their working careers as clerks are more likely to be promoted to better paying positions (outside clerical work) than are those starting as skilled manual workers. It will become apparent that this is the most telling of Hamilton's points. In this regard the higher average earnings of young clerical workers than young artisans found by MacKenzie is interesting, and we shall later suggest an explanation different from the one he gives.

Certain writers, while accepting the income trend, have stressed that an appreciation of market situation must take account of more than mere income. They have been at pains to counter the argument of class convergence by arguing that the economic convergence is more apparent than real. Runciman (1966, pp. 82–4), for example, has argued that in order to obtain an income on a par with clerical workers, the manual worker 'was obliged to work considerably longer hours'. At the same time, 'he was less favoured in terms of holidays', while 'the white-collar worker remained much better placed for retirement', and 'in amenities at work . . . remains clearly favoured'. Lastly '[promotion] is perhaps the biggest difference in the class situation of the manual and clerical worker'. Throughout his discussion of class situation Runciman uses 'clerical worker', 'non-manual worker' and 'non-manual grouping' as more or less synonymous. Many of the advantages claimed for non-manual workers scarcely apply to routine clerks, and he frequently seems concerned to establish merely that, taken as a whole, manual and non-manual employees do not share the same market situation. For example, in arguing that even income figures can be misleading, he quotes an average weekly wage of £14 17s. in April 1960 for weekly paid administrative, technical and clerical workers, but an average weekly wage of £23 15s. 4d. for monthly paid administrative, technical and clerical workers. Whereas the former figure is less than the average earning of all manual workers, the latter, he (1966, p. 84) points out, 'is more than the earnings of manual workers in even the best paying industries'. Indeed it is, but by no stretch of the imagination can this grouping be thought to consist solely, or even mainly, of ordinary clerks. Surely no one doubts that non-manual employees in general enjoy an economic advantage; the question is rather whether recent changes in economic conditions have led to a blurring of the manual/non-manual distinction. Certainly it does need to be made clear that if some manual workers are merging with the middle class, it is only at the lowest levels, but this does not invalidate the convergence thesis. Even Mayer (1963, p. 466), while arguing that many manual workers are being absorbed into the middle class, which in turn is 'losing its class character', sees the new order as 'differentiation without stratification'.

Similar reservations have been raised by Goldthorpe, Lockwood *et al.* (1969). They address themselves particularly to what they call the *embourgeoisement* thesis. Briefly this holds that changes in economic and work circumstances are leading to the progressive incorporation of manual workers into the middle class. Old class barriers are disappearing as the working class adopt middle class values and life-styles. In their study of relatively affluent manual workers they find that considerable differences still exist between their sample and even routine clerical workers, and that *embourgeoisement* has not progressed to the extent frequently argued. They believe the 'proponents of the *embourgeoisement* thesis have exaggerated the effects on class structure of higher wages'. In part this is because of a failure to realise the conditions under which high wages may be achieved by manual workers. The (1969, pp. 157–8) argue that:

Obtaining earnings sufficient to support a middle-class standard of living may well mean taking on work of a particularly unrewarding or unpleasant kind—work, that is, which can be experienced only as labour. And indeed for men in most manual grades the achievement of affluence is likely to require some substantial amount of overtime working on top of a regular working week which is already longer than that of white-collar employees. Finally, it is evident that many types of industrial work, and often those that afford high earnings, exert a seriously restrictive effect upon out of work life; in this respect again shifts and overtime are major factors, and the impact of the former at least will become more rather than less widely felt. Thus, it may be claimed that ongoing trends of change in modern industry are not in fact ones which operate uniformly in the direction of reducing class differences and divisions.

It should be noted, however, that (as the authors are aware) these arguments apply much more to non-skilled manual workers than to artisans. Yet the *embourgeoisement* thesis in its formal presentation has been much more concerned with the latter. The debate on income trends reported above, involving Mayer, Hamilton and MacKenzie, concerned the relative incomes of clerks and artisans. Indeed Mayer (1955, p. 42), who may be taken as one of the leading proponents of *embourgeoisement* has written:

In many respects, therefore, the line which sets off 'aristocracy of skilled labour' from the bulk of semi-skilled and unskilled manual labourers is more significant sociologically than the dividing line between skilled craftsmen and low and middle class white-collar workers which has become increasingly blurred in recent years.

However, the sample of Goldthorpe *et al.* was predominantly not skilled. Craftsmen accounted for 27 per cent, to which we may add a further 11 per cent for the setters, who would usually be regarded as skilled men,[4] but that is all. These two groups were the most highly paid but, in general, were not typical of the affluent workers studied. In these circumstances the authors' (1969, p. 16) claim that their sample 'was drawn from a population whose social characteristics and social setting were such as to favour, in almost every respect, the validation of the *embourgeoisement* thesis, following the logic of the arguments advanced by its various proponents,' reads rather strangely. What it was well designed to do was test the 'vulgar' thesis couched simply and solely in

---

[4] There is considerable difficulty in defining the category of skilled men, which further aggravates the problem of cross-national comparison. For instance the British OPCS uses a very wide definition which includes most of what would usually be called semi-skilled jobs. The only jobs on which there is general agreement are those of craftsmen (though they need defining), and it is these men who have been at the centre of the debate.

terms of the effects of high wages, which they were able to demolish completely.

While we would agree that it is necessary to extend the debate about market situation to include factors other than the level of income, there can be no doubt that, especially since the Second World War, the trend in job security and fringe benefits has been in favour of manual workers. Government intervention has improved the situation with regard to redundancy and retirement pensions, and schemes to secure income during sickness have become more extensive. Even in the area of work experience, changes of attitude are apparent. Though it has not progressed very far, there is a movement towards modifying the most unpleasant and unrewarding types of manual labour. In general then it would appear that here, as with income, the gap between manual and clerical workers has been narrowing.

INCOMES, LIFE-STYLES AND THE DIFFERENCE FROM MANUAL WORKERS

The issues involved in the convergence of the middle and working classes are, however, very much wider than these economic considerations. Thus, for example, the main thrust of the argument against *embourgeoisement* by Goldthorpe and his associates (1969, p. 164) is not, in fact, the continuing difference in relation to work which we have just discussed; it is the failure of affluent workers to adopt, or even to want, middle-class styles of life, including social relationships of equality with non-manual workers. The real issue is the relevance of the economic changes for these other aspects of stratification, and it is significant that their findings 'can lend little support to the idea of the 'middle-class' worker'.

In short, the considerable and continuing interest in the manual/nonmanual division is not primarily a consequence of changed market circumstances. Rather it is due to an apparent failure of these new economic circumstances to overcome pre-existing stratification patterns in other areas of life and so become securely and unequivocally embedded in general social experience.

In the 1950s there was a tendency, while acknowledging discrepancies between income and life-style, to look towards a rapid reconciliation. Mills, writing in the early 1950s, foresaw an imminent intensification of change in social circumstances. The 'narrowing of the income gap' would lead to an elimination of education differences upon which the special claim to prestige by white-collar workers rested. This in turn would lead to a 'status panic', as they sought to maintain separate consideration by seizing upon 'minute distinctions as bases for status . . .' which would 'lead to estrangement from work associates, and to increased status competition'. (1956, p. 254). Mayer (1955, p. 42) went even further in suggesting that a resolution of the problem, albeit of a different form, had already been achieved. The quotation from his work given above comes directly after the following two sentences:

> A large part of the working class shares a 'white-collar' style of life and accepts middle-class values and beliefs. This is especially true of craftsmen, foremen, and skilled mechanics, whose high wages nowadays exceed the salaries of many lower middle-class white-collar employees and even small businessmen.

Neither Mills nor Mayer have been borne out by subsequent events and research. A 'status panic' has not occurred and the evidence of many studies conducted both in the United States, of which Mayer is writing, and in a diversity of other countries both capitalist and socialist, does not support his asserted resolution. There has been a rise in white-collar unionism, particularly in terms of increased militancy, which has attracted much attention. But this is a very different phenomenon from a 'status panic', and anyway it has been occurring at all levels of non-manual employment. Furthermore, this development of class action in employment[5] does not seem to have been matched by changes outside work. Despite similar income trends in most advanced industrial societies, in each case clerks, without an economic advantage, appear as a group to follow life-styles much closer to higher middle-class groups than do skilled manual workers. For example, they marry the daughters of more prestigious and affluent parents. In our 1974 British general sample we see that 24 per cent of clerks had married daughters of professional or managerial workers compared with only 8 per cent of craftsmen (including foremen), while 31 per cent of clerks and 46 per cent of the skilled men had married daughters of non-skilled workers. When we take account of income levels the result is little different: among highly paid craftsmen 11 per cent were married to the daughters of professional and managerial workers, while the proportion who had married daughters of non-skilled workers is still 46 per cent. Among

---

[5] In the sense of specific instances of collective action of the employed against their employers, rather than action on behalf of the proletariat in general.

highly paid non-skilled workers the corresponding proportions are 11 per cent and 58 per cent. (See also Oldman and Illsley, 1966 for UK, Lauman, 1966, pp. 74–7 for USA.) Clerks also live in better neighbourhoods than manual workers (Duncan and Duncan, 1957, Lauman 1966, p. 73–4), place greater value upon education and have higher educational aspirations and expectations for their children (for a review of the relevant literature, see Banks, 1971, Chapters 4 and 5).

In the patterns of their friendship choices they stand between upper white-collar groups and artisans, but much closer to the former (see e.g. Lauman, 1966, pp. 64–70, and MacKenzie, 1973, Chapter 7 for USA; Stewart *et al.*, 1973, p. 416, and Chapter 2, above, for UK). At the end of a discussion of patterns of social interaction, MacKenzie (1973, p. 152) concludes that 'perhaps my most important finding' is that in relational terms clerks and artisans are quite different groups and, as a consequence, 'it is not sociologically meaningful to regard these people as members of the same social class'.

EDUCATION

Perhaps the initially most puzzling feature distinguishing clerks from artisans is the continued superior education of the clerical grouping. Despite the lack of economic advantage over skilled manual workers, at least in the UK, during this century, and the distinctly lower average income received by clerks since the end of the Second World War, young people are still apparently willing to trade superior educational qualifications for inferior economic returns. That clerical work offers a poor return on education is, once again *apparently*, well established. Apart from the tabular presentation of this discrepancy to be found in many works, Hodge (1962) has demonstrated, using regression techniques, that clerks in the USA earn less than would be expected on the basis of returns to their educational level in the population at large. This applies over the whole age range.

Yet clerical positions continue to attract the educationally advantaged. In our white-collar sample 59 per cent of those under 30 years of age who began their careers as clerks had attended either grammar or independent schools approved as efficient, while in the school population at large in January 1965, only 21 per cent of all boys aged 12–15 (i.e. excluding those beyond leaving age) were in such schools.[6] This

---

[6] Taken from Statistics of Education Part I 1965, London H.M.S.O. 1966, Table II(6).

latter figure is typical of the whole period of secondary schooling of those under 30 in early 1970.

Of those aged under 30 at the time of interview who were still in clerical jobs, over 55 per cent had attended such schools. It is interesting to compare this figure with that given by Lockwood (1958) for the portion of his sample aged between 18 and 29 in 1949, bearing in mind the differences in the two sample populations.[7] He reports that 50 per cent of his young clerks had attended either grammar or boarding secondary schools. These figures are probably fairly closely comparable. It is true that education of this type was more available to our sample of clerks than to Lockwood's, but how much more available is not completely clear. Lockwood gives a figure of 14.6 per cent of the total male population aged 18 or over as having received such an education in 1949. The clerks in his sample aged 18 and 29, however, must have been drawn from a cohort with a larger proportion in such education as there was a continual expansion of provision throughout the century. On the other side we have not included in our calculation the clerks in our sample who attended comprehensive schools. Since some of these clerks are likely to have followed grammar school-type courses, we have probably underestimated the numbers with this type of education. In addition, our sample is rather biassed towards industry as against other areas of clerical employment, and there is a greater concentration of clerks with secondary modern backgrounds in industry. All in all the figures can hardly be said to show a tendency towards the recruitment of less well educated candidates to clerical positions over the two decades separating the samples.

We shall return on other occasions to the education of clerks. Our present purpose has been merely to illustrate that apparent discrepancies between economic returns and other stratification factors not only may be observed now, but have persisted and may be more stable than has generally been supposed. In this respect it should be remembered that clerks have enjoyed no income advantage over skilled manual workers this century. Thus the assumption that before about the mid-1930s clerks were fairly easily identified as belonging to the middle-class must be set against the fact that they maintained their position, apparently, without the help of a superior income, though their fringe benefits may have been greater. The apparent discrepancy between income and life-styles is, therefore, older than is frequently

---

[7] Lockwood's sample is part of the sample of Glass (1954) which is there analysed in Ch. 4.

realised, but then so is the general problem of the class position of clerks.

CLERKS AND THE ARISTOCRACY OF LABOUR

Indeed, it is not easy to identify a time when clerical work was unequivocally superior in terms of either prestige or income to skilled manual work. Hobsbawm (1972, p. 297) argues that in the early part of last century the 'aristocracy of labour', comprised largely of artisans, enjoyed a position in the stratification system close to the 'masters' for whom they worked. In the latter part of the century, as the capitalist system developed and gave rise to the extension of general education, new market conditions prevailed in which 'a wedge of white-collar workers and to a lesser extent technicians and independently recruited managers (was driven) between the labour aristocrats and the 'masters', reducing their relative social position and limiting their chances of promotion'. Yet it would appear that from the mid-nineteenth century forward, there has been difficulty in arriving at an adequate categorisation of class arrangements, with an appropriate distinction between skilled manual and certain types of non-manual workers. Thus in Bolton in the 1890s the aristocracy of labour was held to include 'the best paid clerks, bookkeepers, managers and the better sort of working folk' (Clarke, 1899), while in Salford at about the same time it was held to include 'commercial travellers . . . clerks, lithographic printers, joiners, cabinet makers, grocers' assistants and down to colliers'. (Interdepartmental Committee of Physical Deterioration, 1904, XXXII, pp. 4, 422–4. Both this and the last quotation taken from Hobsbawm, 1972, p. 273.)

When the division of the working population into social classes first appeared in the reports of the Census of England and Wales, for the 1911 Census, the problem was again evident. Eight social classes were identified, one non-manual and seven manual. Of the non-manual class, Stevenson (Census of England and Wales, 1911, XIII, Part II, LXXVI), who was responsible for the report, wrote:

Class I—the Upper and middle class—includes all occupation groups of which the majority of members as tabulated at the census could be assumed to belong to these classes. It covers such occupations as commercial and railway clerks and insurance agents, but aims at excluding the artisan, even though his wages may be higher than the clerk's

That both clerks and artisans have to be particularly accounted for in this way suggest a genuine problem in the minds of the assessors about the position of both groups.

Thus we can see that the process of change in the occupational structure had not set clerks unambiguously above skilled manual workers before the First World War. It would seem therefore that if a manual/non-manual division placing clerks on one side and artisans on the other, which has been accepted by most commentators, did exist it was in the 1920s and 1930s. Certainly the greater security of employment for clerks during the depression would have emphasised differences from even skilled manual workers though, as we have seen, clerks enjoyed no income advantage. However, we shall return to this later, when we shall go on to challenge the assumption that such a division was ever unproblematic. We see it as part of a long-standing misinterpretation of the relationship between occupation and social stratification.

RECONCILING THE INCOME/LIFE-STYLE DISCREPANCY

Whatever conclusions are to be drawn about the past trends, it is the present incongruence between income and life-styles which commentators seek to explain or accommodate in their accounts of stratification systems. The pressure has been towards multi-dimensional models of stratification within which the discrepancies can be allowed. In the history of sociology there have been many theories arguing for a diversity of ordering principles not wholly in agreement with each other. Individuals, it has been said, have access to different and diverse sources of market power and social honour. Sorokin (1967, p. 292), for example, has written:

The stratified pyramids of the unibonded groups never consolidate in such a way that all their strata coincide and create one integral consolidated social pyramid, in which all the tops of the unibonded pyramids make one integral top and all the middle and lowest strata consolidate into one integral middle or lowest stratum. The actual 'skyline' of the total stratification rather takes the shape of the skyline of a mountain range with several peaks of different pyramids not entirely merged.

Yet even a casual reading of attempts to describe and account for stratification systems attests to the strength of implicit assumptions that there are strong forces bringing all aspects of stratification experience into balance. Perhaps Aquinas invoked the strongest force, arguing the correctness of income being in line with status as part of natural law, but others have seemed no less sure of the outcome. We have already mentioned the strains of imbalance seen by Mills and the simple resolution presented by Mayer, but this assumption is clear even in more recent works. MacKenzie (1967, p. 38) for example writes:

> As a result of the disappearance of economic differentials between craftsmen and white-collar workers, it follows that the class situation of the former group can also be expected to change. The questions that now remain to be answered are how fundamental this change will be and what direction it will take.

Although we have pointed out that the evidence does not bear out these views, we would suggest that the fault lies not so much in the seemingly intuitive belief in the consistency of the stratification system as in the conceptualisation of the relations between aspects of stratification.

In general, however, the development of theory to account for apparent contradictions between income and life-styles among clerks and artisans has involved a movement towards a more and more rigid division of stratification into discrete analytical and structural categories. This process is easily identified, and we shall outline some of the stages, but what is never clear is the extent to which the imbalanced positions derived from different influences upon stratification are to be regarded as stable. More is usually claimed in this respect by commentators than can be found in original writings. Perhaps it is prejudging the issue to call the positions 'imbalanced', but the attention they receive in the literature reinforces the view that some sort of special explanation is required. Despite frequent assertions that there are diverse sources and different dimensions of stratification position, the independence of the factors identified is not usually well established in theory. That they correspond to real differences in social experience is not usually in doubt, but the extent to which they are, in the longer or shorter term, free to vary independently is seldom established or even adequately discussed.

Lockwood was very influential in establishing the process. In seeking to explain the differences in class identification and class action of manual workers and clerks, he rejected the so-called 'false-consciousness' explanations which sought to account for the class behaviour of clerks in terms of an incorrect identification of their interests. According to the proponents of this view, clerks occupied essentially the same class position as manual workers while identifying with their employers (see especially Klingender, 1935). Lockwood (1958, p. 14) argues that between the wars writers and activists, disappointed with the failure of clerks to join a common class struggle with their manual brothers, turned to disparagement of clerical workers. He writes of the period:

> Indeed, if there is one consistent recurring theme which can be taken as the *leitmotif* of the present study it is that of the 'snobbishness', the 'self-deception' and the 'false-consciousness' of the clerk. The contemptuous term, 'white-collar proletariat', was coined specifically in the inter-war years to emphasise the pathetic self-deception of the blackcoated worker who was seen as indulging middle-class pretensions on a working class level of living.

He (1958, p. 213), on the other hand, holds that, 'to explain variations in class consciousness it is necessary to look for variations in class position', a stance with which we wholeheartedly agree, but, as will become apparent, we offer a rather different account of class positions. In pursuit of his aim of reconciling consciousness and structural position, he separates 'class position' into three areas of experience:

> First, 'market situation', that is to say the economic position narrowly conceived, consisting of source and size of income, degree of job-security, and opportunity for upward occupational mobility. Secondly, 'work situation', the set of social relationships in which the individual is involved at work by virtue of his position in the division of labour. And finally, 'status situation', or the position of the individual in the hierarchy of prestige in the society at large.

The first two areas, he (1958, p. 15) argues, 'comprise what Marx essentially understood as "class position"', while 'status position' was added to the analysis of stratification by Weber. While changes are occurring in each of these areas of experience, they are not necessarily occurring at the same rate, and a degree of independence is possible among them.

Though the components of class position are seen as distinct, the degree of independence to be accorded them is never entirely clear. Certainly, they are seen as closely interrelated, especially market situation and status. Lockwood (1958, p. 100) writes:

> The tie between economic situation and social status is a close and obvious one. What is often forgotten, however, is that the relationship is frequently a reciprocal one. Economic advantage does not simply confer social status; in many cases traditional social status is a ground for perpetuation of economic differences.

A number of interesting implications arise from this statement. The strain towards consistency is obvious: economic advantage confers, presumably appropriate, social status, while traditional status differences serve to maintain economic differences. But further, there is no independent account of the generation of status. The phrase 'traditional social status' strongly suggests its genesis in previous economic circumstances, which would agree with its source in Weber, and this is strongly supported in another passage by him (pp. 208–9):

> In actual fact, however, class and status differences are closely related. There is nothing strange in this association. A dominant class has never existed which did not seek to make its position legitimate by placing highest value on those qualities and activities that come closest to its own.

There is nothing in this formulation which allows for the perpetuation of differences in class and status in the long term. The forces are all towards a reconciliation of such differences.

This being so, it is not surprising that Lockwood is rather guarded in his statements about discrepancies. He is careful to emphasise that his findings, relating consciousness to the positions on different class components, are for the situation current at the time of writing. Though 'work situation' may be somewhat more independent, there is a strong implication that economic and status factors cannot remain in imbalance forever, and when we consider the process of reproduction of the class system, in particular the way in which recruitment to occupations is maintained or varies, we may conclude that the reconciliation is likely to be accomplished in the shorter term.

It should be noted that Lockwood writes of *three components of class position*, emphasising their interrelatedness, but later writers have moved further towards identifying independent 'dimensions' of stratification. Runciman, for example, makes a more rigid differentiation into 'class', 'status' and 'power'. In doing this he, in part, uses Lockwood's work as justification and so, by implication, suggests for it a more general applicability than is claimed in the work itself.

Despite his insistence that the dimensions of stratification are analytically and substantively distinct, Runciman is well aware that they are closely related. By giving them separate histories and separate accounts of their contemporary states, he reinforces assumptions of their independence which, in the long term, is not well established. In general, the question of independence is a problem of all multidimensional approaches to stratification.

We earlier noted the continued ability of clerical work to attract well qualified entrants. With separate components of stratification identified, this apparent discrepancy between education and income has frequently been solved by a simple formula: the rewards lacking in class (income and conditions) are compensated by higher status returns (social honour or prestige). Such a resolution is against all evidence. It is true that Lockwood, for example, argues differences in class and status situation, but perhaps the most important basis of the higher status of clerks in his writings is *their superior education*. In fact, Lockwood (1958, p. 126) argues for a status ambiguity in the position of clerks which he explains in the following way:

> To speak of ambiguity of status, then, is to recognise that the prestige of an occupation may be determined by many criteria which are not always consistent with one another. If, as a result, clerical workers are divided among themselves on the question of their proper position in the social hierarchy, then we may speak of status ambiguity. Or if the grounds on which they generally claim a higher status than manual worker are regarded as inadmissible by the latter, so that an expectation of respect is met with contempt, then this again is a sign of status ambiguity. In both senses the social status of clerical work has become increasingly ambiguous.

The particular instances he gives of status ambiguity are as follows:

> In terms of social background, education, working conditions, proximity to authority and opportunity of upward mobility, clerks can still perhaps claim a higher status than most manual workers. In

terms of productive contribution, income, skill, masculinity and group loyalty, they may be accorded a lower status.

This lies at the very heart of the problem. It will be noted that the second group of characteristics, upon which clerks do worse than artisans, are all characteristics of the particular *job situation*. Productive contribution and skill define the occupational task; income is related to conventional assessments of the market situation of the occupation both in the labour market and the market for the product; masculinity is determined by conventional judgements of the specific job tasks; only group loyalty falls into a different category. This group of status characteristics come very close to his own defining characteristics of *class* position.

On the other hand, the claims to superior status are to a large extent based upon characteristics not of the jobs but of the *incumbents*. This being so, it is hard to see how the status can be said to be a reward of the job. Social background and education are aspects of the status of 'the clerk', only in so far as clerical work is afforded status on the basis of the prestige (due to these characteristics and obtained independently of the job) of those who are clerks. When superior educational achievements are taken as a component of the status of 'the clerk', we must either understand this person as an abstract construct standing for the aggregate characteristics of the population of clerical workers, within which there are considerable variations of education level, or by some process all individual clerks (represented by 'the clerk') take on an identical status for at least identical components in their overall status) by virtue of their membership of an occupational category with a certain distribution of educational qualifications among its members. The first possibility is at best a weak device, using a known social fiction, which does not imply that the status in any way derives from being a clerk. The second has a limited plausibility, along the lines that 'a better class of people' become clerks and so anyone who is a clerk shares in the general image. This may help to make it a socially acceptable occupation for those from high status backgrounds. However, in terms of actual status rewards, insofar as the argument is not circular it is largely implausible.

Those determining the status are the clerks themselves, so the argument turns on there being a shared 'average' status from pooling individual differences. However, it would seem sensible to suppose that if those employed as clerks can be readily differentiated collectively from other workers in terms of their backgrounds and education, they can also be differentiated as individuals. In any case, even if the argument is correct it means that only those clerks with lower status backgrounds and education can benefit from status of the job, while the better educated and those from higher status backgrounds are, apparently, losing out on status as well as economic rewards.

The basic flaw is to regard clerical work as the defining characteristic of the social position of those employed in it, to regard 'clerk' as a social reality of the stratification system. The flaw consists in equating people and jobs. As we shall see, the change in income relativities between skilled manual and clerical work and the changed distribution of clerical incomes do not mean that any identifiable group of people need have suffered erosion of their position in either market or status terms. The unfortunate habit of writing about 'clerical employees', 'clerical workers' or 'clerks' when what is really being discussed are trends associated with clerical jobs has been grossly misleading. Examples are numerous, but perhaps two will serve to illustrate the point. When Giddens (1973, p. 190) writes, 'it is not only in terms of income, however, that clerical employees have seen their economic circumstances lessened as compared with blue-collar workers', we may forget that in the absence of information about patterns of recruitment, promotion and general movement into and out of the category, no such lessening of circumstances can be established. The present relatively deprived population of clerks may not be in any real sense the same as, or the equivalent of, the previous relatively advantaged population. Again when Lockwood writes 'as regards income relativities, the clerical worker more or less kept his position vis-à-vis the wage earner until the late thirties', we understand that, since he is writing of the period from 1900, he is not writing of any actual clerical worker or group of clerical workers; but the style of presentation suggests an equivalence between the population of clerks in 1900 and that in 1939 which has not been established by detailed argument.

This curiously ageless, abstract creature, 'the clerical worker', serves to simplify the relationships between individuals and occupations by creating a false identity between them. What we must do is separate individuals and jobs and give a more coherent account of the relationship between them.

It will be noted that Lockwood differentiates clerks from artisans in terms of their promotion prospects. Yet if opportunities for advancement out of clerical work are extensive and if they are predictable on the basis of characteristics of individuals, for example educational qualifications, then the meaning of clerical work will not be the same for all engaged in it. Mere employment as a clerk will neither define expectation of work career nor tell us in an unproblematic way the social meaning of identical work tasks. We shall go on to demonstrate that there are diverse routes to clerical work and diverse destinations from it. What we are suggesting is that the very questions 'what is the class position of clerks?' is invalid, because 'clerks' does not define a meaningful reality in stratification terms.

5 The Clerical Workforce

At this point it is necessary to take a closer look at 'the clerks'. We need a clear view of the composition of the clerical workforce and changes that have taken place. In order to understand the processes involved and their relevance for stratification we must move from the general consideration of the abstract 'clerical worker' to a more detailed examination of the data.

CHANGES IN THE AGE STRUCTURE OF THE CLERICAL WORKFORCE

Viewed from the 1950s there is a certain plausibility about assumptions of change in clerical careers. Some of the data available to Lockwood, for example, would be consistent with an interpretation which argued for extensive promotion prospects in the 1920s and 1930s gradually declining until in the 1950s promotion had become comparatively rare. In Fig. 5.1 the age profiles of male clerical workers in the Censuses of 1921, 1931 and 1951 are presented. Because of changing definitions, and practices of aggregating detailed job categories, between the various censuses these are not identical categories. For example the figures for 1921 are for clerks and draughtsmen excluding clerks in local and national government, who are included in a different category with all government officials. The 1931 figures do not include draughtsmen and do include government clerks who were for that census distinguished from their senior officials. The 1951 definitions are close to those of 1931. All three sets of figures include some persons with supervisory responsibility with titles such as 'supervising clerk' or 'head clerk'. However, the differences in definition are not too disturbing in relation to our purpose. We are not concerned at this stage to make detailed arguments around precise job definitions, but rather to show the outlines of the main trends in the data.

These curves presented in Fig. 5.1 were constructed by calculating the proportion, expressed as a percentage, of the total population of male

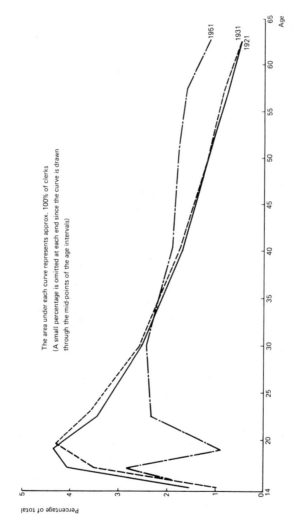

The area under each curve represents approx. 100% of clerks
(A small percentage is omitted at each end since the curve is drawn
through the mid-points of the age intervals)

FIG. 5.1 Age distribution of male clerks: 1921, 1931 and 1951, England and Wales

clerks in each census occurring in each age grouping. These age groupings also vary from census to census, but as far as possible we have constructed equivalent categories for each curve. This has involved a mixture of one, two, five and ten year groupings. To facilitate a visual presentation we have drawn the curves through points in the middle of the age ranges, these points having been given the value of the mean percentage per annum of the category. Although this procedure blurs certain trends in the data, the main outlines may still be observed.

At early ages we were not able to create exactly equal age bands, or rather to have done so would have involved producing one very wide category which would have hidden important trends. However, the differences are not great. First, the 1951 figures show 15 as the youngest age category, whereas for 1921 and 1931, 14 and 15 is the youngest grouping. The 1951 and 1921 figures are grouped 18 and 19, and 20 to 24, while the 1931 figures are grouped 18, 19 and 20, and 21 to 24. Thereafter all sets of figures use the same age bands.

Despite the lack of identity in the occupations included, the curves for 1921 and 1931 are very similar. There is some tendency for apparent recruitment at older ages in 1931, but the differences in the peaks of the curves is possibly to some extent an artifact of the different age bands. Apart from these differences the age profiles, separated by ten years, look remarkably similar. It should be stressed that draughtsman, like clerk, has been recognised as an entry occupation from which movement out into other jobs occurs as careers develop. Certainly these figures are entirely consistent with the view of classical clerical careers in which large numbers of young men took clerical jobs upon first entering the labour market, and as their careers developed moved out into other forms of employment. Bearing in mind the inclusion of senior clerical staff in all sets of figures, the movement out of the area of ordinary clerical work was probably even greater.

The similarity of the curves for populations ten years apart argues strongly for stable processes rather than differential recruitment as determining the figures. However, we should note that the figures are not entirely free from the effects of recruitment. Immediately after the First World War there was a fairly high level of recruitment which, coupled with the effect of men returning from the war to their old jobs, meant that there was a rapid increase in the number of clerks. Not all those resuming their careers were young, but it is probable that this added slightly to the peak in the younger years. When the hoped-for expansion turned to depression, the expected opportunities for promotion did not materialise, leaving some clerks without much chance of promotion in later years.[1] By 1931 the high recruitment had already stopped, of course, and the slightly older distribution of clerks is in keeping with these developments. On the other hand, the overwhelming similarities of these curves ten years apart indicate that, at least at that time, the basic pattern of movement out of clerical work had not changed.

By 1951 the situation has changed substantially. It is clear from Fig. 5.1 that the decline in numbers with age is no longer nearly so dramatic. In fact the decline in the proportions of clerical workers by age is not much greater than the decline in the proportions of the total male working population by age. Superficially this may seem to suggest that promotion prospects had declined from the early 1930s, leaving a larger and larger proportion of those starting in clerical jobs in similar jobs throughout their work career. We have seen there is an element of truth in this, but it is far from sufficient to explain the changed age distribution.

At least one source referred to by Lockwood contained information which should have suggested that such an explanation was very inadequate. A study by Thomas collected data on present occupations and occupations on first entering the labour market for men aged 18 and over, in gainful employment in May/August 1949. This study shows that the number then currently employed as clerks was only just over half the number who started their careers as clerks. Furthermore, a substantial proportion of the present clerks had started in other jobs, while of those who had started as clerks only about a third remained in clerical work and 38 per cent had already been promoted. Thus, two years before the 1951 Census, against which Lockwood's sample is justified, the net movement out of clerical work had been very considerable in the male working population.

This suggests that the more equal distribution of the proportions of male workers in clerical jobs by age cannot be explained by low levels of promotion from clerical work among older workers. It is clear that the numbers in clerical work up to age 20 in the 1951 Census were uncharacteristically low. From Fig. 5.1 the dip in the figures around age 20 will be noted. To some extent this may be a consequence of interrupted war careers which, on return to the civilian labour force, were taken up at the point at which they were left. This created a glut of clerks in the early career stages leading to limited recruitment of school-leavers in the immediate post-war period. In addition it is likely that

---

[1] See, for example, Blackburn (1967) for an account of the position in banking.

recruitment and career patterns were disturbed by the arrangements to have jobs covered by older personnel or women during the war years. To this we would add some basic points. Between 1931 and 1951 there was a decline of some 13 per cent in the male working population aged under 30 years, and in the age group 15 to 20 years the fall was 20 per cent. When we set this against an overall growth of nine per cent in the population, we see that a very substantial change in recruitment pattern is to be expected. Controlling for this demographic factor would do much to restore the curve to the shape of earlier years. At the same time the demand for clerical labour was growing, but it was met by increased recruitment of women and, to a much smaller extent, by the recruitment of men from manual work. Altogether there are strong grounds for seeing a change in the pattern of recruitment. However, undoubtedly the most important factor was conscription; at that time National Service took many young men away from their normal work, particularly in the 18–20 age range where we see the sharpest drop in Fig. 5.1. Whatever the explanations, the 1951 figures are a departure from the past, and it should be quite clear that blocked promotion does not account for them.

The situation of fairly even distribution of male clerks by age does not occur in later census reports. By 1961 the pattern of very much larger numbers in the youngest ages, peaking at about age 20, was re-established and continued in the 1966 Sample Census and the Census of 1971 (see Fig. 5.2). Thus the Census of 1951 is out of line with both previous and later censuses in this respect, and when we consider this alongside the information on careers in the Thomas data, it would appear that if there was a low level of recruitment it was of fairly short duration. Fig. 5.2 presents the distribution of male clerks by age in the 1961 and 1966 Censuses of England and Wales and the 1971 Census of Great Britain. We have followed the same practice as for Fig. 5.1, drawing the curves between mid-points of age ranges which have been given the mean percentage distribution of the population per annum of the range.

It is immediately apparent that the variation in numbers by age is in each case rather different from that found in 1951, though the data for 1966 and 1971 are more markedly different than those for 1961. However, the smooth, continuous decline in numbers with age exhibited in 1921 and 1931 is not re-established. Rather we now see a more sudden drop in numbers in the years between approximately 20 and 30, followed by a gradual rise which in turn leads to a final decline as we move towards the age of retirement. The differences between the curves

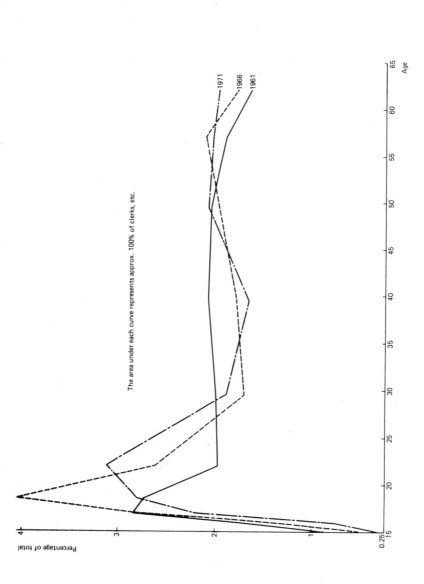

FIG. 5.2 Age distribution of male clerks, senior clerks, office managers and office machine operators, 1961, 1966 and 1971, England and Wales

would suggest that the situation is not entirely stable. It would seem likely that there were different rates of recruitment at the different times. In particular the numbers under 20 in 1966 would seem to be exceptionally high. In part this, again, is probably a reflection of general population trends as it coincides with the results of the immediate postwar so-called 'baby boom'.[2] The later peak in the 1971 figures would suggest that this increased recruitment is taking some time to work through the system.

There may also be different rates of movement out of clerical work, but such arguments are much more difficult to establish. Again the definition of this area of employment has not been stable over the period. In 1961 clerks were not distinguished from either office managers, head clerks, managing clerks, etc., or from office machine operators. In 1966 the last group was given separately and in 1971 all three groups were distinguished. The figures we have presented include all three groups for each census, but we are not confident that the reconstructed categories are entirely comparable.

That office managers and such like are included means that the profiles underestimate the concentration of ordinary clerks in younger age groupings, since promoted positions are typically occupied by older employees. In any case it should be noted that even without subtracting these groups from the figures, differential recruitment will not explain the general shape of the curves. The peak of the 1961 figures is not maintained in the 1971 figures for respondents ten years older.

We have presented the debate about changes in the class situation of clerks in an international setting, and before proceeding it would seem appropriate to establish that figures of this general form are not solely a feature of the situation in England and Wales. International comparison of occupations is very difficult if one wishes to examine issues in great detail, as definitions vary even more from country to country than in the same country at different times; and even where detailed definitions are shared, data presented in public sources, like census reports, may be the consequence of different practices in aggregating the detailed classifications. The international data we present are for the USA Census of 1970 and the Australian Census of 1971. In general the reports on the former are far more detailed than those on the latter, and we have been able to create a category of clerks in the USA which we believe is fairly close in definition to that we have used in our White-

---

[2] Note the dips as the low point in population noted earlier works through the range on successive graphs.

Collar sample. The Australian data are compiled from the various State Census reports. These give a more detailed breakdown of the population by occupation than do the reports for the Commonwealth as a whole and allow us, for example, to separate clerks from more senior personnel. In the Commonwealth reports fairly senior officials are included in the same category as clerks. This is especially true of government service where the distinction between the various grades has been minimal in published statistics.

In Fig. 5.3 we present the age profiles contained in the American and Australian data with those of both the 1971 Census of England and Wales and the clerks of our own White-Collar sample. In this case the data from the Census of England and Wales do not include the category of 'Office Manager', thus excluding the more senior people with supervisory responsibility, but it is not possible to separate out the 'office' or 'clerical supervisors'. Also included are a number of occupations, such as door-to-door money collector, which are not usually regarded as clerical. These did not feature in our White-Collar sample, and although supervisors were included, we asked directly about supervisory responsibility and were therefore able to assign respondents to the categories with considerable accuracy. The higher peak in the younger ages in the White-Collar sample and the smaller proportions of older ages may be partly a consequence of these differences in the data. Certainly if we include 'Supervising Clerks' and 'Office Managers' in both sets of data, the bias towards younger ages in the White-Collar data disappears. For example, the proportion of these combined groups under 35 years of age in the White-Collar sample is 38.6 per cent and in the census data 40.5 per cent. We believe that, in fact, our figures underestimate the numbers at the youngest ages. At the start of the interviewing programme we applied a policy of interviewing only those between the ages of 21 and 65. For various reasons, theoretical and logistical, this practice was abandoned, but not before a small part of the programme had been completed. The distortion is probably not great though we have no direct comparison with national data for precisely the period of our interviewing programme.

The same practice as in earlier figures has been followed in Fig. 5.3 though in this case the age categories are broader at younger ages. This was necessary because of the way in which the Australian figures are presented. The similarities in the general outlines are clearly illustrated. In each case there is an early peak, a rapid decline and a later smaller increase before a final decline.

To some extent the dip in each profile may be explained by the

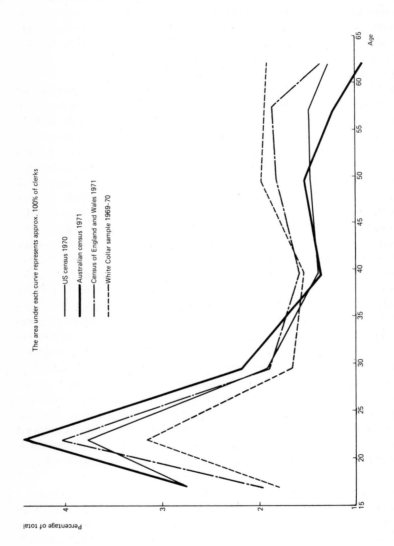

FIG. 5.3 Age distributions of male clerks: comparing three countries and the White-Collar sample

distribution of males in the population in general (as we have already suggested for England and Wales). In each society the age profiles of the male population show a peak in the early to middle 20s in 1971 (1970 in the case of the US) and a dip which reaches its lowest point between 35 and 40, thereafter rising to a second peak between 45 and 50. As we shall see, however, there are other factors affecting the distributions of clerks by age.

The second peak is more pronounced in the British data, but we have reason to believe that the bi-modal distribution in our White-Collar data is not exaggerated. Though they do not remark upon it, Bowen and Shaw (1975) present data on the age distribution of male clerks in a number of industries which is very similar to our data for manufacturing. The male clerks in their sample are drawn from a universe of 437 clerks of whom 35.7 per cent were aged below 30, 15.1 per cent were between 30 and 40 and 49.2 per cent were aged over 40. The equivalent figures for clerks employed in manufacturing in the White-Collar sample are 31.3 per cent, 16.4 per cent and 46.6 per cent. Westergaard and Resler (1975, p. 82n) also discuss figures which support the general shape of the age distribution for England and Wales, and the movements they reflect. They write:

'Calculations from unpublished information for 'office and communication' workers (which was kindly made available to us by the Department of Employment from its 1970 survey) suggest a considerable net outflow of men in their thirties from clerical into other jobs involving a net loss of perhaps 30 per cent or more of clerks of that age group. . . . They also appears to be a net inflow (proportionately perhaps on the same scale) into clerical work at higher ages—of men in their fifties'.

It should be noted that the ages during which outflow is greatest in the Census and White-Collar data, the 20s, are missing in the above statement. By comparison the outflow in the 30s is modest.

OCCUPATIONAL BACKGROUNDS OF CLERICAL WORKERS

So far we have been concerned primarily with clerks as an undifferentiated group of employees, but we now turn to an examination of differences of occupational experience among clerks, and try to establish patterns of movement into and out of clerical work. For the most part this analysis will rest upon data from our White-Collar sample, but we shall also draw upon wider sources where appropriate. We have shown already that the clerks in our White-Collar sample show a similar age distribution to clerks in the UK, the USA and Australia, and we should now like to show that they are also similar in more general characteristics. We have mentioned above the study by Thomas relating first jobs to current jobs of the male working population aged between 18 and 64 in Great Britain in 1949. There also are available similar studies for both the USA and Australia. The data for the USA come from a publication of the Bureau of the Census in the series entitled 'Current Population Reports'.[3] The figures presented there are for males, 25 to 64 years old, in the experienced civilian labour force. The Australian data were collected by Broom and Jones and their colleagues in 1973. Their figures cover men at work aged 30–59. Provisional figures were presented to the Mathematical Social Sciences Board Seminar in Toronto in 1974. The figures we present are somewhat different, as they subtract from the clerical category those with supervisory responsibility (who had been included in that category in the Toronto presentation) and include only those who began their careers, and are currently, in the civilian labour force.

In Table 5.1 we have extracted from these three studies, and from our White-Collar sample, data on the first jobs of those currently employed as clerks, separating these jobs into three areas of employment: manual work, clerical work and other white-collar work.

TABLE 5.1 Movement from first to present job: clerks, other non-manual and manual workers (Data for White-Collar sample compared with UK, USA and Australia)

	UK 1949 Ages 18 + %	W-C 1969/70 18 + %	USA 1962 25–64 %	W-C 1969/70 25–64 %	AUST 1973 30–59 %	W-C 1969/70 30–59 %
Currently Clerks						
First Job: manual	32	33	50	43	43	50
clerical	66	52	31	44	43	39
other non-manual	1	14	20	13	14	11

[3] Its title is 'Lifetime Occupational Mobility of Adult Males, March 1962' (Bureau of the Census, 1964).

Since we are concerned with the movements out of and into clerical work with age, we would obviously have preferred the three studies to cover the same age range in the population. The variations by age were very marked in Figure 5.2. As a result the differences between the three national samples are likely to be a confusion of structural differences and different views of similar structural processes, and it will be impossible to separate these completely. In an effort to go some way to overcoming this difficulty we have presented our White-Collar data in three different ways so as to match the three different age ranges. Considering, first of all, only the White-Collar data, certain processes associated with age are apparent. Thus, for example, ex-manual workers form approximately 33 per cent of all current clerks over the age of 18, but of all clerks between 25 and 64 they form approximately 43 per cent, and between 30 and 59 they form exactly 50 per cent. The proportion of clerks who started their careers in manual work, therefore, increases with age. This being so, a sample which includes younger ages will give an estimate of fewer in this category than a sample which omits this younger group. The differences then between the Thomas data and the US and Australian data are, no doubt, partly explained by these differences in age ranges. Certainly the White-Collar data treated in the different ways show differences in the direction of such an interpretation. Thus it would seem that the composition of the category of clerical work changes with age in such a way that progressively larger proportions of ex-manual workers and smaller proportions of those who started as clerks are employed. Those who started in other white-collar jobs also form a declining proportion with advancing age.

Too much should not be made of the differences between the proportions of clerks whose first jobs were clerical in the Thomas data and the White-Collar data. The Thomas data follow the census practice of the time and include promoted positions in the clerical category. Like the 1971 Census category, but to a greater degree, this also includes jobs other than strictly clerical ones. In fact it excludes only managerial and professional work. Certainly there is no great difference between the proportions of ex-manual workers in clerical employment in 1949 and 1969/70 on the basis of these figures.

It would appear also from these figures that the recruitment of manual workers to clerical positions is more marked in the USA in 1962 than in either Britain in 1949 or Australia in 1973, although this type of recruitment is very marked in all three countries.

Having established the main outline of employment in clerical work with national data, we would like to pursue the issue in more detail in our White-Collar data. The general structure of employment experience by age is well illustrated by the profiles in Fig. 5.4, which shows the distribution of clerks over all ages up to 60. With fairly limited numbers for this sort of task, we have chosen to present these as moving averages over five years. It should be remembered that this slightly affects the distribution by age. Also plotted in Fig. 5.4 are the distributions by age of current clerks whose first jobs were in clerical work and those currently clerks who began work in non-manual jobs or in manual jobs.

The by now familiar bi-modal distribution of clerks by age with the second peak at around 50 years of age is well illustrated, but it can be seen to be the result of different trends in the data. The first peak is due to the large numbers of early recruits to clerical work while the second peak is largely the result of growing numbers of ex-manual workers. Those from other areas of non-manual work first rise and then decline.

We have explained the distribution of ex-manual workers in our sample as due to an increasing movement into clerical work with age. However, it could be argued that it is a consequence of a once-for-all recruitment in the early post-war years which is taking its time to work through the system. Though our data do not allow us to determine exactly how long these clerks have been in clerical work, the answers to certain parts of our questionnaire provide an adequate refutation of such a view. We asked each respondent to outline the first job he held on joining his present firm and the date at which he joined the firm. We also asked the length of time he had held his current job. Thus we have the occupation of each respondent upon joining the firm and his length of service in both the firm and his current job. These data allow us to make an estimate of the longest and shortest possible time spent in clerical work for those who changed to this in their present firms, and the shortest for those who entered the firm as clerks. It is clear that many have become clerks fairly recently and indeed the impression given by these estimates is that most have been clerks for only a very short time.

Since this cannot be due to a recent upsurge in the recruitment from manual jobs (see the Thomas data for 1949 in Table 2.1), the most likely explanation is that employment in this area is relatively unstable. It seems probable that early entrants from manual work tend to move on into better jobs as do the clerks recruited directly from full-time education. The older the age of recruitment, the less likely is promotion to higher positions. Our data show a declining tendency with age for ex-manual workers to be recruited *to come into the firm* as clerks. At the same time we find that the proportions of clerks who are ex-manual

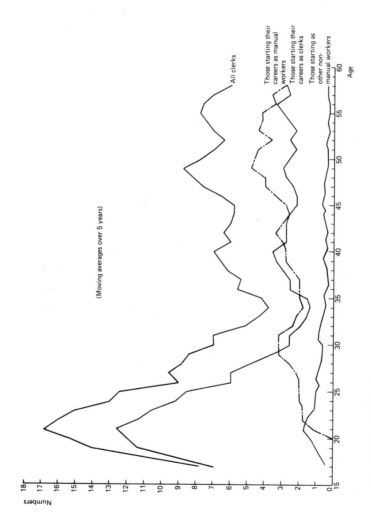

FIG. 5.4 Age distribution of male clerks who started their careers as clerks or in other occupations

workers in each age group do not show an equivalent decline, though, on the other hand, the numbers are not large enough to suggest a mere accumulation of ex-manual workers in clerical positions with advancing age. Some at least must be leaving clerical work with the passage of time. This would seem to be true especially of those who enter at relatively young ages. No one aged 45 or over, who started in manual work and entered the firm as a clerk before the age of 30, is still employed as a clerk; those who first entered the firm at ages above 30 are well represented in the older age groups of clerks. These figures would support extensive movement out of clerical positions for those who entered when young, and some of this movement at least is likely to be in an upward direction.

When we look at the group who joined their present employers as manual workers, the patterns are rather different. While the recruitment of clerks who are ex-manual workers from outside the firm declined with age, for this group there is a general increase in recruitment by age of entering their present clerical jobs. Since we would not normally expect increased job mobility with age, this does suggest a particular process of change to clerical work. This group have generally very long service with their firms; 61 per cent have been with the firm for longer than ten years, and a number have been with the same employer since leaving school, while of those who joined their firms as clerks only 27 per cent have served for more than ten years. Among those with long service, the clerks who joined the firms as manual workers have spent less time in their present jobs. It would seem, therefore, that the two groups are rather different, and a presumption that the latter enter clerical work at later ages, while not absolutely demonstrated, is strongly implied.

The general picture of male clerical employment, then, is of large numbers of young men recruited straight from school or very soon afterwards, who in the earlier years form a large majority of clerks. They then move progressively to other employment, especially during their 20s and after age 30 form a smaller proportion of all clerks than do ex-manual workers. These latter are fairly rare at younger ages, but gradually their numbers increase to a peak between ages 50 and 60. Recruits from other areas of non-manual work are much less common than ex-manual workers. They are in greatest numbers between 20 and 30, falling thereafter to a very small proportion. This is consistent with a view that many of them after moving into this area of employment subsequently move out again as their careers develop. To some extent we would expect that the younger ex-manual workers would follow a similar pattern, that for them entry to clerical work is the route to a more successful white-collar career rather than a final resting place. Such an interpretation is supported by evidence of differences between younger and older ex-manual workers which we shall shortly present.

VARIATIONS OF OCCUPATIONAL EXPERIENCE BY INDUSTRY

This general picture is, as we would expect, the consequence of aggregating rather different experiences in the different areas of employment, and we should like to present figures for the three rather different areas of employment we have distinguished in our data, namely Public Service, Insurance and Manufacturing Industry. Before proceeding to an analysis of the White-Collar data, however, we should like to establish once again, that they are not atypical of the male clerical working population in these areas of employment. Tables presenting areas of employment by occupation and age are not, at the time of writing, available for the 1971 Census, and the comparisons we shall make are with figures from the 1966 Sample Census.

Once again we face the problem of the ways in which the Census data are aggregated. We believe, however, that the data used in these comparisons, though not as close as would wish, are adequate to our purpose. To match the area of Insurance in our figures, we have chosen 'Insurance, Banking and Finance' in the 1966 figures, which, although a much larger category, is predominantly clerical throughout. Our clerks in local and national government departments are matched by the 1966 category of 'Public Administration and Defence', and our clerks in Manufacturing Industries are matched by an unweighted combination of the figures in the 1966 data for the various industries in which our sample were employed. Though our clerks do not represent a random sample of clerks in these industries, we believe that to have used weighting to render the samples more similar would have been an unnecessary sophistication given the other difficulties of matching the data.

Figs 5.5, 5.6 and 5.7 contain the age profiles of the clerks in our sample and those in the 1966 sample census for the three areas of employment. We have followed the practice in our previous figures of plotting the percentage of the total sample in each year of age by taking the mean percentage in each age range and drawing the curve through the mid-point of the range. We should stress once more that speculation

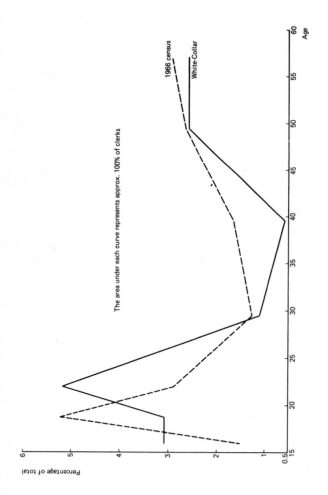

FIG. 5.5 Age distribution of male clerks in manufacturing industry: sample and national percentages

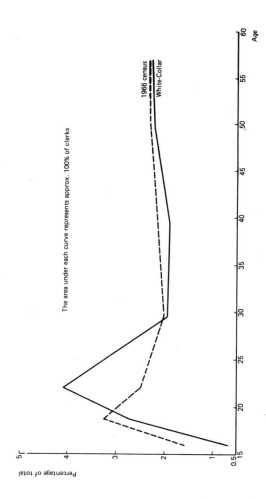

FIG. 5.6 **Age distribution of male clerks in public service: sample and national percentages**

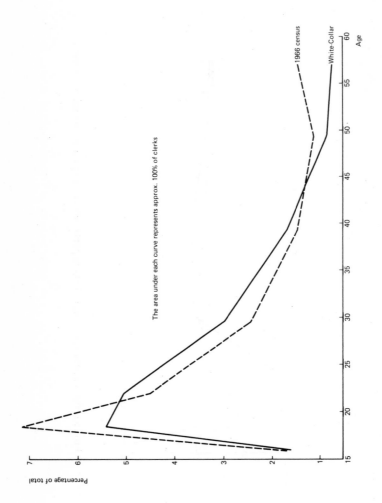

FIG. 5.7 Age distribution of male clerks in insurance: sample and national percentages

about detailed differences may be less than fruitful because of basic differences in the data. What we are concerned with are the general shapes of the curves.

Looking across the three figures it is clear that the bi-modal distribution found in the total sample of clerks is determined chiefly by the age distribution in manufacturing industry. There we can see that in both the White-Collar sample and the 1966 Census data there are peaks followed by fairly deep troughs with substantial recoveries of numbers at later ages.

We have already noted that the youngest ages are probably underrepresented in the White-Collar sample, which helps to account for the differences in the ages of the early peaks. However, it is probable that a more important reason relates to the later date of the sample and the effects of the 'baby-bulge' of the immediate post-war years, which was approaching the age of 20 in 1966. It seems likely from all the evidence that there was a higher rate of recruitment to all areas of employment as a consequence of entry of this unusually large cohort to the labour market. It would also seem that the effects of the increased recruitment were taking some time to work their way through the system and that earlier patterns of movement out of clerical work had been disturbed. At any event the peaks in the distribution of the white-collar clerks in both Manufacturing Industry and Government employment occur later than the peaks of the 1966 Census samples. In Insurance, though the peaks coincide, there are more clerks in their earlier 20s in the White-Collar data. It will be remembered that the latter were collected between three and four years after the 1966 Census.

The profile in Fig. 5.6 shows that in government employment there is a fall in numbers after an early peak and thereafter a slow, but sustained rise. Insurance, however, shows an age distribution of clerical employees quite unlike the pattern in the overall figures. The main characteristic is an early peak and a subsequent continuous decline in numbers, though in the case of the census data there is a small upturn at the most advanced ages. These curves for Insurance are similar to the curves for the total populations of male clerks in the 1921 and 1931 Censuses which we outlined in Fig. 5.1. It would seem that in this area the stereotype of clerical work between the wars as providing steadily increasing opportunities for promotion with advancing age still applies.[4]

---

[4] The slight upturn in the census figures for the age group 55–9 is most probably the last trace of the recruitment 'bulge' after World War I. The

Having established that in essential characteristics the age distributions in our sample are not dissimilar to the population as a whole, let us now turn to a more detailed examination of the composition of the clerical workforces of the three areas.

Table 5.2 presents data on the composition of the clerical workforce, in terms of type of first job by age, for each area of employment separately. We have used the same system of classification of first job as that used before in Table 5.1, the categories being Manual, Clerical and other Non-Manual. The heavy concentration of ex-manual workers in manufacturing industry is immediately apparent. Approximately 81 per cent of all those currently clerks, at ages less than 60, who started their working life in manual work are employed in manufacturing industry. Of course this is partly because our sample comes predominantly from manufacturing industry, but when we allow for this, the pattern is still overwhelmingly clear. Of all clerks in manufacturing industry, ex-manual workers form approximately 45 per cent, in government employment they account for only 24 per cent and in insurance a mere 12 per cent.

There is a marked tendency in all three areas of employment for ex-manual workers to be in the older age ranges. In each case roughly four fifths lie in the age range between 30 and 59. Since clerks who began their careers in clerical work are concentrated in the early ages, ex-manual workers come to form an increasingly large proportion of all clerical workers with increasing age. Thus in manufacturing they form only about 21 per cent of all clerks under 30, but 60 per cent of clerks between 30 and 59. The equivalent figures for government service are approximately 10 per cent for ages under 30, and 40 per cent for ages from 30 to 59. These figures, of course, reflect the lower concentration of ex-manual workers in this area of clerical employment while the figures for insurance show even lower levels, being 4 per cent for the younger ages and 24 per cent for the older group. Looked at in this way, the concentration of ex-manual workers in the older age groups is inversely related to their overall proportion in the sector of employment. Thus the ratios of the proportion of clerks over 30 who started in manual work to the proportion under 30 are 3:1, 4:1 and 6:1 for manufacturing, public administration and insurance respectively.

---

combination of the 'bulge', the Depression and World War II meant that some men who might otherwise have been promoted became 'too old' and were passed over in favour of younger men. At that stage they would probably find it difficult to leave insurance and get as good a job or better.

TABLE 5.2 First job by age: clerks in three areas of employment

Age	Insurance First Job				Public service First Job				Manufacturing First Job				Total First Job			
	Manual	Cleri-cal	Other White-Collar	Total	Total Manual	Cleri-cal	Other White-Collar	Total	Total Manual	Cleri-cal	Other White-Collar	Total	Total Manual	Cleri-cal	Other White-Collar	Total
15–19	0	12	1	13	0	10	0	10	1	14	1	16	1	34	2	37
20–4	1	19	1	21	0	13	1	14	9	30	5	44	10	62	7	79
25–9	1	16	0	17	3	2	0	5	8	18	0	26	12	36	0	48
30–9	3	13	4	20	0	2	0	2	20	11	2	33	23	26	6	55
40–9	2	5	0	7	3	4	0	7	34	22	3	59	39	31	3	73
50–9	3	4	0	7	7	7	2	16	29	18	0	47	39	29	2	70
Totals	10	69	6	85	13	38	3	54	101	113	11	225	124	218	20	362

No such clear patterns emerge for the age distributions of clerks who began their careers in other areas of non-manual work. In any case the numbers in our sample are very low, and overall they represent less than 6 per cent of all clerks under 60. Though too much should not be read into it, the distribution is bi-modal with a concentration at very young ages (below 25) and between 30 and 40. It would seem likely that the younger group are not greatly different from those who started in clerical jobs in terms of their career prospects.

In each sector, the number of those who started as clerks declines sharply with age after the early 20s. The rate of decline is steepest in government employment and least in insurance, but in neither of these areas do the numbers increase again in the older age range. In manufacturing industry, after an initial decline, the numbers rise again sharply in the range 40–9 and more or less hold the level in the age range 50–9. We shall go on to argue that this is to some extent a consequence of a return to non-manual work by those who started as clerks and subsequently moved into manual jobs.

OLDER CLERKS

Let us now examine in more detail the characteristics of clerks aged over 40, among whom the ex-manual workers are concentrated. We choose aged 40 as the cut-off point because we believe that below that age those entering clerical work from manual work may be passing through to higher positions. The patterns of distribution to different occupations of those who began their careers as clerks, which we shall examine in detail in Chapter 6, strongly suggest that by that age, recruitment out of clerical work is substantially complete. We shall compare the educational characteristics of clerks with that group of our respondents in the same age range who began their careers as clerks and are now employed in other areas of white-collar work. It will become clear later that the different areas of employment recruit clerks with different backgrounds, and we have therefore limited the comparisons to groups employed in manufacturing industry, where most ex-manual workers are employed. We could have strengthened our case by including government service and insurance, where clerks appear to be recruited with better educational qualifications. This procedure would have increased the contrast between the groups of ex-manual workers and the group who started in clerical work and are now in other white-collar jobs, but we believe our decision provides a better critical case.

From Table 5.3 it will be seen that clerks aged over 40 who began work as manual workers overwhelmingly attended elementary or equivalent schools and do not possess any formal qualifications. This is true whether they worked in skilled or unskilled jobs. In fact the educational experience of the two groups of ex-manual workers is remarkably similar. By comparison clerks in the age range who began their careers as clerks are better educated, but still a sizeable majority fall in the category of elementary school with no formal qualifications. We know that many people who start their working lives as routine non-manual workers move between such jobs and manual jobs, and it seems likely that many of this group of clerks will have spent a considerable part of their working life in manual jobs.

By way of contrast, both groups in Section B of Table 5.3 have minorities in the lowest educational category. This is more marked for those who started in clerical work. However, a more detailed examination would show that there are proportionately more ex-manual workers than ex-clerks with the higher levels of formal qualifications, often attained through part-time education after leaving an elementary school. In the case of both groups, the patterns of education are clearly distinguished from those of older clerical workers.

In Table 5.3 there are exactly equal numbers of ex-manual workers, currently employed as clerks, with first jobs in skilled and unskilled occupations. Since we collected information only on first job, first job in the firm and present job, we have no way of knowing of early changes in the jobs held. Thus we do not know how many began, but did not complete, apprenticeship, or, on the other hand, how many began in unskilled work and went on to take apprenticeships. However, it is clear from these figures that movement into clerical work for the groups in this age range is not a consequence of obtaining formal qualifications after entering employment. Their educational background, and that of those who began as clerical workers, supports the view that clerical jobs in industry are routine jobs which do not call for much in the way of skill or specialised training.

Among the clerks aged less than 40 who are ex-manual workers there are important differences by level of skill. There are not many of these clerks, and they are almost all employed in manufacturing industry—38 out of 43, of whom 21 began in skilled jobs and 17 in unskilled. Both groups show a tendency for fewer of their members to fall in the least educated category distinguished in Table 5.3, but for the unskilled the change is relatively small in that a large majority, 65 per cent of the total, still fall in this category. For skilled workers the difference is greater. Only one-third fall in this lowest education category. This is consistent

TABLE 5.3 First job by education: clerks and other white-collar workers aged 40–59 in manufacturing industry

	Attended Elementary or Equivalent School		Attended Grammar or Equivalent School		Totals
	No formal qualifications	School Certificate or higher qualifications	No formal qualifications	School Certificate or higher qualifications	
A. *Presently Clerks*					
1. Started as unskilled manual workers	25 81%	5 16%	1 3%	0 —	31 100%
2. Started as skilled manual workers	25 81%	4 13%	2 7%	0 —	31 100%
3. Started as clerks	23 61%	3 8%	8 21%	4 11%	38 100%
B. *Presently in Other White-Collar Jobs*					
1. Started as clerks	26 29%	26 29%	19 21%	20 22%	91 100%
2. Started as manual	74 43%	53 31%	14 8%	30 18%	171 100%

with the view that some of these latter, at least, are at any early stage of a white-collar career which will take them eventually out of clerical work.

If we turn briefly to other aspects of the background of older clerks, a similar picture emerges. In terms of fathers' occupations when they left school, there is little difference at the younger ages between those who started in clerical or manual work. 34 per cent of the former and 29 per cent of the latter under the age of 40 had fathers whose occupations were non-manual at a higher level than clerk. However, the difference is much more striking over the age of 40. The proportion with higher status fathers rises to 43 per cent among those who started as clerks, but falls to 23 per cent for ex-manual workers. The first figure suggests a reluctance to 'move down' to manual work, and the second is further indication of the different sort of clerk who comes from manual work late in his career.

With regard to housing, the pattern of householding is more or less the same for both groups under 40 and for the over 40s who began as clerks. Roughly 60 per cent are owner occupiers and just over 20 per cent are in council houses, with the remainder renting privately— though, as we might expect, rather more of the older clerks had moved out of private rented accommodation. On the other hand, among the older ex-manual workers only 48 per cent owned their own home and 39 per cent were in council properties. Again we see the greater affinity to their former manual-worker situation.

For the most part, then, older clerical workers cannot be seen as having been 'proletarianised'. A minority of those who started as clerks and a very small minority of those who started as manual workers might have expected more successful careers, but overwhelmingly in terms of background and occupational experience these older clerks have always been 'proletarians'.

OLDER CLERKS AND WHITE-COLLAR TRADE-UNIONISM

We have elsewhere (Prandy *et al.*, forthcoming) discussed white-collar unionisation in considerable detail, and all that we propose here are a few findings and brief comments. It will be recalled how closely the proletarianisation debate has been tied to the issue of white-collar union membership, or rather lack of membership. For writers such as Klingender (1935) in the 1930s the problem was the failure of the white-collar proletariat to recognise their objective conditions and join in the common struggle with their manual brothers. In common with Lockwood we have argued that the objective conditions of clerical workers are not always similar to those of manual workers, though the bases of our arguments are different from his. Clerical work and semi-skilled manual work may offer similar conditions and rewards, but included in the objective situation are the conditions under which the jobs are held. We have demonstrated that there is no single market situation for clerical labour and that the apparent strain between market situation and status, which so many writers have observed and have sought to explain, is a consequence of misinterpreting available data. How then does the trend towards the recruitment of manual workers to clerical positions affect trade-union commitment and membership?

Before going on to suggest possible answers to this question, we should make it clear that in terms of white-collar unionism our sample is far from typical, at least as far as private manufacturing is concerned. In the country generally this is the area of employment with the lowest completeness of trade union membership. Bain (1970, p. 28) reports that in 1964 only 12 per cent of white-collar employees in manufacturing were members of trade-unions as against, for example, 84 per cent in local government. Clerical workers were even less organised, according to Bain, with only 10.5 per cent in unions in manufacturing industry. It should be remembered that Bain's figures include women and that the mass of these women would be typists and secretaries, who are much less unionised than men. In addition, he excludes internal organisations such as staff associations even where these organisations conduct collective bargaining. These considerations, together with the general growth in the completeness of white-collar unionism between 1964 and the date of our interviews (Bain & Price, 1972), suggest a suitably adjusted figure might be nearer 20 per cent. Nevertheless, this is in contrast with our White-Collar data where 40 per cent of clerks belong to some form of representative body. The difference is due to the way the White-Collar sample was constructed. We chose firms carefully on the basis of a balance between those who did and those who did not recognise trade-unions. In achieving this balance we have included rather more of the former type of employers than in the population at large, and this is sufficient to give bias to the figures on membership, since there is a fairly strong relationship between employer recognition and completeness of membership. However, we have no reason to believe that these characteristics of the sample seriously distort the nature of the relationships between trade-union commitment and membership and occupational experience.

If, initially, we simplify the situation and divide our clerical workers into younger and older, those below 30 and those 30 and above, and into those who started their working career as clerks, those who started in other non-manual jobs and those who started as manual workers, then certain clear trends in trade-union membership emerge. These data appear in Table 5.4. As we would predict, ex-manual workers are more likely than those who started as clerks to belong to trade-unions. Overall 48 (46 per cent) out of 104 ex-manual workers are members as against 38 (33 per cent) of the 116 who started as clerks. Only 13 clerks started in other non-manual jobs and of these 6 (46 per cent) were members, the same proportion as for ex-manual workers though the numbers are too small to be significant.

TABLE 5.4 Clerks in private manufacturing industry: trade-union membership by age and first job

| | Age | | | | |
| | Under 30 | | 30—59 | | |
First Job	Non-Member	Member	Non-Member	Member	Totals
Manual	11	6	45	42	104
Clerical	45	13	33	25	116
Other non-manual	4	3	3	3	13
Total	60	22	81	70	233

Among those who started as clerks there are significant differences by age. Of the 58 in the younger group only 13 (22 per cent) are members against 25 (43 per cent) out of 58 in the older group. A similar trend applies to ex-manual workers, though the numbers in the younger group are rather small. In that group 6 (35 per cent) out of 17 are members, while in the older group 42 (48 per cent) out of 87 belong to trade-unions. Clearly, among those from both occupational backgrounds, trade-union membership is associated with age. This result is not unexpected. We would anticipate that younger clerks, with expectations of advancement, would be less likely to be union members. The older clerks, who have either suffered blocked promotion (and in our general study of trade union experience we find this a most important factor determining a turn to trade-unionism) or have brought over from manual work a habit of commitment to union membership, are more likely to be union members. It should be remembered that many who started as clerks and are currently clerks probably spent a large part of their working life in manual jobs and are, in that respect, very similar to those who started in manual work.

It would seem, then, that the trend towards employing older men from manual work is likely to have had the effect of increasing trade-union membership. Certainly, Bain (1970, p. 33) reports the largest gains in membership in manufacturing industry. Whereas white-collar membership of trade-unions grew by 34 per cent overall from 1948 to 64, the increase in manufacturing was 77 per cent. In addition, this was the one area of employment where unionism more than kept pace with the increase in numbers employed. More recently membership has grown faster than employment in most areas, and because of the greater potential, this has probably been more marked in manufacturing (Bain and Price, 1972). Although the completeness of unionisation remains, in general, low, it has grown by a few percentage points. Of course this growth is not exclusively confined to clerical work, but neither are the general trends towards recruiting older manual workers to white-collar jobs. Although technicians are generally more skilled and better paid than clerks, there are fairly large numbers under that job title who are doing simple tasks and have been recruited late from manual work.

It is evident, therefore, that the growth in white-collar trade-union membership is not indicative of a new middle-class commitment to class action. Those young clerks following traditional careers in manufacturing industry, where the current growth of trade-unionism is largely concentrated, are still weakly unionised and the very much higher membership among older clerks (and other groups) is less likely to represent a new radicalism than a carrying over of the commitments and identifications of a lifetime by 'proletarian' ex-manual workers. Insofar as there is a general growth in support for collective action, it probably reflects changes in conceptions of industrial relations at a societal level rather than new militant values. Here it is important to recognise the nature of trade-union attachments. Membership need not imply hostility to employers, even when it is allied (and in certain cases especially when it is allied) to a strong identification with the working class.

As we have stressed in the past[5] unionism is not merely a question of membership, but also of character—the character of trade-union behaviour and the character of members' commitment. In previous work we have introduced the concept of unionateness as a means of measuring the character of representative organisations. In the earliest formulation (Blackburn, 1967, p. 18) an organisation was to be described as more or less unionate 'according to the extent to which it is

---

[5] See Blackburn and Prandy, (1965); Blackburn, (1967); Prandy *et al.*, (1974).

a whole-hearted trade-union, identifying with the labour movement and willing to use the powers of the movement'. Later research (Prandy *et al.*, 1974, pp. 430–1) led to the division of the concept into two related components, enterprise unionateness which 'refers to those aspects of the behaviour of an organisation which are concerned with the pursuit of the interests of its members as employees through collective action', and society unionateness which involves 'a recognition by the organisation of the similarity of its interests to those of other organisations and a willingness to ally itself with them'. Society unionateness is concerned with identification with the wider trade-union and labour movement. Though the concepts are presented as measures of organisational character, we have used them also as measures of individual commitment to unionism by asking repondents about preferred types of representation, and it is with this aspect that we are most concerned for present purposes.

Within the non-manual field changes have been taking place in the characters of representative associations, which we would suggest are at least as important as changes in membership. Insofar as these reflect changes in commitment to class action, they must involve the commitment of individual workers. However, our aim is not to describe changes in organisations or individuals but, more fundamentally, to examine some issues concerning the nature of individual commitment.

In addition to the measures of unionateness we will make use of two other scales. The first is a scale of attitude to management. This was constructed from three items, scored from one to five, which dealt with attitudes of workers to the management of their firm. The higher the score, the more positive the attitude to management. The second is a measure of involvement in representative bodies. This runs from none through a minimum of knowing of an organisation and various levels of approval, membership and attendance at meetings to being currently an officer of the association. The associations concerned vary in their character from fairly mild internal staff associations to trade-unions affiliated to the TUC and the Labour Party. Most are in fact trade-unions. (Both of these measures and the methods of their construction are more fully described in Prandy *et al.*, forthcoming.) Before presenting data using the measures, we should like to outline the debates to which our arguments are addressed.

We find in the discussion of class conciousness and industrial relations the same sort of voluntaristic assumptions that we have been criticising in other areas of social theorising. The central theory, which is generally felt to be wrong and is thus subject to considerable attack, is moral consensus theory. In an action perspective the only alternative to a true consensus as the basis of stable social relationships in a system of inequality is some sort of deficiency of understanding. Unless there is consensus, deprivation cannot coexist with knowledge of its production without at least the desire for change. Furthermore, if societies were truly constituted in interpersonal production, then the apportioning of blame would always be potentially appropriate; and though efficient oppression by force might inhibit open opposition, such a situation would be inherently unstable. Thus the lack of agitation for change on the part of the deprived has to be based upon either a moral consensus or upon some form of ignorance of true social processes.

This explains the emphasis, in recent writings on class consciousness, upon the deficiencies of understanding on the part of the working class. Their consciousness has been characterised as either limited or fragmented or false. In some cases the presumed ignorance of the class extends to very basic information about social conditions. Scase (1977, p. 33), for example, in comparing the 'social structures of Britain and Sweden' writes:

Fulcher, in fact, has argued that the structure of trade unionism in Sweden is such that it constitutes an institutionalised form of class conflict. If this is so, it can be suggested that it is conducive to resentment among manual and lower-grade white-collar workers, if only because they are aware of the higher rewards accruing to other occupational groups. Indeed, such attitudes are likely to be more pronounced in Sweden than among those in countries where patterns of trade unionism are less consistent with occupational divisions. In such countries, it might be expected that there will be less awareness of *class* inequalities and limited resentment over economic rewards.

However, this sort of ignorance has not been found in most empirical studies. We reported earlier, in Chapter 3, our finding of accurate knowledge of income and other differentials among a small sample of unskilled manual workers, and other studies support this. It is true there has been discussion of the extent to which perceptions of economic inequalities can be interpreted as an awareness of class division and opposition, but few have doubted the ability of the working class to perceive such inequalities. Moorehouse (1976, p. 490), for example, after a survey of various British studies, concludes that 'the "money model of society" . . . (provides) . . . an extremely *accurate subjective perception of the objective* reality of the class system in Britain'.

Yet Moorehouse's interpretation of his findings is another testimony to the strength of voluntaristic assumptions. In seeking to dispel a belief in the ignorance of the working class, he has to confront the implications of knowledge for social attitudes. His solution is to argue that the factual differentiations the working class make are, in reality, evaluational differentiations—that when they say that people are richer or poorer, they are also implying that lying behind differences of income or wealth are differences of competence or power, and that the rich maintain their privilege through active oppression. This latter is an assertion rather than a finding, though it is a reasonable assertion if, but only if, social institutions are directly produced in action. The alternative would be a moral consensus and there is no evidence for that. The flaw is the action assumption.

Though arguments which stress working class ignorance of basic divisions recur fairly regularly, a more usual emphasis is upon ignorance of the true nature of social processes, arguing for some version of capitalist hegemony. Hegemonic theories vary, some implying false or forced consensus, i.e. an acceptance similar to that found in consensus theory, but based upon some manipulated failure to recognise the true nature of interpersonal relations. Others go some way towards the sort of explanation we would accept, arguing for a dominance among the deprived of conceptions of general principles of social life, which principles are understood, or tacitly accepted, as lying outside personal competence. However, the action perspective remains in the view that conditions are truly constituted in action, in the power of the oppressors.

Another illustration of the power of action assumptions is the way they underlie theories which in certain respects strain to avoid them. One such theory is that of 'pragmatic acceptance' put forward by Mann (1970, p. 425), though he has subsequently modified his position. He argued that the deprived individual 'complies because he perceives no realistic alternative', but the nature of the forces acting upon him remains for him obscure and contradictory. Interpretations of their social life by the deprived are limited and fragmented, to correspond with the fragmentation of their experience, but once again in this theory the true fabric of society is the competent action of individuals. The acceptance is one of choice, though based on the experience of external constraint and not necessarily implying any moral approval. He continues (p. 435), 'When we consider whole complex societies, it is not clear that all social members can be considered as parties to the social contract . . . only those actually sharing in societal power need apply consistent societal values'.

It is the powerful who have the knowledge and coherent values to exercise control. This point is taken further, by adding manipulated understandings to the explanation. Thus, Mann (p. 437) writes, 'For the reason most working class people do "accept" (in whatever sense) their lot and do not have consistent deviant ideologies, we must look back to the historical incorporation of working class political and industrial movements in the 19th and 20th centuries within existing structures. Dahl's historical analysis would lead to the same conclusion as that of Marcuse, that the institutionalisation of class conflict has resulted in a closing of the "political universe". But, of course, whereas Marcuse stresses that this process was itself dominated by manipulative practices of the ruling class, Dahl has stressed its elements of genuine and voluntary compromise. Clearly, the historical as well as the present-day theory must be a "mixed" one.' The 'mixed' theory is of true and false consensus; both are voluntaristic explanations. While the first is clearly so, the second has two action components. Firstly the commitment of the deprived is from their perspective a true consensus, and secondly the process is dominated by a competent ruling class.

There is a long tradition in British writings on class consciousness which stresses the limited ability of the working class to form coherent, abstract accounts of the social world. In itself this view is un-objectionable though hardly remarkable (indeed, if it were not so, there would be no need for sociologists to struggle to form such accounts). Difficulty arises when it becomes the basis of an argument where the elements of experience, independently of the context in which they are understood, are given centrality as the source of values. From Hoggart (1957) onwards, writers have expressed views which Mann (1971, p. 436) summarises succinctly. 'We have seen that two types of deviant values are widely endorsed by working class people: firstly, values which are expressed in concrete terms corresponding to every day reality, and secondly, vague simplistic divisions of the world into "rich" and "poor".'

The problem of class consciousness then becomes the problem of generalising the conflicts of everyday life, of providing coherent views within which common interests of the working class, in opposition to capitalists, can be recognised and acted upon, and of locating specific conflicts in more extensive understandings. Lane (1974, p. 268), for example, writing of working class politics and trade-unionism argues, 'The working class was possessed of a collective consciousness, but it was rooted in the work place because it was only there that it came up against capitalism as an immediately experienced reality. The social relations of production in particular workplaces generated an "us" and "them" consciousness which daily encounters with work discipline and authority served only to reinforce [There was a] tendency for consciousness to "end" at the factory gates.'

This seems to us to be almost the reverse of the truth. A 'trade-union consciousness' is not one limited by an inability to concern itself with more than employment issues, but rather an understanding of the total system within which struggles of labour and capital as factors of production are rendered meaningful. The conflict is over the appropriate distribution of wealth created by labour and capital acting together. This is the form of explanation that is generally available and accepted in our society—'there is no quarrel about the baking of the cake, only the way it is divided'—and it serves to limit rather than promote conflicts on the shop-floor. The acceptance of the 'facts' of economic life entails an understanding that individual capitalist undertakings are constrained by external economic laws just as are workers. Their particular relationships are seen not as direct productions, but as reflections of external truths. As Marx (1973, p. 164) expressed it, the '*conditions of existence* are independent of the individuals and, although created by society, appear as if they were *natural conditions*, not controllable by individuals'. It is true that Marx (1973, p. 165) believed that such understandings would be 'consolidated, nourished and inculcated by the ruling classes by all means available', but in general his emphasis is upon the pervasiveness of these ideas as understandings rather than as values. They are understandings for those whose interests they serve no less than for those they oppress. His long debate with the classical economists was not a struggle for a new value orientation alone; it was an attempt to provide new, more adequate, understandings of social and economic realities. If, as he believed, there are contradictions in capitalist society which lead to the exploitation of man by man, then the development of society around these contradictions will lead to the failure of current practical understandings; and the evolution of evaluative standards which have contributed to the dominance of current ideas will be at the centre of the process by which they are undermined.

The 'them' and 'us', 'rich' and 'poor' oppositions characteristic of the working class are unlikely to relate directly to practical, everyday friction, as Lane suggests, but more to a vague general desire for change which cannot be located in practical action. There may be occasions, strikes for example, when individual managements can be metaphorically blamed for capitalism, but for the most part the issues of class relations are distinct from the issues of day to day conflict. We are not suggesting that all workers have clear conceptions of the operation of the capitalist system (and to the extent that they do not, oppositional statements implicating immediate managements are likely), but the understandings available for the extension of practical problems are inhibiting and apparently inescapable.

If the basic character of the system is accepted, as we have argued, there remains the issue of location within it. We have argued that all parties believe their relations to be governed by practical, external truths, but their experiences within the system are various and an identity must be formed in relation to the system. Both issues of class (the basic nature of the system) and of personal identity can have a bearing upon industrial relations and trade unionism.

In order to illustrate this, we have tried, as far as possible, to isolate two groups of clerks who share very similar present circumstances, but who have different work histories. We shall see in the next chapter that promotion out of clerical work is substantially completed by the time entrants are in their mid-30s, and we have noted a little earlier that trade-unionism is concentrated among older clerks. We have chosen, therefore, clerks aged 35 and over who are currently employed in manufacturing industry in firms which recognise some form of white-collar representation. These latter conditions are necessary to give us groups that are sufficiently similar in terms of their current employment. Within this general category we have distinguished two groups of clerks. The first are those whose experience, so far as we can tell, has been principally in manual jobs. Both their first jobs and their first jobs with their present firms were manual jobs. In the second group are those whose first jobs were white-collar, as were their first jobs with their present firms. We realise that this does not give us a completely accurate division between the groups in terms of experience, but it is the best possible given the limitations of the data. For simplicity we shall refer to the groups as 'ex-manual' and 'white-collar'.

The arguments we are putting forward are largely about difference of identity and their consequences for industrial relations. We believe that both groups accept the facticity of the capitalist system and understand, however vaguely, the external exigencies which any capitalist undertaking must face. Industrial relations are conducted within that acceptance and involve, for the most part, marginal issues over which the immediate actors are believed to be competent. The desire for a more just and equitable system does not find resonance in practical possibilities and is relegated to a vague hope of future political change.

However, the groups have different identities—different conceptions of their appropriate social locations. The ex-manual workers are more likely to see themselves as working class and to see their current earnings and status as not inappropriate. The white-collar group are conspicuous failures. The vast majority of those with whom they entered white-collar employment are now in promoted positions. (How large a majority can be seen in the next chapter.) To the extent that they continue to identify with former peer groups, their present income and status will appear inappropriately low. Furthermore, their promotion rests on decisions by managers, against whom feelings of aggression can sensibly be directed.

Unless there are particular reasons (and most industrial relations issues are particular we have argued) which bring the ex-manual workers into conflict with their management, we would anticipate that they are better disposed towards them than are the white-collar group. Many of the ex-manual workers will have been given the lighter clerical jobs for reasons of health or age and thus have particular reasons to be grateful to their management.

In fact the data support these predictions, as can be seen from Table 5.5. The ex-manual group have a mean score of 7.33 on the attitudes to management scale while the white-collar group have a mean of 6.39. On a difference of means test, the one tail probability of these groups being drawn independently of the attitudes from the same population is 0.002. The white-collar group also have a higher mean score on enterprise unionateness, showing a greater desire for strong representation in their direct employment situation, though in this case the one tail probability is 0.1. Thus we see that, as hypothesised, the white-collar group have generally more aggressive attitudes towards their own management.

We would not anticipate that these aggressive attitudes would be translated into an identification with trade-unionism as class action. Indeed the very basis of their particular disaffection with their management is that they are truly White-Collar employees whose advancement has been blocked. To the extent that they accept working class status, the source of this disaffection is somewhat undermined. On the other hand, the ex-manual group, we have argued, are more likely to identify with the working class, and so we would expect them to have higher society unionateness scores. That this is so can also be seen in Table 5.5. The ex-manual group have a mean of 17.62 while the white-

TABLE 5.5 Differences between 'ex-manual' and 'white-collar' clerks in union involvement, unionateness and attitudes to management

	Mean	Probability (Sig. of difference)	Eta
Union Involvement			
First Job white-collar	4.56	0.35	0.04
Ex-manual worker	4.79		
Enterprise Unionateness			
First Job white-collar	30.54	0.10	0.14
Ex-manual worker	26.90		
Society Unionateness			
First Job white-collar	16.21	0.03	0.22
Ex-manual worker	17.62		
Attitude to Management			
First Job white-collar	6.39	0.002	0.32
Ex-manual worker	7.33		

NOTES
$N = 78$, comprising 39 in each group.
Probability is derived from a 1-tail t test with 76 d.f.

collar group have a mean of 16.21, with a probability of less than 0.05 that the difference arose by chance.

Because of the way the groups were chosen, their levels of involvement in representative organisations do not differ greatly, but the way in which the other variables relate to involvement and to each other reinforces the general interpretation. From Table 5.6 we can see that, for the white-collar group, while involvement in representative bodies correlates 0.54 with society unionateness, it has virtually no correlation with enterprise unionateness. Society and enterprise unionateness have only a weak, non-significant relation to each other. Thus for this group, acceptance of working class identity and militant attitudes in employment appear to be largely independent of each other, even though both are related to negative attitudes towards management. Hostility to management is also associated with involvement in representative bodies, but this is fairly weak and may be explained by the relationship between society unionateness and involvement. If we think of attitudes to management and unionism jointly determining involvement, the effect of the former is negligible, as is that of enterprise unionateness (in both cases path coefficients are small and negative). It seems that

TABLE 5.6 Correlations between union involvement, unionateness and attitudes to management: 'white-collar' and 'ex-manual' clerks

	Union involvement	Enterprise unionateness	Society unionateness	Attitude to management
		First Job White-Collar		
Union involvement	—	0.02	0.54	−0.19
Enterprise unionateness	0.36	—	0.18	−0.43
Society unionateness	0.40	0.49	—	−0.35
Attitude to management	−0.08	−0.03	−0.06	—
		Ex-Manual Workers		

NOTES
N = 39 in each group.
Significance: coefficients<0.2 are not significant, p>0.10
all other coefficients are significant, p<0.02

hostility to management is associated with trade union involvement only in so far as it is combined with identification with the labour movement. Indeed, such identification is the crucial factor in determining whether this group resort to trade unionism. Where their unsatisfactory situation produces a desire for strong representative action within their employment situation, this does not lead on to involvement in trade unions.

The ex-manual group show a quite different pattern of relationships. Their attitudes to trade unionism do not appear to be associated with attitudes to their immediate management. They are likely to have been formed in a longer history of trade-union involvement. This is confirmed by the fact that enterprise and society unionateness are well related, and both are associated with union involvement, yet there is no significant association between involvement and attitudes to their present managements. If we apply to this group the model of attitudes to unionism and management determining present union involvement, we again find the effect of attitudes to management is negligible (path coefficient small and negative), but enterprise unionateness does have an influence here, though still less than society unionateness. We can also see now why the mean enterprise unionateness of this group is not more clearly below that of the white-collar group, since it is a result of past experience and not a response to the present situation.

It is not sensible to see trade-unionism purely as a response to direct employer-employee relationships. It is evident that for clerks who have come from manual occupations, it is much more likely to reflect a general commitment to the working class. While for white-collar clerks the frustrations of the work situations may lead to desire for industrial action, they need not produce a commitment to trade-union action and membership. Indeed the conflicts may reflect a strongly held conception of not being working class.

To reverse the position adopted by Lane, trade-unionism in certain of its aspects starts only beyond the factory gates. It can represent a general class commitment though one which is not immediately associated with strong practical consequences for social change. Though practical struggle is over distribution within the system, a desire for more radical change cannot be doubted, and the 'class' nature of relevant change is probably recognised, at least implicitly, and embodied in class identity. It is perfectly possible to recognise the necessity of a transformation of class relations involved in significant social change without being able to identify procedures which would effect the changes. We have argued that these procedures are much more closely related to the practical exigencies of social life than with some abstract value orientation to a better future. The *conditions of existence* must be transformed, and in the process value perspectives will both contribute and be changed. A reorientation of values is not sufficient. The action perspective, with its emphasis upon values, misleads in its identification of problems of class identity and class action. Whether or not consciousness is fragmented is not the most crucial issue for social change, as a coherent account of class divisions and class conflict is available within the dominant understanding of the operation of the capitalist system.

6 Clerks and Promotion

It should be clear from the evidence that we have presented so far that there must be very considerable promotion out of clerical work. We should like now to address ourselves to this problem directly, as it is crucial to the debate about changes in the class structure.

Evidence bearing on this problem is not extensive and, such as it is, often relies to an extent upon misconception of the career process, as we shall shortly demonstrate. Of course, previous writers on the subject have not been unaware that some clerks do get promoted, but they do not appear to have recognised the implications of this for treating 'clerks' as a category of stratification. Apart from Lenski (1966), they appear to regard promotion prospects simply as possible future movement out of the present category to a better stratification position, rather than as *a part* of the individual's present position. Perhaps this reflects the concern with blocked mobility. If indeed promotion out of clerical work were rare, the usefulness of the category as a description of stratification arrangements would be greatly enhanced, and this is an assumption that has been made by a number of authors. In their attempt to evaluate the factors influencing promotion to management, the authors of the Acton Society Trust report (1956) rates having a first job as a clerk as a positive disadvantage, only marginally less of a handicap than starting in a manual job. Lockwood (1958) has argued that part of the reason for the growth of clerical unionism is the blockage of promotion chances in the modern, bureaucratic office. Sykes (1965) apparently has shown trends in this direction in a steel company, and Mills (1956) claimed to find such trends in the USA. Most recently MacKenzie (1973, p. 30) seems to believe that opportunities have virtually ceased. He cites the three sources above to support the following view:

> I am suggesting, therefore, that in terms of the level of promotion possibilities inherent in the occupational role, lower level clerical workers are fast approaching the level of *stasis* that has, in the past, been the lot of the blue collar worker.

If indeed this were the case, we should have to accept both that there had been great changes in stratification arrangements and that 'clerk' was a meaningful and useful category with which to describe stratification experience. However, the statement cannot be accepted at any level. Neither has promotion of clerical workers declined drastically, nor is there any evidence that blue-collar work ever failed so completely to provide opportunities for advancement.

A less extreme view of changes in promotion prospects, which appears to be widely held, is that career avenues have been cut off for clerical workers with the extension of facilities for full-time education and the increasing rigidity of qualifications requirements for recruitment to senior positions. The argument is that, whereas in the past clerks could work their way up through the organisation, they are now prevented from doing so as the senior positions are the preserve of those leaving the full-time education system with higher qualifications. In the following chapter we shall throw doubt on the extent to which such a process has been occurring.

In any case the view of changing mobility patterns has not been entirely one-sided, and not all authors have agreed with the arguments of diminished opportunities. Lockwood actually considers various factors tending to increase or decrease promotion, though he ends up presenting the closing off of the promotion channels as the salient outcome. Others have simply not shared the orthodox view. For example, Crozier (1971) found no evidence of declining promotion in French insurance companies, and Mumford and Banks (1967) argue that as a consequence of the increase in the employment of women in the most routine clerical positions, men have been freed to fill the increased number of promoted positions. One of the present authors (Blackburn, 1967, 1968), writing of men in banking, has argued that there has been a post-war increase in opportunities. Whereas many men in the past could expect to complete their careers at the clerical level, it would now be a reasonable expectation for a man to get at least some sort of promotion. As we shall see, the data of our White-Collar sample strongly support the arguments of this latter group of writers. However, before entering a detailed examination let us once again set the discussion in an international context. Table 6.1 is similar to Table 5.1 in that we have placed the data from the White-Collar sample against data for the UK, the USA and Australia, taking account of the different age ranges in these data. The sources of these data are the same as in Table 5.1.

In it we have calculated, for those whose first job was in clerical work, the proportions currently employed in three areas, manual, clerical and

TABLE 6.1 Movement from first to present job for those starting as clerks: data from white-collar sample compared with UK, USA and Australia

	UK 1949 Ages 18 + %	W-C 1969/70 18 + %	USA 1962 25–64 %	W-C 1969/70 25–64 %	AUST 1973 30–59 %	W-C 1969/70 30–59 %
1st Job Clerk						
Currently manual	28	(28)	31	(31)	26	(26)
clerical	34	25	19	17	23	14
other non-manual	38	47	51	52	51	60

non-manual. Since our White-Collar sample does not include those currently in manual work, the figures are in these cases estimates, and are given in parentheses. We have no direct way of estimating the proportion of those who started as clerks and are currently in manual work, but in order to compare our figures with those of the three national samples, we have assumed in each case that the proportions in our sample are the same as the proportions in these samples taken individually. This is the most useful assumption for purposes of comparison.

However, we did attempt to check it from an analysis of our general sample, with appropriate weightings for respondents in the three occupational categories to match the national distribution. The derived estimates are quite similar to the White-Collar figures except that the proportion who had moved to manual work is actually lower than the estimates in Table 6.1. These figures range from 22 per cent for all over 17, to 17 per cent for the age range 30 to 59. In the younger age ranges, the lower number of manual workers is offset by more clerks, but at older ages by more in promoted positions. Thus, for all those over 18, the estimate of promoted men is again 47 per cent with 31 per cent clerks, but in the age range 30 to 59, the estimate is that only 18 per cent are still clerks while 65 per cent are promoted. Apart from the lower proportion going from clerical to manual work, the estimates for this age range are very close to the White-Collar data. Overall then, this checking exercise suggests that the data in Table 6.1 are a reliable guide for the comparison made, though they somewhat overestimate movement into manual work and underestimate promotion prospects for those starting as clerks in England.

Looking only at the White-Collar figures, it is apparent that the more

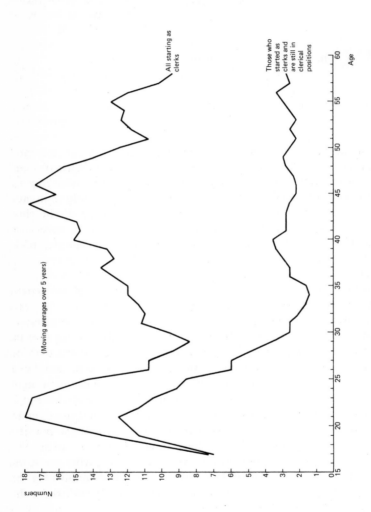

FIG. 6.1 Age distribution of those starting their careers as clerks

advanced the age covered, the smaller the proportion still currently in clerical work, which strongly suggests promotion with increasing age. Thus the apparently lower levels of promotion in the Thomas data when compared with both the USA and Australia may well be a consequence of the inclusion there of younger ages and the more general nature of the clerical category. It may also be a consequence of the different dates of the data. We have already noted that clerks at that time had been affected by something of a dip in promotion prospects, at least in the UK, and the subsequent revival of opportunities is apparently reflected in the 1969/70 figures of the White-Collar sample. The White-Collar figures are very close to those for the USA, but appear to show greater promotion than the Australian figures. It should be remembered, however, as we have pointed out above, that the Australian figures probably contain some more senior non-manual employees in the clerical grouping and as such may underestimate promotion. In any case the figures are sufficiently similar to warrant the comparison, and we shall now turn to a fuller examination of the White-Collar data. Fig. 6.1 contains the age profile of all those respondents in the White-Collar sample who started their careers as clerks. We have also included the profile of those currently clerks who started as clerks, which appeared in Fig. 5.4.

The curves are, as in Fig. 5.4, formed from moving averages over five years, which serve to smooth out the more violent fluctuations due to the rather small numbers.

A striking feature of the profile of all those starting as clerks is the trough following the early peak and the second peak at older ages. Why should the numbers starting as clerks and currently in the white-collar labour force show this sort of distribution? Is it merely a peculiarity of our sample? While we cannot show that our sample is not to some extent distorted, there are strong reasons for expecting a dip of this sort. In the first place it matches the decline in recruitment we noted in the 1951 Census figures for the under 20 age group, which had moved on in the 1966 Sample Census and is now 20 years older in the 1971 figures. We would, therefore, expect the dip in the number of those who started as clerks at that time to be greater than that for all employed men. In addition it overlaps with a rather shallower decline in the figures for the male employed population.

The distribution of the male employed population in 1971 alongside the distribution of those starting as clerks in the White-Collar sample is illustrated in Fig. 6.2. The age intervals are the same in each, but the White-Collar respondents are actually one year younger in each age

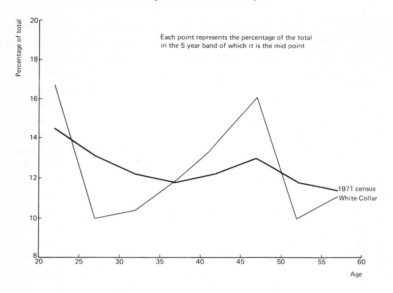

FIG. 6.2 Age distribution of all males in employment (1971) and those starting as clerks (White-Collar sample)

grouping to offset in part the interval between the collection of the two sets of data. We have not included ages below 19 in the White Collar sample and 20 in the Census data because individuals leave full-time education and enter the labour market at different ages. As a consequence the proportion of the total male population at each age formed by the total male *working* population rises from the minimum leaving age until about the mid-20s. Occupations vary in the patterns of their recruitment by age and so, taken individually, are likely to be poor reflections of overall trends. For example, the professions recruiting at relatively advanced ages will have lower proportions of their members in young age groups than will be found in the working population at large, while unskilled manual work recruiting early will have larger proportions. Clerks probably lie between these extremes, but as an entry occupation probably have a smaller proportion than the working population at large in the very youngest age groups. It seems safer, therefore, to exclude the youngest ages.

Though the second peaks of the two profiles coincide in Fig. 6.2, the general outlines are rather different. Not only is the trough more extreme in the white-collar data, but it reaches its lowest point far earlier. Bearing in mind that our sample consists solely of men who are in non-manual jobs now, this pattern is consistent with a fairly extensive movement out of clerical work and out of the area of white-collar employment at relatively young ages, and a subsequent return to white-collar work at later ages. In keeping with this interpretation we find there is a similar dip in the total White-Collar sample which is greater than in the overall national figures but, as we would expect, not quite so marked as for clerks. Furthermore, just such findings are reported in a number of previous studies. Lipset and Bendix (1959, p. 180), for example, write of their Oakland sample: 'Individuals whose occupational career is predominantly non-manual quite often spend some of their occupational career in manual positions, generally briefly, and generally early in their career.'

Hodge (1966), reanalysing figures gathered by Palmer (1954) and Goldstein (1958) and using Markov techniques, produces results which suggest the same tendency. Analysing the jobs of respondents at three points at five-year intervals, it is apparent that holding a non-manual job at the first point affects the likelihood of holding a non-manual job at the third point, independently of the effects from first to second and from second to third.

It is not our contention that differential recruitment may not have contributed to these figures. On the contrary once again we believe that this is a factor in the explanation. To some extent the strikingly low numbers in the mid-20s to early 30s may be seen to reflect the difficulty in recruiting male clerks which some employers experienced in the 1950s. In an expanding economy, with a relatively low number of school leavers and a popular belief that clerks were losing ground to manual workers, some employers found it useful to reorganise their work to employ less men, or women instead of men (see Mumford and Banks 1967), or to take on older men from manual employment. However, whatever the difficulties, the expansion of clerical employment continued in this period, including a growth in the number of men employed (though the growth in female clerical employment was far faster). It is hardly conceivable, then, that this factor is sufficient to explain the contrast in the curves, and it should not be allowed to obscure the regular features of movements between occupational areas which are strongly suggested by the figures.

The more rapid decline in our figures after the second peak may be in part a consequence of our sampling procedure. We excluded from our sample members of the boards of directors of the companies employing our respondents, and we most probably underrepresented the highest level of management in major companies. Such positions are not usually reached until fairly late in a man's career. For example, in Copeman's

(1955) study the mean age of Directors is 55, and more recently Stanworth and Giddens (1974) report that 60 per cent of company chairmen had been working at least 30 years before attaining the office. The absence of these people from the sample is likely to be felt at fairly advanced ages. Again there is some evidence in our figures tentatively supporting such an explanation. Public service does not have boards of directors and there we took the most senior people available. the numbers who started as clerks and are currently in white-collar jobs in public service show no decline from the ages 40–9 to the ages 50–9; in fact there is a slight increase in the figures. On the other hand, both of our other areas of employment, insurance and private manufacturing industry, where there are boards of directors, show a marked decline in numbers between the two age ranges.

We stress these arguments because at some point we must estimate the numbers who, starting as clerks, enter and remain in manual work if we are to be able to assess promotion prospects. If our arguments are indeed correct, then the various figures given in Table 6.1, for those currently in manual work, having started as clerks, will be under-estimates of the numbers who have some experience in manual work (since they include younger and older groups in which manual work is relatively rarer), but they may also be overestimates of those whose careers are predominantly in manual work or who will complete their careers in such work.

At this point we may note that when we come to consider promotion prospects directly, we are faced with the problem that it is not easy to give them a precise definition. Prospects, so long as they are understood as an aspect of the present job, are clear enough as a concept—it is in the evaluation of promotion that the difficulty lies. Are we, for example, to take any experience, however short, of better paying, more interesting work as promotion? Or are we arbitrarily to decide that we shall take the last job held in the labour market for comparison with the first as the basis of determining occupational movement? It takes little reflection to show the poverty of the latter approach. It would seem from various studies that it is a fairly common practice in the few years before final retirement for those in responsible positions to move to less onerous and time-consuming jobs. In these cases final occupations are poor indicators of the main outlines of careers. However, it would take very extensive data over very long periods of time to establish in a satisfactory way the outlines of movements and anticipated movements over the whole period of working lives, and even when these are established, the meaning of promotion can still be debated. Our data will allow us only a very general approach to this problem, and we shall suggest only limited and temporary indications of promotion prospects.

Let us return now to the main current of the argument. It is obvious from a comparison of the two curves in Fig. 6.1 that the movement out of clerical work is very extensive. After age 30 current clerks form only 19 per cent of all those who started their careers as clerks. Since 'clerk' is the lowest earning occupation in our White-Collar sample, it might be true to say that over four-fifths of those who began their careers as clerks and are now employed in white-collar work are currently in higher positions. For the most part a fairly unproblematic meaning could be given to such a statement, but two significant reservations need to be considered. The first point is that these figures are dependent on the composition of our sample, which does not include, and cannot be regarded as representative of, the whole range of non-manual employment. Nevertheless, in view of the way the sample was drawn, it seems likely that they are a good approximation and certainly give a reasonable guide to the general trend. The second point specifically concerns an occupation which is included, namely foremen, and for the 44 ex-clerks who became foremen of manual workers, a little more discussion is advisable.

In general it is accepted (and confirmed by our analysis (in Chapter 2 above)) that the statuses of the occupations covered by the term 'foremen' are similar to those of the occupations over which they exercise control. Thus these occupations are usually seen as a somewhat superior form of manual work. When placed in relation to working careers, they are traditionally associated with manual work because incumbents have been recruited from such work and in many cases return to such work. Though it may be the first step from the shop floor into management, this is by no means normal practice, and those manual workers who enter higher paying non-manual jobs in most cases by-pass such positions, moving, on the basis of qualifications, to the early positions of white-collar careers. In career terms, therefore, 'foreman' more frequently represents the terminus of the journey rather than a stage on the route. As such, when careers are being compared, foremen may be seen as having lower status than young clerks, many of whom, as we shall see, are on an early staging point of much more rewarding careers. However, when the occupations are compared, in terms of interest, responsibility, authority and extrinsic rewards, 'foreman' is generally superior to 'clerk'. For example, the mean income of the foremen among our ex-clerks is £1611, while that of those still clerks over the age of 30 is £1322. It would therefore seem sensible to regard the foremen as occupying promoted positions even if their careers have been, in terms of normal expectations, disappointing.

As usual the overall figures presented in Fig. 6.1 are a consequence of aggregating somewhat different trends in the three areas of employment of our clerks. Table 6.2 contains figures for the three areas of employment separately. The different patterns of numbers and proportions promoted by age are apparent, but it is clear that in all areas very considerable numbers are promoted. It should be remembered that the areas of employment are for current occupations and that we have not collected information on the area of employment of first job. We do not, therefore, have information on movements between areas of employment, and we do not know the extent of continuous employment in one area. However, insurance is an area where, traditionally, clerks have tended to make their careers within the one industry and our figures are consistent with this. It would seem that, as is almost certainly the case nationally, there has been a gradual increase in the numbers of youngsters engaged as clerks. There would also appear to be a steady increase in the numbers promoted up to about age 50. Insurance, we have written above, is the area in our figures which best represents the traditional clerical career patterns. We have already seen that figures for current clerks in this area follow a similar pattern to those found for all clerks in the 1921 and 1931 Censuses, and it would seem on the basis of this table that traditional conceptions are well borne out. Over four-fifths of the age group over 40 are in promoted positions.

In government service, promotion would seem to arrive more quickly and be more certain, but this may be illusory. The sharp decline in the numbers employed in the area after the mid-20s and subsequent rise in numbers from about the age of 40 should be noted. This could be due either to differential recruitment so that there were few competing for promotion in the young ages, or to movement out of this type of work, which would be more likely among those not promoted, followed by a return or new entry by clerks who began elsewhere; or as we suggested earlier it could be due to a combination of both. Whatever is the case, almost nine-tenths of those who started as clerks, who are aged 40 or over and employed in this area, are in promoted positions.

Manufacturing industry presents an even more complicated pattern. A similar drop in numbers from the mid-20s to the 30s is evident, and a similar increase from then until around the age of 50 occurs. The drop in the numbers is not quite so marked, and there is a further decline in the 50s, but the distribution is roughly similar to public service. However, the pattern of the proportions in promoted positions is quite different. It

TABLE 6.2 Promoted clerks by age

Age	Insurance			Public Service			Manufacturing			Total		
	Started as clerks	Now in promoted positions	% promoted	Started as clerks	Now in promoted positions	% Promoted	Started as clerks	Now in promoted positions	% Promoted	Started as clerks	Now in promoted positions	% Promoted
15–19	12	0	0	9	0	0	16	2	13	37	2	5
20–4	25	5	20	18	4	22	46	21	46	89	30	34
25–9	22	5	23	6	4	67	26	12	46	54	21	39
30–9	44	30	68	15	12	80	64	57	89	123	99	80
40–9	39	32	82	28	25	89	91	71	78	158	128	81
50–9	21	17	81	29	26	90	60	40	67	110	83	75
Totals	163	89	55	105	71	68	303	203	67	571	363	64

starts earlier, then rises more sharply than that for insurance and less sharply than that for public service at early ages, but reaches an earlier peak than either. In ages between 30 and 39 nearly nine-tenths are in promoted positions; thereafter the pattern shows a marked decline in proportions promoted.

Without additional information we cannot give a definitive account of these trends, but a few relevant observations may be made. It will be remembered that when discussing the overall figures we mentioned that members of the boards of companies were excluded from our sample and some other top-level managers were probably left out. We speculated that to some extent the decline in figures after ages in the late 40s might be due to their exclusion. We have also stressed earlier that there is evidence for a return to non-manual work at later ages by those who started as clerks, but then moved into manual work. If we take these two factors into account we may go some way to explaining the figures for manufacturing industry. Let us imagine that those successful careers which start from clerical jobs and end on the boards of companies[6] are reaching their peaks in ages between 40 and the mid-50s. During the ages between 30 and 39, before they have reached board level, most will still appear in our figures, but at later ages progressively more will have passed out of the sample. That something like this process operates can be deduced by the rapid fall in the number of graduates employed in manufacturing industry in our sample as we move to more advanced ages. Between ages 30 and 39, 29 per cent of our managers are graduates, while between 40 and 50 only 8 per cent hold degrees, and between 50 and 59 there is not a single graduate. This fall is much more extensive than would be predicted from the increase in the numbers of graduates in the post-war period, and is also out of line with other studies such as that by the Acton Society Trust (1956) and that of Clements (1958), which include directors.

As people pass out of the top positions in our sample into directorships, so others who started as clerks and have been in manual work return to the lower positions in the non-manual area. During ages in the 40s these movements most closely coincide in our figures, and from then on a combination of return to clerical work and differential movement out of the sample may explain part of the fall in the proportion of those who started as clerks who were in promoted positions as we move to the oldest age groups.

---

[6] If it should be doubted that those starting as clerks reach board level, see e.g. Clark (1966) which shows 27.9 per cent of directors with this background.

An alternative explanation is that promotion prospects were better for the cohort aged between 30 and 39 than for older cohorts. Once again we come to the dip in the number of economically active males in this age group, and the low level of recruitment of young clerks after the war. The high proportion promoted may reflect less competition and so better chances. If this is indeed the case it is interesting to note that this cohort was just entering employment when the sample was drawn for the study used by Lockwood in his analysis. They were still in their teens or early 20s in the period when various observers 'discovered' their declining promotion prospects. These clerks were supposed to be the ones who would not be promoted!

It would appear that the chances of promotion in all areas of employment have been excellent, though we must keep in mind that these data relate only to those who are currently in white-collar employment. We have seen that there is a significant movement into manual occupations in the younger years; and although it seems to be the case that many return to non-manual employment, there must be an unknown small proportion who end up as manual workers, who may well outnumber those promoted out of our sample at the top. This appears to be very rare for those starting in insurance, but is probably less so in the other sectors. Bearing this in mind, it still seems unquestionably clear that promotion chances in each area have been extremely high, though perhaps somewhat less overall in manufacturing industry.

EDUCATION AND PROMOTION

To some extent the differences between manufacturing and the other sectors may be explained by the nature of the recruitment to the separate areas of employment. We have already remarked that government service and insurance recruit clerks with better educational backgrounds, and the larger proportions in promoted positions in ages above 50 may reflect this. In order to examine this question and also to look at the relationship between education and promotion more carefully, we present Table 6.3. This table shows, for various age groupings, the numbers in each industry starting their careers as clerks, who now hold foremen's, clerical or promoted white-collar positions, by types of educational experience.

It is immediately apparent that insurance recruits clerks with better educational backgrounds. 81 per cent of all who started as clerks in that

TABLE 6.3 Education by job by age of those starting as clerks in three areas of employment

| | Government | | | | Insurance | | | | Manufacturing | | | |
| | School 0 | | School 1 | | School 0 | | School 1 | | School 0 | | School 1 | |
	No quali-fications	'O' level	No quali-fications	'O' level	No quali-fications	'O' level	No quali-fications	'O' level	No quali-fications	'O' level	No quali-fications	'O' level
Age −30												
Foreman	1	1	0	0	0	0	0	1	2	0	0	0
Clerical	8	5	7	3	8	4	10	12	25	6	16	8
Promoted (W-C)	0	1	4	3	0	1	1	8	4	7	6	13
Age 30–39												
Foreman	1	0	0	0	0	0	0	11	3	3	0	0
Clerical	0	0	1	1	0	0	4	5	2	3	2	2
Promoted (W-C)	1	2	0	9	0	3	3	21	13	11	8	13
Age 40–49												
Foreman	0	0	0	0	0	0	0	0	9	2	3	4
Clerical	2	1	0	0	2	0	2	0	12	1	3	3
Promoted (W-C)	3	8	6	7	5	4	7	19	17	14	9	11
Age 50–59												
Foreman	0	0	0	0	0	0	0	0	7	0	5	1
Clerical	4	1	2	0	0	0	1	2	8	1	4	1
Promoted (W-C)	2	4	5	11	0	0	8	9	9	6	8	0
Totals	22	23	25	34	15	12	36	78	111	54	64	65

NOTES
School 0 = Elementary, Secondary Modern, Comprehensive.
School 1 = Grammar, Public, Private.
Qualifications were '0' level, School Certificate, or higher levels.

industry attended either a grammar-type school or a private or public school, and 64 per cent of them had at least 'O' level or equivalent qualifications. On the other hand, of those employed in manufacturing industry who began their careers as clerks, only 36 per cent went to schools of this type, and only about 34 per cent of them had any formal qualifications. Government service lies between these two with 57 per cent having attended grammar-type, private or public schools and 55 per cent possessing some form of formal qualification.

We again run into the problem of how to interpret the position of foremen, and in line with our previous decision, we shall regard them as promoted. Not only do they earn more than clerks, but they also earn as much as many in supervisory clerical positions, which have been taken as promoted positions. On this assumption manufacturing industry has slightly fewer in promoted positions though the differences are not great. If we assume that foremen are not in promoted positions, then industry does rather badly in terms of the proportions it might expect to be promoted on the basis of education. Table 6.4 is derived from Table 6.3 and presents the percentages of various educational groups aged over 40 who are in promoted positions by employment area. The figures assume foremen to be promoted, but we have given in parentheses, for both manufacturing industry and the total figures, the percentages assuming foremen to be unpromoted. From this table it is clear that promotion prospects for clerks with any formal qualifications have been excellent. Far from having virtually ceased as MacKenzie argued, it is fairly well assured for those of even modest educational attainment.[7]

So far we have established that the prospects of being promoted are high for those who start out as clerks. In this sense there has clearly been no decline, but we have not looked at the distances they rise. It might be argued that in contrast to former times, they can now only attain relatively low-level positions. However, we shall postpone answering this argument until the following chapters, when we shall be looking in detail at occupational careers and associated incomes. At this point we want to continue the consideration of clerks with a provisional look at the more limited topic, of what has been referred to as their 'income careers'. This has been another element of the proletarianisation myth.

---

[7] Interpretation is again subject to the reservations arising from the nature of our sample, which we discussed earlier. In particular we do not have data on those currently manual workers who started as clerks. However, evidence from our general sample suggests it is extremely rare indeed for anyone with qualifications to start as a clerk and be in unpromoted manual work after age 40.

TABLE 6.4 Education and promotion: those whose first job was clerk and who were aged between 40 and 59

| | Percentage in Promoted Positions | | | |
	Government service	Insurance	Manufacturing industry	Total
Secondary modern school and no formal qualifications	45	71	68 (42)	65 (45)
Secondary modern school and at least 'O' level or equivalent	86	100	92 (83)	90 (86)
Grammar school etc. and no formal qualifications	85	83	78 (53)	81 (68)
Grammar school etc. and at least 'O' level or equivalent	100	93	86 (70)	92 (86)
Either type of school and at least 'O' level equivalent	94	94	89 (75)	92 (86)
All levels	89	82	74	79

NOTE
Figures in parentheses are percentages assuming foremen to be unpromoted.

THE 'INCOME CAREERS' OF CLERKS

The term 'income career' has been lightly used by both MacKenzie (1967) and Parsler (1970). By it they mean merely the median income of successive age groupings. The implications of the use of the term are, in these circumstances, very interesting. Presumably they do not mean by 'income career' the actual pattern of earnings that has occurred for older clerks or will occur for younger clerks. The inflation of the post-war era in the industrialised nations of the Western world and the general rise in living standards over the past few decades ensure that the actual patterns of either money or real incomes by age are specific to the period in which they are gathered. It seems unlikely that either author was unaware of these facts, so something rather different must be implied by the term 'income career'. In fact it would appear that both have a conception of clerical work as providing a progression of income with age for succeeding cohorts of clerks. The younger and older groups are related within a common structure in that the younger occupy earlier career positions and will progress to the later career positions.

Income then becomes an indicator of relative position within a coherent career structure, and the 'income career' is not an actual or anticipated experience of earnings with increasing age, but *the present distribution of earnings to career positions.*

In general we believe this view of a career is justified. Indeed in many areas its application is obvious. Take, for example, the position of university lecturer. There is a scale of annual increments which means the individual's earnings increase with age.[8] In terms of seniority, or career position, the distribution of earnings by age will, in this case, be a more or less adequate account. Though there are difficulties with promotion to higher positions, over certain age ranges the incomes are good indicators of age-related career positions, because the term university lecturer encompasses a career. Clerk on the other hand is not, as we have shown, a term which encompasses a career. There is some excuse for MacKenzie assuming that this is the case, as he (wrongly) believes promotion from the clerical category to be rare, but other writers, such as Parsler (1970), Lockwood (1958) and Giddens (1973), who are aware of the greater promotion prospects of clerks than manual workers, should have avoided the reification of 'clerk' as a meaningful description of career experience. Since the occupational experience of those either employed as clerks or who began their careers as clerks typically crosses boundaries into other jobs, age bands of clerks cannot represent coherent stages in income or any other form of career.

Before going on to show the consequences of assuming 'clerk' is a career category, we should like to establish that our data, treated to match the 'income career' data of other studies, will produce similar results. Since Parsler's data are, as we argued earlier, for a rather broad band of inadequately specified white-collar occupations, we shall confine our comparisons to MacKenzie's data from the 1960 US Census, although the Census category he chooses, 'Clerical and Kindred', is far from being straightforwardly clerical workers. It contains many groups that in Britain are classified as manual (see Levison 1974), but at least it does not contain promoted personnel.

The US Census data and our White-Collar data were collected almost a decade apart in different countries, and we do not argue the merits or otherwise of the levels of income in the separate circumstances. We are

---

[8] We realise not all universities have the Cambridge system of an age-related scale which is fairly rigid in its application, and elsewhere lecturers may take up posts at different points, in relation to their ages, but there is a fairly clear age-salary pattern nevertheless.

concerned only to show that in general outline the patterns of median incomes by age are similar. Table 6.5 gives MacKenzie's figures and our figures together with some comparisons with data from the New Earnings Survey, 1970. From these latter it would seem that our clerks probably earn about as much as semi-skilled workers in the engineering and building industries in terms of overall median earnings when we bear in mind that the New Earnings Survey figures include both skilled and non-skilled manual workers. They would seem to lie in income terms a little above the category of Intermediate Clerical and so fairly in the middle of the clerical range in their data.

TABLE 6.5 Median earning by age of male clerks, England and USA

Age group	Clerical workers US 1960 census (Males $)	Percentage of overall median	Clerical workers White-Collar survey England 1969/1970	Percentage of overall median
Under 20	—		558	46
20–4	4000	77	956	78
25–9	4800	92	1189	97
30–4	5230	101	1327	109
35–9	5370	103	1418	116
40–4	5640	108	1346	110
45–9	5620	108	1382	113
50–4	5420	104	1304	107
55–9	5000	96	1285	105
20–59	5200	100	1221	100
Over 21		New Earnings Survey		
Senior clerical			1534	126
Intermediate clerical			1206	99
Routine clerical			1004	82
Skilled and non-skilled manual in engineering and building			1399	115

MacKenzie's income figures and our figures follow the same general pattern of an early rise and a late fall, as may be readily seen. Indeed they follow a very similar pattern. Since the currencies are proportional while national levels of earnings differ, the most stringent—and probably most appropriate—test of their similarity is the extent of a linear relationship between the two sets of median income figures. The high level of this is indicated by the product moment correlation coefficient of 0.93. Also included in Table 6.5 are the earnings of the different age groups in both our data and the US Census data expressed as percentages of their respective overall medians. In the White-Collar data the median earnings of clerks between 20 and 59 (£1921) has been used to make the data directly comparable with the US data. We can see that the pattern of earnings with age are very similar in the two situations though the American data form a smoother curve, which suggests that the irregularities in our data may be due to the relatively small numbers in each category upon which median earnings have been calculated.

Instead of using clerical income by age, a better guide to 'income career' for the group in our data who started as clerks would be their current earnings by age irrespective of occupations. Though we cannot show that succeeding cohorts have had or will have identical occupational and relative income patterns, the data in our section on promotion would suggest that recent modifications of experience have not decreased promotion prospects or income expectations. We shall, in the next chapter, look at the issue of careers in much more detail. For the moment we are concerned merely to dispose of the previously accepted basis for the income component of the 'embourgeoisement' or 'proletarianisation' thesis.

Table 6.6 contains figures on the mean incomes of various age groupings of those who began their working life in clerical positions in our White-Collar data. In the first column we present the mean incomes of those currently employed as clerks. In general they follow the pattern of earnings of all clerks, presented in Table 6.5 above, though they are slightly higher at all ages and they do not decline so rapidly in the ages between 40 and 59. In the second column are earnings of the 39 respondents in our sample who, having started as clerks, are currently foremen of manual workers. They earn rather more than those currently clerks, though their earnings are much lower than those of the group in other promoted positions which are presented in column three. This group shows a fairly rapid rise to about age 40 and thereafter a rather irregular pattern of earnings, though the general trend is still upwards. Finally in column four we present the figures for all of those who started their careers as clerks, irrespective of current occupation. These figures clearly show that the earnings of those who started as clerks are very much greater than the earnings of current clerks. Thus the rates of earnings of clerks by age cannot be used as a guide to the rates of earnings of those starting as clerical workers.

We do not argue that column four gives an account of the 'income

TABLE 6.6 Mean incomes* of those starting as clerks by age (Number in parenthesis)

| | | | *Present Job* | | | | | |
| | Clerk | | Foreman | | Other non-manual | | All who started as clerks | |
	£	(N)	£	(N)	£	(N)	£	(N)
Under 20	558	(35)		(0)	615	(2)	562	(37)
20–4	949	(57)	1023	(3)	1260	(29)	1053	(89)
25–9	1217	(33)	1430	(2)	1547	(19)	1341	(54)
30–4	1370	(10)	1421	(6)	1862	(40)	1727	(56)
35–9	1535	(14)	1756	(3)	2102	(51)	1970	(68)
40–4	1324	(14)	1624	(6)	2206	(55)	1995	(75)
45–9	1470	(12)	1928	(12)	2218	(59)	2068	(83)
50–4	1421	(13)	1520	(7)	2209	(40)	1958	(60)
55–9	1443	(13)	1668	(6)	2396	(33)	2073	(52)
All	1106	(201)	1628	(45)	2038	(328)	1680	(574)

* Gross annual earnings

careers' of clerks; indeed we shall go on in the next chapter to show that these data contain various diverse career patterns, but as an aggregate guide to past trends and future trends in relative income expectations, column four is much more satisfactory than the income by age of current clerks.

If we compare the figures of columns two, three and four of Table 6.6 with the figures for manual workers earnings given above in Table 6.5, it is very clear that those starting as clerks earn very much more than those whose whole career is in manual work. Clerk is not a well-paid position, or even a highly regarded position, but it is an early stage on relatively lucrative and highly regarded careers. As such it attracts those with relatively high educational qualifications and middle class aspirations and expectations. The assumption that their middle class life styles are maintained with incomes untypically low for the middle class is unfounded, and we shall return to this point later. However it should, by now, be clear that the image of blocked mobility and non-increasing incomes is far from accurate.

7 The Myth of Declining Opportunities

In this Chapter we shall address ourselves, at rather less length, to a myth that is the obverse of proletarianisation, the myth of declining opportunities or truncated careers. It has been extensively believed that opportunities to rise from the ranks into managerial positions have seriously declined in recent years. As Little and Westergaard (1964, p. 302) put it, 'As professionalisation, bureaucratisation and automation of work proceed, so access to occupations of the middle and higher levels increasingly demands formal educational qualifications. Career prospects and social position come to depend less on experience and training acquired on the job than on the education obtained in childhood and adolescence.' Goldthorpe (1964, p. 108) similarly has argued, 'To the extent that education becomes a key determinant of occupational achievement, the chances of "getting ahead" for those who start in a lowly position are inevitably diminished. This fact is most clearly demonstrated in recent studies of the recruitment of industrial managers. These show that as the educational standards of managers have risen, the likelihood of shop floor workers being promoted above supervisory level has been reduced.'

We have shown that promotion chances for clerks remain excellent, but it could be argued that though this is true, the avenues of promotion do not lead so far. For example, the massive influx of female labour to routine clerical employment may have improved male chances of promotion, but only to relatively low level supervisory positions. The higher positions, to which clerks previously aspired, it may be argued, are now beyond their reach. That this is so would seem to be established by various studies of the careers of managers, such as those mentioned by Goldthorpe above. These same studies also show, apparently, a declining tendency for managers to be recruited from other low-level jobs. We shall examine the results of these studies in some detail, comparing their results with those of our White-Collar study. For this purpose we shall be especially concerned with the studies by the Acton

173

Society Trust (1956) and Clark (1966). The authors of both works purport to show that successive cohorts of managers draw more and more upon directly recruited trainees with high educational qualifications and less and less upon those started their careers as clerks or other low-level employees. They do this by selecting from among their managers different age bands for which they present the proportions who started their working lives in different occupations. The Acton Society Trust (1956, p. 18) claim that their figures 'show a fairly clear trend away from starting working life as a clerk. The proportion who started their working life officially as trainees has increased considerably.' Lockwood (1958, pp. 60–1) took up the same theme, quoting this material as evidence that those who began their careers as clerks were forming a declining proportion of managers. Clark (1966, pp. 145–6) similarly feels that promotion channels are becoming blocked. He writes:

> With the growing emphasis being placed on academic achievement, specially technical and scientific prowess, it might be expected that there would be an increase in the proportion of managers starting their careers in jobs demanding these skills, and this proves to be the case. And this movement has, of course, led to a decrease in the proportion of managers who started their careers in apprenticeships or manual work . . . . At the same time, there is also a corresponding drop in the proportion who started their careers in a clerical capacity . . . a considerable increase in the proportion of managers who started as trainees indicates once again managements' awareness of the need for well trained and usually highly-educated recruits.

However, contrary to what the authors believe, neither of these studies can, on its own, address the problem of trends in the recruitment of managers. The different age groupings of managers are not equivalent to succeeding cohorts. The evidence from various countries is that a very small proportion of those employed as managers start their careers in management. As a first job category it is very small indeed. For example, in Thomas's (1949) figures for the UK the category of current managers is almost 17 times as large as the category of those starting work in managerial positions. In the 'Lifetime Occupational Mobility of Adult Males' report put out by the US Bureau of the Census (1964), proprietors of small businesses are included in the figures, but the category of current manager is still almost nine times as large as the starting category. In Broom, Jones *et al.* (1974), data for Australia show the ratio is almost 15 to 1. Thus managerial employment has to draw massively from other starting occupations, and the proportion of a cohort in managerial positions increases with age. It should be obvious, therefore, that those who start as trainees represent a category which not only may decrease in size with age as its members move into other areas of employment, but in any case cannot increase, and as a consequence must at succeeding ages form·a declining proportion of a rapidly growing occupation. Clerks and other low-level employees, on the other hand, will only slowly reach their maximum penetration of the category as careers develop with age.[1] As a consequence, in order to show a decline in promotion prospects one would have to consider samples taken at different times rather than different ages within the same sample.

Management is a term that covers a very wide variety of specific jobs. It cannot really be viewed as a single occupation, and it is not a set of occupations in a single career. There are careers in different forms of management, some prestigious, some routine and poorly paid. Although in our sample we have only managers in relatively large establishments, this scarcely improves the homogeneity of the group. The crucial variable is not size of establishment. In fact, large establishments need certain kinds of low-level managers, doing special- ised tasks, who are not found in smaller establishments. Here we shall deal with managers as if they were a single group, but we hope in a future work to look at this question in more detail with improved coding schemes and more information on background and expectations than is at present available to us. At least viewing managers as a single category allows us to compare them with previous studies which have covered all levels of management.

In Table 7.1 we present such a comparison. At the outset we should make it clear that the studies used different techniques for gathering data from different sampling frames and that they cannot be regarded as entirely equivalent. For example, they do not display the same mixture of industries. In addition different coding practices make it difficult to reproduce identical categories of occupation. However, with these limitations in mind we can at least dispose of certain arguments which are not supported in the data and can give some estimate of the processes that actually apply.

[1] Lockwood (1958, p. 61) actually notes this key error in the Action Society Trust argument when he says 'Clerks take longer to work their way up into managerial positions' but he fails to follow through the implications and draws the wrong conclusions.

The Acton study was carried out in a sample of very large firms, each employing over 7000 people. They included all managers above the level of foreman and below the level of executive director. The firms were all in private manufacturing industry and spread throughout the country.

Clark's study was of a sample of private and public enterprises with more than 600 employees in the Greater Manchester area. For the purpose of comparison only those managers employed in private industry are included in Table 7.1. Clark allowed his firms to define a 'manager' and his study includes directors. From the data he presents, it is not possible to extract directors from the figures for the different age groups. They could have been extracted from the total figures, but we felt these figures should be, as far as possible, an aggregate of the figures for the age groupings. In any case the overall distribution of occupations of directors is very similar to that of the remainder of the sample, there being only a slight tendency to begin work in higher status jobs.

The White-Collar data, as we explained in the introduction, were collected in establishments within a 60 mile radius of Cambridge. In private manufacturing establishments, which have been selected for this table, the minimum number of employees was 500. The definition of manager used was very close to that of the Acton study,—above the level of foreman and below board level. We have noted earlier, however, that we believe our sample underestimates the most senior managers who are not directors.

The Acton study was conducted in 1954, and although Clark does not give precise information on the date of his study, from internal evidence it would appear to have been conducted in 1963. The White-Collar sample were interviewed between autumn 1969 and spring 1970.

If the trends towards blocked promotion, that both Acton and Clark claim, were genuine, we should expect them to have operated in the period between the studies. In fact the figures in Table 7.1 support almost none of their conclusions about managerial recruitment. If we consider only the Acton and Clark data, we can see that though the proportion who began as clerks has fallen in the latter, the proportions who began as manual workers or apprentices have increased in both age groups. Sales workers have increased overall, though they are less common in the younger age group. Trainees form a smaller proportion in Clark's data at both age ranges, and though there are small increases in the proportion of managers and professionals, these are not large enough to offset a net loss of all ages when these two categories are combined. The strong trend that both studies purported to find towards direct recruitment to management or management training of well-

TABLE 7.1 Percentage distribution of first jobs by age of managers in manufacturing industry in three studies

First job	Acton society trust[1] Age			Clark[2] Age			White Collar Age		
	−39	40+	All	−39	40+	All	−39	40+	All
1. Manual workers	12.3	23.4	21.0	3.8	11.9	9.0	16.7	17.1	16.9
2. Apprentices	5.7	3.8	⎱	13.4	16.1	15.2	13.6	25.0	19.7
3. Laboratory assistants			⎰ 4.4	20.1	14.1	16.3	13.6	18.4	16.2
4. Draughtsmen and technicians	33.9	26.3	28.4[3]	24.7	13.5	17.3			
5. Clerks	23.6	31.7	29.5	18.4	29.4	25.5	24.2	30.3	27.5
6. Sales	2.8	3.1	3.1	2.1	5.8	4.5	0	3.9	2.1
7. Trainees	18.7	7.8	10.8	13.4	5.6	8.3	15.1	3.9	9.2[4]
8. Managers and professionals	3.1	2.9	2.9	4.2	3.6	3.9	16.7	1.3	8.5[5]
Total	100	100	100	100	100	100	100	100	100
N	750	2002	2752	239	446	689	66	76	142

NOTES
1. Taken from table A.4, p. 92.
2. Taken from table 15, p. 170.
3. This includes 'Senior Clerical' some of whom are minor professionals.
4. This includes managers and trainees.
5. This category may include some who would appear in category 4 in the Acton Study.

educated entrants is, in fact, reversed in the comparison of the studies.

Whether there is an overall tendency to recruit from those starting at higher or lower levels largely depends on the interpretation of the movement towards higher proportions of laboratory assistants and manual workers and lower proportions of draughtsmen and technicians. In the first place we should note that the change may be less than it appears. It is to be expected that many of the draughtsmen and technicians actually began as apprentices and the distinction between manual and non-manual is not always clear at the start of such training. Thus, although the category of apprentices is intended to contain only manual workers, and is actually combined with the manual category in the Acton data, there is probably some ambiguity in the classification of those starting in apprenticeships which led to their becoming draughtsmen. Differences in coding practice could, therefore, go some way to explain the higher proportion of draughtsmen and technicians and the lower proportion of manual workers in the Acton study. However, this still leaves to be explained the increase in the proportion starting in laboratories at the expense of the draughtsmen and technicians group.

Nothing in Clark's study suggests that this is a movement towards employing better educated personnel. For example, in his data 86 per cent of those starting as draughtsmen and technicians attended grammar or private schools as did 83 per cent of those starting as laboratory assistants. It would seem that these groups are similar at point of entry to employment, and if we combine them they come close to forming the same proportions in the two studies, though it should be remembered that, in addition to any who might have been classed as manual apprentices in the later study, the Acton study included 'senior clerical' with draughtsmen and technicians. It may well be that the high proportion of laboratory assistants in Clark's study is due to a peculiarity of his sample. In any case it cannot be taken as a movement towards higher status recruits when compared with draughtsmen and technicians. Thus the general pattern is one of considerable stability for both age groups, while if anything it appears that overall there was an increased rather than a decreased tendency to rise from the bottom between 1954 and 1963 on these figures.

Since Clark presents a comparison, similar to that of the totals in Table 7.1, between his data and those of the Acton study, his adherence to age bands as the basis of trends in recruitment is puzzling. This is especially so as some of his arguments for trends in education are based upon differences between his study and previous studies in terms of their aggregate data. It is true that he also makes the mistake of looking for education trends by selecting differing age groups, and it may be that once perceived the flaw is obvious, but that until then the simplicity of the method makes it hard to resist.

Comparisons with the White-Collar data present rather more problems. We are not able to reproduce exactly the occupational categories of the two previous studies. We have noted above the difficulty of separating manual apprentices and apprentice draughtsmen when the groups share a common early apprenticeship. This may go some way to explaining the somewhat higher proportion who started as apprentices among managers in the White-Collar study and the lower proportion of draughtsmen, technicians and laboratory assistants, though it cannot completely account for this difference which does seem to rule out a growth in recruitment from laboratory assistants which might be inferred from Clark's data. Furthermore it would not explain the very much larger proportion of manual workers, though it is worth noting in passing that even larger proportions of managers are recorded as starting as manual workers in samples of general populations.

Thomas (1949), five years before the Acton study in the UK, found 59 per cent of managers and proprietors drawn from manual workers. The OCG figures of the US Bureau of the Census (1964) show 54 per cent for the USA in 1962 and Broom, Jones *et al.* (1974) found 45 per cent in Australia in 1973. The studies use somewhat different definitions of the managerial category, and in the case of the US and UK data in particular, the category is an extremely wide one, including the proprietors of small businesses for whom there is a great deal of data suggesting heavy recruitment from manual work. In addition, all of these works include managers in small enterprises who appear in none of the studies being considered here. We cannot say how typical our sample is of managers as a whole in this respect, though Clark's study also suggests trends, if more modest, towards the recruitment of more skilled and unskilled manual workers if these groups are taken together.

There is a larger proportion of professionals in the White-Collar data than in the other two studies. It is probably exaggerated in the White-Collar data as we think it likely that some of those who are listed as starting in professional jobs in the White-Collar sample would have been described as higher clerical or technical employees in the Acton Study. Nevertheless there is a significant increase which, taken with the modest increase in the Clark study compared with Acton, may suggest a trend, though the fact that the high proportion in the White-Collar sample is confined to the younger age group suggests it may be more a matter of different age distributions. Once again, just as with Clark's study, there is a decline in the proportion of management trainees between Acton and White-Collar. The much heralded growth of this type of recruitment seems to have failed utterly to materialise.

Overall in Table 7.1 there is very little tendency towards a blockage of recruitment from below; indeed, if anything, opportunities appear to have been increasing. The details of actual processes concealed within these data will only be revealed in a much more intensive analysis which will have to disaggregate the category of managers. We hope to conduct such an analysis at a later date on the data from our general sample, but we have not yet exhausted the White-Collar data in terms of indications that might be given for the direction of such a later analysis.

It will be recalled that the arguments about decreasing promotion opportunities to management were predicated upon a tendency for the direct recruitment of better educated personnel and that the availability of such personnel was due to a general increase in educational provision within the community. That such a change in provision occurred cannot be denied, but the effects of the change are not easy to estimate. The extent of the increase over the whole age range of managers is not easy to calculate. In Chapter 4, when dealing with clerks, we quoted Lockwood as saying that 14.6 per cent of the total male population aged over 18 in 1949 had attended either private or selective secondary schools. By the mid-1960s between 20 per cent and 25 per cent were receiving these types of schooling. Grammar school education has grown continuously in the post-war period, though the largest increase was due to the reorganisation which followed the 1944 Education Act.

Over the same period management as a category of male employment was growing proportionately, from 4.4 per cent of the male working population in 1951[2] to 9.1 per cent in 1971.[3] This increase, which was at the expense of lower occupational groups, would tend to affect adversely the position of management in competition for those with higher school backgrounds. Reviewing the situation in 1960, i.e. shortly after the studies by Acton and by Lockwood and just before that of Clark, McGivering (1960, pp. 62–3) *et al.* observed:

A feature of the post-war years has been the sudden realisation of the shortage of persons fitted to become managers. . . . There has

[2] Table 1 Census, 1951, England and Wales, Occupation Tables (London: HMSO, London, 1956).
[3] Table 6, Census, 1971, Great Britain, Qualified Manpower Tables (10 % Sample), (London: HMSO, 1975).

been a demand not only for more, but for better qualified, managers. . . . There has been no increase in supply to match the increased demand. . . . When one considers that full employment and a high level of demand have led to increased requirements for educated manpower in other sectors of the economy, it will be realised that industry has had to take special measures to recruit its customary, let alone an increased share of the available supply.

The supply of people with educational qualifications has increased since then, but so has the demand for managers.

Finally, there would appear to have been a tendency towards the recruitment of managers at younger ages. This can be seen by an examination of the numbers in each age group in Table 7.1 above. In the Acton study 27.3 per cent of the sample were aged below 40, which compares well with another study of managers conducted at about the same time by Clements (1958). His figure is 29.1 per cent. In Clark's study the proportion was 34.9 per cent and in White-Collar 46.5 per cent. We believe this last figure is too high—we have already discussed our suspicion that we have underestimated senior managers, who tend to be older—but not sufficiently to negate the trend. The effect of a tendency towards younger recruitment, coupled with the expansion of education, is to concentrate recruitment in better educated cohorts.

Taking these three factors together (the growth of selective secondary education, the growth in management as an area of employment and the trend towards recruitment at younger ages), it is difficult to predict precisely how patterns of secondary education would be changed for an assumption of a constant discrimination in favour of higher level schools in management recruitment. Comparisons with other studies are also complicated by differences in coding practice. In the Acton study they distinguish elementary schools from what they call 'Ordinary Secondary' schools. In this category they place 'senior elementary' and the selective secondaries of the pre-1944 period which were not grammar schools, as well as post-1944 secondary modern and secondary technical schools. They further distinguish grammar schools and two categories of private/public schools, all of which we have combined. Clark would appear to have followed a practice similar to that of the Acton study. We, on the other hand, in creating a dichotomy between selective and non-selective schools, coded senior schools and elementary schools, which were the same, with secondary modern and secondary technical schools, but coded intermediate and central schools, which were selective secondaries before the 1944 Act, to the same category as grammar, private and public schools. Another study which distinguished selective secondary schools of the pre-1944 era was that of Clements (1958) conducted in the years 1954–5. Clements, like Clark, confined his study to managers in private manufacturing industry in the Greater Manchester area, but his firms varied more in size. Of the 26 cooperating firms, the smallest employed 32 people and the largest six employed between 3000 and 10,000. He included directors, and although he had no strict definition of a manager he used a minimum salary of £800 as a guide, though several managers included earned less. In general he seems to have biassed his sample towards senior management, though a higher refusal rate among directors may have offset this somewhat. We did not introduce comparisons with Clements' study earlier because he does not include data on first jobs of his managers.

Table 7.2 shows the distributions of types of schools in the four studies of managers. What is immediately obvious is that Clark's figures seem to show an increase in selective secondary education when

TABLE 7.2 Schooling of managers in four studies

	Acton[1] (1954)	Clements[2] (1954/55)	Clark[2] (1963)	White-Collar (1969/70)
Private and grammar type schools	48.1	61.6	67.6	59.2
Elementary, secondary modern and technical schools	51.9[4]	38.4	32.4[4]	40.8
Total	100	100	100	100
N	2650	620	689	147

NOTES
1. Appendix II, table 1A, p. 91.
2. Appendix 2, table 3, p. 174.
3. Appendix II, table 3, p. 158.
4. These figures probably overestimate the numbers in non-selective secondary schools for the reason outlined in the text.

compared with the earlier studies. However, it would appear that his figures are uncharacteristic in this respect. Since he uses definitions close to those in the Acton study it is most useful to compare his data with theirs. If we select the group aged 30–44 in the Acton study and compare it with the group aged 40–54 in Clark's study, conducted about nine years later, we find that 54.2 per cent of the Acton group went to grammar or private school against 68.1 per cent of Clark's group. Now in both studies there is a pronounced tendency for mean schooling to decrease with age as those who have worked their way up enter management, and as a consequence we would expect a decline in the proportion who had attended the higher schools between Acton and Clark's study. That we see a large increase strongly suggests that these studies are not dealing with equivalent groups. It may be that in allowing the firms to define managers Clark tapped rather fewer junior personnel than appear in the Acton figures.

If this is indeed the case it has rather interesting implications. That the two samples should differ so much on schooling, yet be so similar in the distribution of first occupations, suggests that these entry occupations are very broad and include persons of diverse educational backgrounds.

There is other work that suggests that Clark's figures cannot be compared directly with the Acton figures. Lee (1968), for example, in comparing figures for the 1951 and 1961 Censuses, showed that in terms of the age of leaving school, the position of the category of managers in large establishments had changed no more than would have been anticipated on the basis of trends affecting the population as a whole in the period between the Censuses. There had been an overall trend towards later leaving, and apparent changes in recruitment to managerial positions were a reflection of that general trend. At least in terms of extra years of schooling there had been no tendency towards a higher level of positive discrimination for those staying on among recruits to management.

If Clark's figures are overestimates of those in higher secondary schools, the White-Collar figures are possibly underestimates. Although it would appear from the table that from Clements' study to the White-Collar study there has been a decrease in managers from the higher type of schools, the White-Collar under-representation and Clements' over-representation of senior management probably account for this. Clements' managers are generally better educated than those in the Acton study conducted about the same time, and the differences are no doubt due to the different nature of the samples and the different data gathering processes. Our older managers probably have fewer senior men than the other studies, and this is reflected in lower mean levels of education. This is very true of university education where only four out of 76 managers in our sample aged 40 or over have university degrees. At the younger levels our education variables are not so far out of line.

With these limitations in mind we cannot point to very definite trends in schooling, but we can say that there is no strong evidence for an increased discrimination in favour of the products of higher schools, and a very substantial proportion of managers in the White-Collar sample had only the most rudimentary secondary schooling. Just over 23 per cent attended non-selective state schools and left at the earliest opportunity. A further 6.8 per cent attended such schools and left after only one year's schooling beyond the minimum. If we add those who attended private schools or selective state schools and left at the first opportunity or after only one extra year, the figure is 48.6 per cent of all managers on whom we have information on schooling and years of leaving. It will be seen, therefore, that a very large proportion have 'risen from the bottom'.

Secondary schooling and full-time further education are not the only, or even the most frequent, sources of qualifications relevant to employment. In all of the previous studies the importance of part-time education, especially evening classes, has been stressed, but there have been general assumptions that this route to qualifications has declined as the provision of formal full-time education has increased. Before looking at this proposition in detail, let us look at the sort of qualifications brought to the job by managers of different schooling and occupational experience.

Tables 7.3 and 7.4 present data on qualifications by type of first job for managers who attended non-selective state schools and those who attended grammar-type schools or private schools, respectively. Each person is recorded once only, under his highest qualification. The measurement of qualifications is discussed in detail in Chapter 9, and a scheme for the General sample is used which is rather more detailed than that for the White-Collar data. Here we simply set out the main qualifications which occur in each category of the latter scheme:

O = No Qualifications
1 = General Qualifications of a low level
2 = 'O' Level and Equivalent Qualifications
3 = 'A' Level, Ordinary National Certificate and Equivalent Qualifications
4 = Higher National Certificate or Diplomas
5 = Minor Professional Qualifications
6 = Major Professional Qualifications
7 = Degrees and Higher Degrees

As one would anticipate, managers from the different types of schools differ both in the jobs they first held and in the qualifications they possess. A comparison of Tables 7.3 and 7.4 shows that whereas 24 out of 82 managers who attended the higher secondary schools (29 per cent) began their careers as managers or professionals, this was true of only one out of 60 managers from non-selective schools. Slightly over half of all managers from these latter schools began work as unskilled manual workers or as apprentices, while this was true of only just over one

TABLE 7.3 Qualifications by first job for managers who attended non-selective secondary schools

	Qualifications*								
	0	1	2	3	4	5	6	7	Total
Non-skilled manual	5	0	1	3	0	2	0	2	13
Skilled manual	6	1	1	4	2	3	1	0	18
Draughtsmen and technicians	4	0	0	2	0	2	1	0	9
Clerical	7	0	1	3	2	4	0	0	17
Sales	1	0	0	0	0	1	0	0	2
Managers	0	0	0	0	0	0	0	1	1
Professional	0	0	0	0	0	0	0	0	0
Totals	23	1	3	12	4	12	2	3	60

NOTE
* See the text for the types of qualifications indicated by the numbers.

TABLE 7.4 Qualifications by first job for managers who attended grammar schools or private schools

	Qualifications*								
	0	1	2	3	4	5	6	7	Total
Non-skilled manual	4	0	0	3	1	0	2	0	10
Skilled manual	2	0	0	1	5	2	1	0	11
Draughtsmen and technicians	3	0	1	2	1	3	0	4	14
Clerical	10	0	2	0	3	1	4	2	22
Sales	1	0	0	0	0	0	0	0	1
Managers	4	0	0	1	1	1	0	5	12
Professional	0	0	0	0	1	0	1	10	12
Totals	24	0	3	7	12	7	8	21	82

NOTE
* See the text for the types of qualifications indicated by the numbers.

quarter of those from higher schools. Those from the lower schools also tend to have lower qualifications. Ordinary National Certificates or 'A' levels and minor professional qualifications are by far the most common. Though we have not distinguished them in these data, it is likely that ONC is a more usual qualification than 'A' level among those from the lower schools, as is the case in our General sample. Only one person with this level of qualification stayed on at school long enough to have taken 'A' levels before leaving. Taken together with HNC and minor professional qualifications, they make up about three-quarters of all qualifications in the lower school sample. Those who went to the upper schools are more likely to hold a degree than any other qualification. Degrees and membership of a major professional association account for half of all qualifications for the higher school sample.

In both samples a substantial proportion of managers possess no formal qualifications. The figures are 38 per cent for the lower group and 29 per cent for the higher, though we believe that the latter figure is too high, for reasons we shall discuss shortly, and several included in it have low-level qualifications. Of all managers, only those who started in professional jobs are not represented among the unqualified. Those starting as clerical workers are slightly more likely to be in this group, though the differences between them and other groups, excluding professionals, are not significant. On this evidence the route to management involves the acquisition of qualifications for a majority of each group. Those who start in manual jobs are just as likely to hold qualifications as those who start in non-manual jobs, other than professionals. How then are these qualifications acquired?

In the studies with which we have compared our White-Collar sample of managers, there was an assumption that full-time formal education as a route to qualifications was replacing part-time education, especially evening classes. The image of the man leaving school early, and working his way up by the acquisition of specialised skills, supplemented by part-time study, was taken to be a characteristic of the past, now rapidly in decline. As Clements puts it, 'The growth of specialisation in administration and techniques, the necessary demands for qualifications and the increases in technological complexity may mean that the recruitment of managers from the bottom will continue to decline. Specialisation by narrow experience and night school studies are not enough.' It seems the belief is not confined to these commentators but is widely held. For instance Sykes (1965) found that clerical workers in a steel company no longer believed in the possibility of rising to senior positions through evening classes because of an increasing tendency to recruit directly from among those with qualifications from full-time study.

Our data do not confirm this trend, and it should be noted that Clements' arguments are based upon the usual flaw of regarding age groups as cohorts. In Tables 7.5 and 7.6 we show types of educational experience by the level of qualifications held. The importance of part-time education can be deduced from the figures in both tables. In Table 7.5, among those who attended the non-selective schools, only one man out of 60 had only full-time further education and three combined full-time with part-time. Of these three, the two with degrees probably used part-time education in the earlier stages of their post-secondary education. Both left school at the first opportunity and took non-skilled manual jobs. Their full-time education was not a continuation of their school careers. At the other end we have 12 men with no recorded further education, though one of them has a minor professional qualification and probably engaged in some sort of part-time study, by correspondence course, which we have not coded, or by private study. It would appear, therefore, that of the 37 managers from non-selective schools who possess formal qualifications, part-time education played an important part for 34 (92 per cent) of them and was the only form of further education for 31 (84 per cent). None of the qualifications shown was received at school, though one or two of the more highly qualified may have obtained low-level qualifications while they were at school.

TABLE 7.5 Qualifications by type of further education for managers who attended non-selective secondary schools

	Qualifications*								
	0	*1*	*2*	*3*	*4*	*5*	*6*	*7*	*Total*
1. Full-time further education only	0	0	1	0	0	0	0	0	1
2. Full-time and part-time further education	0	0	0	0	0	1	0	2	3
3. Evening class only	9	0	1	5	2	6	0	0	23
4. Day release only	1	0	0	2	1	1	0	1	6
5. Evening and day release	3	0	1	5	1	3	2	0	15
6. No recorded further education	10	1	0	0	0	1	0	0	12
TOTAL	23	1	3	12	4	12	2	3	60

NOTE
* See the text for the types of qualifications indicated by the numbers.

T ABLE 7.6 Qualifications by type of further education for managers who attended grammar-type schools or private schools

| | Qualifications* | | | | | | | | |
	0	*1*	*2*	*3*	*4*	*5*	*6*	*7*	*Total*
1. Full-time further education only	0	0	0	2	3	0	1	12	18
2. Full-time and part-time further education	0	0	0	0	0	1	0	7	8
3. Evening classes only	17	0	3	1	5	2	2	1	31
4. Day release classes only	1	0	0	0	2	2	1	0	6
5. Evening and day release classes	2	0	0	3	2	0	3	1	11
6. No recorded further education	4	0	0	1	0	2	1	0	8
TOTAL	24	0	3	7	12	7	8	21	82

NOTE
* See the text, p. 184, for the types of qualifications indicated by the numbers.

The overwhelming importance of part-time education as a means of obtaining qualifications for managers with this type of school background is very clear.

Turning to those from the higher type of schools, the most noticeable feature of the table is the extent to which full-time and part-time study are alternatives. The mutual exclusiveness is not complete as eight men did engage in both types, but in the case of the seven who were graduates, it would appear that the part-time study was in pursuit of particular specialised knowledge after they had taken their main qualifications.

We believe that 'A' and 'O' level GCE results are probably underestimated in this table. Though our questions about qualifications did not seek to tie them to specific courses of study, they were asked directly after questions on the type and duration of further education. We believe that some respondents thought we were asking about qualifications from these types of courses, and failed to report qualifications they took at school. Some support for this comes from the fact that there is a slight tendency for the years spent at school beyond the minimum to be negatively correlated with the possession of formal qualifications, if we exclude those with the highest level qualifications. For example, the four men who reported no qualifications and no further education all spent at least three years at school beyond the minimum leaving age, and two were recruited directly as management trainees. On the other hand, of the seven in this table who possess 'A' level or equivalent qualifications, only three had stayed at school long enough to have taken them there, and two of these had also some experience of full-time further education, and their qualifications may well have resulted from that.

If we make the least favourable assumptions, that all with full-time further education received their qualifications primarily by that route, that all 'O' level or equivalent qualifications were taken at school and that the man who stayed at school and has 'A' level or equivalent qualifications received them at school, then 26 (45 per cent) of the 58 qualified men in this table still received their qualifications primarily from part-time study. It would seem therefore, that even for those from the higher-type schools, part-time study remains a very important route to qualifications, and is quite possibly the most important route.

In both tables the most frequent type of part-time study is evening classes. Those for whom evening classes are the only type of further study form 38 per cent of the total sample of managers and 43 per cent of those with some form of further education. However, evening classes seem to be the type of further education least tied to qualifications. Everyone who had some full-time further education has some formal qualification, and of those with day-release experience, alone or in combination with other types of further education, 32 (82 per cent) out of 39 possess a qualification, while of those who attended only evening classes the proportion drops to 28 (52 per cent) out of 54. It may be that to some extent the courses followed provided specific vocational training without formal qualifications at the end, such as evening classes which supplement on-the-job training in apprenticeships, but it also seems likely that some taking evening-classes start towards qualifications that are never completed.

Overall it would appear that part-time study is not declining much among managers. In Clements' study 79 per cent of all managers had had some part-time vocational training, including correspondence courses. Nine years later 73 per cent of Clark's rather better educated sample had still undertaken some form of part-time study. In our sample at least 76 per cent had some part-time experience, though this omits any who took correspondence courses and had no qualifications, who were included in both the other studies. Day-release courses, though still covering only a minority, became more important throughout the period, and they seem much better predictors of success in obtaining qualifications than evening classes. However, the major boost in day-release education came from the Industrial Training Act which came into force too late to affect our sample of managers. The Act changed the character of day-release education by encouraging the provision of much lower level courses, often of a short duration, not attached to significant qualifications.

In general then, part-time study still seems to be the major route to qualifications and promotion to management, though there also appear to be entirely internal methods of promotion which remain without the need to be formalised in external qualifications. As yet any movement towards higher levels of education substantially completed before entry to the labour market has made little inroad into the traditional patterns. Most of our managers have, in one way or another, worked their way up, having started with jobs and educational backgrounds from which promotion is certainly not guaranteed.

In this chapter we have not been able to give the sort of definitive accounts of managerial careers which would be appropriate for incorporation in adequate accounts of the reproduction of the occupational system, but we have been able to dispel certain myths and point to lines of development. We have shown that studies arguing for declining opportunities have misread their data and built spurious arguments. We have also shown that on available evidence the general trends they sought to establish are not borne out. Opportunities to rise into management from below have not decreased in the post-war era, and direct recruitment into management has not increased as predicted. There would appear to be no disproportionate rise in the educational experience and attainment of managers. In fairness, there does seem to have been a recent modification of the position generally adopted by writers, which we outlined at the beginning of the chapter. Westergaard and Resler (1975, p. 325) are much more tentative about trends in their recent book than were Little and Westergaard earlier (1964). They write, 'It is probable, in short, that social mobility through promotion—and perhaps demotion—over part of the range of occupations has become rarer; while the acquisition of formal educational qualifications outside work, and usually before entry into work, has become more important as a precondition of occupational success. Too little is known about this shift to set figures to it.' Of the Acton and Clements studies they (1976, p. 326) write, 'There is also evidence consistent with, though not positive proof of, a decline over time in the proportion of managers who started work near the bottom of the ladder, with little formal education in Acton Society Trust, 1956, and Clements, 1958.' This represents a retreat, but not a sufficiently emphatic retreat. The main outlines of the arguments remain, and are no less mistaken, even if they are presented with increased caution.

MYTHS OF STRATIFICATION

In this section the objectives and procedures in our extended treatment of clerks are very well described by the first paragraph of the conclusion of Lockwood's *Blackcoated Worker* (1958, p. 201). There he writes:

It was suggested [in the introduction] that the class consciousness of the blackcoated worker would best be interpreted in terms of general concepts which have been used in the study of working-class consciousness. There was no reason to believe that the outlook and behaviour of the clerk were a function of any psychological idiosyncrasy in his make-up that could not be explained in terms of his peculiar social situation. On the basis of this assumption the intervening chapters sought to provide detailed information on the major features of the social and economic position of the clerk, and particular emphasis was placed on the way in which they differed from those of the manual worker. Thus it was possible to relate differences in attitude and conduct of the two groups to variations in their respective social environments.

However, we have provided rather different accounts of social and economic circumstances. In one major respect our approach differs from Lockwood's from the start. We do not assume that we are dealing with 'the clerk' or that he has a 'peculiar social situation'. Those employed in clerical work come to it from diverse backgrounds and social experience, and while some may complete their careers in this type of work, others will leave to a great diversity of occupational careers. The clerk does not have a peculiar social location. To seek the class position of clerks, as if they were a homogeneous group in their relationship to stratification processes, is to confuse the position (or more correctly, positions) of clerical work in the productive system with the position of those employed in such work in the labour market. In fact the latter has to be separately specified, and clerks are in diverse relationships to the labour market.

The central issue to which Lockwood addresses himself is one which has had great currency in discussions of occupations and the class structure from the 1930s to the present. It is the apparent discrepancy between background, life-styles and aspirations of lower level white-collar employees on the one hand, and the low level of economic returns to such work on the other, what Lockwood describes as status ambiguity. Anyone reading the literature on the blue-collar, white-collar divide may be excused a feeling of *déjà-vu*. In the 1930s Klingender was of the opinion that the economic circumstances of clerks placed them firmly as proletarians, which left the problem of their lack of an appropriate consciousness. Mills in the 1940s predicted a 'status panic' as the customary economic sources of superiority of white-collar workers over blue-collar workers were eroded. Lockwood provided an elegant statement of how practical sources of difference might be found, while still accepting the basic formulation of the problem. More recently both Mackenzie and Braverman have seemed to return to a basic statement of the problem. Each asserts that as a consequence of recent changes in economic circumstances, lower level white-collar workers are now proletarians. The problem of their consciousness remains.

In fact, as we have shown, market circumstances are not as supposed, and we shall see in Chapter 9 that when a more realistic model of earnings is produced, the discrepancies between life-style and economic circumstances disappear. So far as we can tell there are no particular disadvantages to starting a career in clerical work, and the assumption that promotion prospects of men employed in this area have drastically declined in recent years would appear to be the opposite of the truth. With the increasing employment of women and the growth of the white-collar area generally, their promotion prospects have probably improved. We do not have adequate historical data to test this hypothesis, and the data that are available are flawed by the frequent changes in the detailed definitions of clerical work in official statistics; but we can say quite unequivocally that for young men entering clerical employment at the present time promotion prospects are excellent.

It appears from data on the 1921 and 1931 Censuses that, typically, large numbers of young men were recruited to clerical work directly upon entering employment and that there was a regular outflow to other occupations throughout their working careers. Changing definitions make comparisons across censuses difficult in detail, but in the post-war era a change in the nature of employment in this area is clearly indicated. The old pattern of a large number of young clerks and a constant trend out of this type of work is increasingly modified by a second, though much lower, peak in the mid-1950s. We have seen that this type of bi-modal distribution is characteristic of not only Great Britain, but also Australia and the USA. In our White-Collar sample the second peak is clearly attributable to the recruitment of men, later in life, from manual to non-manual work.

From our detailed examination of trends it is evident that the recruitment of manual workers to non-manual work is most characteristic of manufacturing industry. To an extent it occurs in government employment, but it is not an important feature of employment in such traditional clerical areas as insurance and banking. There the pattern is close to that found in the 1921 and 1931 censuses. Even within manufacturing industry the pattern of direct recruitment to clerical work and subsequent movement out is merely overlaid by the pattern of later recruitment. Careers starting in clerical work and moving on to better things remain the dominant feature of clerical employment.

To what extent can the major change in male clerical employment, the recruitment of manual workers late in life, be regarded as a proletarianisation of clerical work? The answer must be to a very limited extent. Certainly the ex-manual workers are not proletarianised; they are, by both past and current experience, proletarian. Those who entered at an early age, for the most part, are not proletarianised. The vast majority leave clerical work, mostly in an upward direction. It may be that the minority who remain will now find themselves employed alongside proletarian ex-manual workers, which was not a likely circumstance pre-war, and this may intensify any crisis occasioned by relative failure, but their circumstances are not otherwise greatly changed.

Our concern in this section has been with the occupations and careers of men, but we cannot ignore the major change represented by the greatly increased number of women in clerical employment. Since their presence has tended to free men from routine tasks and hasten promotion, it can hardly have a proletarianising effect on the male clerks. Whether the women are proletarianised raises complex questions which we hope to examine elsewhere, but it seems the answer must be no. They have always been employed in routine positions, mainly in specifically female jobs. Even those apparently in the same jobs as men have been concentrated at the lower levels, though, if anything, their promotion prospects have improved slightly over the years. They come from diverse backgrounds and follow different life-styles, which are largely determined by factors other than their own occupations.

It may be argued that the work itself has been proletarianised in the sense that its content has, in Braverman's terms, suffered degradation. Certainly Braverman believes so, quoting clerical employees who stress the trivial nature of the tasks they perform, but, as we have seen, clerical work was never well regarded. The Dickensian image of the clerk scarcely presents a man with stature and income. Lockwood (1958, p. 101) quotes the President of the National Union of Clerks, speaking to the assembled delegates in 1910 thus: 'You may not perhaps have realised that clerical work is very generally looked upon as "unskilled" work, not only by employers, but by the skilled artisan as well.' Klingender's (1935, p. 61) analysis, made in the early 1930s is, in places, very close in tone to Braverman's assessment in the 1970s. He writes, for example, 'It is this process (mechanisation) which completes the technical proletarianisation of clerical labour.'

If clerical work has been in any sense proletarianised it is only in the limited sense that proletarians now undertake clerical work which was previously the preserve of those middle-class careers. No actual groups of individuals or type of employee has been proletarianised.

The embourgeoisement/proletarianisation debate depends for its currency upon the reification of occupational categories which cover individuals and groups in diverse relationships to the labour market. The division of class and status, as one of economic and social factors, so characteristic of theoretical discussions of social stratification has depended for its empirical plausibility upon just such reification and confusion. We have indicated some of the detailed processes at work, but it should be recognised that in general there are very great movements between conventionally defined occupations throughout working careers. Aggregate tables of so-called career mobility show very extensive movements of the working population from first jobs to subsequent jobs. Generally the movements shift the population from lower level manual jobs to higher level manual jobs, from low level non-manual jobs, to higher level non-manual jobs, and from manual jobs to non-manual jobs. We have shown how the careers of managers have been misunderstood, but we need to know much more about the general process of occupational reproduction and change. In the next section we shall address ourselves to a general, descriptive model of such processes.

Part Three

Education and Careers

8 Mobility within and between Occupations

In the last section we showed that particular occupations do not define the career experiences of individuals, whether we mean by career merely the occupations held through the entire period of an individual's working life or something more restricted such as Slocum (1966, p. 5) means when he writes, 'An *occupational career* may be defined for this discussion as an orderly sequence of development extending over a period of years and involving progressively more responsible roles within an occupation.' In this chapter we shall be looking more generally at the nature of careers. In so doing, one of our aims will be to examine how occupations have come to be reified into categories of stratification experience, and the consequence of this for studies of stratification.

Slocum's formulation of the relation of 'occupation' and 'career' is interesting in that it is an explicit statement of what remains implicit in many approaches to occupational classification, such as the coding schemes of the OPCS or the US Bureau of the Census. He defines an occupation in such a way as to include the various experiences which go to make up a career. Thus occupation is a very broad term, potentially covering many types of job experience throughout an individual's working life. A career is constituted entirely within an occupation, so on this definition career mobility and occupational mobility are not simply different but completely distinct. The latter describes movement between occupations while the former describes career development within occupations. For various reasons, which will become obvious, Slocum (1966, p. 239) finds it difficult to maintain his definition of a career throughout his analysis. Thus when he comes to define career mobility he writes, 'Career mobility involves moving from one occupational stage to another. This may involve promotion to a more responsible position, demotion, discharge, moving to another organisation, or retirement.' The orderliness of his earlier definition is not maintained here, but what is common to both definitions is the notion of a career as occurring within a single occupation.

Although this view of the relationship of career to occupation has not always been shared by other writers, some of whom have allowed a rather wider notion of career, the essential idea is entailed in much writing on occupational experience. Wilensky (1961), for example, in writing of orderly and disorderly careers, clearly sites disorder in crossing occupational boundaries, and the prominence of similar assumptions in schemes of occupational grading in most countries may be traced, in large measure, to the strength of the general notion. In this country, for example, the OPCS, *Classification of Occupations*, 1970, codes all members of the major professions to the same category, though for socio-economic groupings, it distinguishes between employees and the self-employed. Similarly all apprentices, articled clerks or other trainees, for all manual or non-manual work, are coded to the occupation of the qualified workers.[1]

There is a great deal of sense in regarding the whole of an occupational career in this way. Though there are considerable variations of life-time experiences within the general titles, there is also an integrity of career experience which makes it meaningful to regard all members as occupying more or less the same position in the stratification system. The younger members of the occupation carry their potential with them. Clearly there is a problem in this, in so far as more start than realise the potential to the extent of reaching the highest level. In some cases the main step is simply qualifying, but in others there are clearly defined stages which only a few may reach. For example, those who reach the rank of General in the army are so few and far removed from the mass of officers and men that it is hard to think of them as having the same occupation.[2] However, even in an extreme case such as this, there is a unity in the career structure which makes it meaningful to think of it as a single whole.

The major problem is that the concept does not cover the whole occupational system. Many occupations and typical occupational careers do not fit this dominant pattern. Slocum (1966, p. 226) writes that occupational careers, as he has earlier defined them, 'are restricted

---

[1] The code 032 for Engineering Apprentices may appear to be an exception but is intended for those whose training cannot be attributed to a particular skill—either because of the general nature of training or due to lack of precise information. These same procedures are followed by Goldthorpe and Hope (1974).

[2] We would suggest anyway that, contrary to OPCS classification, officers should be regarded as a separate career, but that is not the prime issue here.

to professionals, managers, skilled carftsmen, technicians, and a few others', but we might take issue even with this list. Though there are undoubtedly career hierarchies in management and technical occupations, these occupations do not typically contain their own lowest career positions. We have discussed, in the last section, how few managers start in managerial positions or as trainees in Britain, the USA or Australia. Technician is, in our data, another occupation that gathers members from other starting occupations. In this case even fewer of our sample, six per cent as against ten per cent, started in their current occupation. These percentages, of course, refer to the proportion of technicians or managers at a point of time, but those who began their working lives as technicians or managers tend to have held their jobs longer, and so form much smaller proportions of all those who have experience of these occupations at some stage in their careers.

If these exceptions to the rule of coherent careers within an occupation involved small proportions of the total working population the situation might not be serious, but in fact a majority of men starting their working lives in non-manual work enter occupations which are conventionally defined as different from those in which they have most of their work experience. Indeed there is, in general, a movement between first occupation and subsequent occupation which shifts the population into better paying, more prestigious occupations across conventional boundaries. In each of the national studies relating first job to present job which we quoted in the last chapter, this tendency applies. The white-collar area grows relative to the manual area between first job and present job,[3] and on either side of the manual/non-manual boundary there is a tendency towards a higher concentration in better occupations. Among manual workers this tendency is more marked in the US data, where movement into skilled manual jobs is rather easier than it is in either Britain or Australia. Nevertheless the pattern, if less marked, is similar in both of these countries.

There are, in fact, few starting occupations in our White-Collar sample. Apart from the professions, four specific jobs cover most people who start their working life in the white-collar area: shop assistant, clerk, draughtsman and laboratory assistant. These are all occupations with heavy net losses between first job and current job, and in the case of clerks we have seen that current holders of the job are not the same as those who started in it.

[3] See also Harris and Clausen (1966), who show that for a sample of men, between the years 1953 and 1963 the non-manual section gained 21.9 % from the manual section while losing only 8.2 %—a net gain of 13.7 % in ten years.

We have mentioned how the non-manual area grows from first jobs to current jobs, recruiting personnel who started their working lives in manual jobs, but if for the moment we leave those people aside and consider only men who started in non-manual work, then 73 per cent in our White-Collar sample started in one or other of these four occupations. A further 20 per cent started in a major professional occupation. However, the distribution to these various first jobs varies considerably between different areas of work, as does the extent of recruitment from manual work.

Among all insurance workers in our sample 84 per cent started as clerks. A further five per cent started in professional jobs and seven per cent started in manual work. If we leave aside these latter, then of our sample of insurance workers who started in non-manual work, 90 per cent started as clerks and 5.5 per cent as professionals. Most of the manual workers joined their present firms as clerks, and for the younger recruits we may regard this as the starting point of a new career. Thus we can see that there is little alternative to being a clerk as a first occupation in insurance.

Public service, in our data, shows a rather different recruitment pattern. A much larger proportion of the work force is recruited directly to major professional occupations, accounting for a quarter of the total sample in this area. Public employers also recruit more extensively from among those who began work in manual jobs, and this group is 23 per cent of the total. If we leave them aside, professionals form 32 per cent of those who started in non-manual jobs. Clerks form 47 per cent of this group and 37 per cent of the total sample in public service, while the other three occupations—draughtsmen, laboratory assistant and shop assistant—between them make up 13 per cent and 10 per cent respectively.

Manufacturing industry shows even greater differences from insurance. In this case ex-manual workers form nearly half of all non-manual employees (48 per cent). Consequently, though clerks form about the same proportion of those starting in non-manual work as they did in the public service area, 45 per cent, they are a much lower percentage of the total, 24 per cent, than in either insurance or public service. Professional occupations form a smaller proportion of starting positions than in public service but higher than in insurance, both in the sample as a whole and among the white-collar starters, the figures being 10 per cent and 18 per cent respectively. Manufacturing is the area, in our figures, where draughtsmen are concentrated, and, together with shop assistants and laboratory assistants, they comprise 14 per cent of the initial occupations of the total manufacturing sample and 28 per cent of those who began in white-collar jobs. This probably underestimates the numbers who start as draughtsmen because, as we have said, there is not always a distinction between draughtsmen and certain engineering apprentices at the outset of apprenticeship. As a consequence some trainee draughtsmen may have been coded to skilled manual occupations.

In general, then, we see that in non-manual work there is a very high concentration of first occupations. Manual work is a very important source of later recruitment, especially in manufacturing industry, though the figures we have presented so far probably overrepresent its importance. To a very large extent ex-manual workers are concentrated in the lowest non-manual jobs in our data—clerk and foreman. We have already argued that a movement from manual to clerical work cannot be seen as having much effect upon class position if it occurs late in life for men with no formal qualifications. Similarly, though foreman is undoubtedly a promoted position, it does not remove the incumbent far from his previous position or far from those over whom he exercises control. We showed in Chapter 2 how, in terms of patterns of social interaction, foremen are very similar to manual workers.

The general conception of an occupation containing career stages covering the whole of an individual's working life is obviously strongly tied to the professions and skilled manual work. In both of these areas the conventional view is that specialist skills are acquired in training, which are exercised in normal work activities. Thus the demands of the job are seen as more or less equivalent to the qualifications of the man, and it is apparently meaningful to identify them both with a specific class or market position. When qualifications are of a less specific nature, when they are relevent to a diversity of jobs, an identity of job and incumbent is no longer so obvious, and the individual is less tied to a particular form of work.

The mistake that is implicit in the general formulation is one which identifies the market circumstances of individuals with the particular occupations they hold. Individuals at very different career stages may be gathered under one occupational title and, in addition, many different types of career may be developed from some general occupations. By reifying occupations we apparently render meaningful such questions as 'what is the class position of clerks?' or 'what is the income career of clerks?' It may be that the occupations conventionally distinguished by the OPCS and the US Bureau of the Census reflect a past set of arrangements where careers were more closely identified with the occupational titles, but if this is the case our data suggest that these arrangements were in the remote past. Managerial positions have been filled from other starting occupations for the whole of this century. In any case, as we have seen, the conventional arguments have been that the process is in the completely contrary direction: that previous 'promotion from the ranks' into management has decreased with the bureaucratisation of managerial careers and that as a consequence movement across occupational boundaries has decreased.

Furthermore, there are standard career patterns crossing occupational boundaries into management. Take, for example, the situation of professional engineers employed in industry. A substantial proportion move from technical jobs to managerial jobs after some time in industry. As this pattern is well established, it seems perverse to label such moves as occupational or social mobility while professional and manual careers are labelled immobility.

In general the conventions of occupational classifications give rise to some rather strange results in mobility studies. Allingham (1967), for example, finds that, rather than the traditional rags to rags in three generations, the process is accomplished in two. He examined the marriage licenses of over 3000 men in New South Wales, Australia and extracted data on the occupations of the grooms. He then contacted a sample and from their birth certificates took their father's occupations at the time of the respondents' birth. In examining these data he found that there was, apparently, what he called a class regression factor operating. The sons of upwardly mobile fathers had not apparently consolidated their fathers' higher positions. In the main they were back in the occupations their fathers had held at the time of their birth. Allingham speculates on a number of reasons why this should be so, but since most of the upward mobility in his data consisted in movements out of what are starting occupations into occupations which are typically held later in life, and since his sample of sons were close to the beginning of their working lives, the most plausible explanation is that the extent of upward occupational mobility of the fathers, and the extent of downward inter-generational mobility from fathers to sons, has been exaggerated. In large part, the differences between their occupations at the time of the son's marriage reflect different stages on standard careers. This is supported by the closer relationship of the sons' current occupations with the fathers' earlier occupations than with fathers' current occupations.

Lee (1968, p. 308) also finds a puzzling result which may be attributed to the movement of individuals across occupational boundaries. In order to examine changes in 'career prospects' he looks at the distribution of the male working population between 'middle class' and 'working class' occupations in the Census of England and Wales, 1961, by the age at which they left school and their current age. His intention is to compare the proportions of those leaving school at different ages in the different age groups to show how the likelihood of holding a 'middle class' job varies by type of schooling. But in setting out his data, a further, to him, surprising result is discovered. He writes:

> That the younger members of *all* T.E.A.[4] groups (and not just the early leavers) should be found less frequently in the middle class is a curious feature of this tabulation; but it is to be expected on account of (a) a tendency for some late leavers to perform manual work for a short time in order to gain experience, (b) a tendency for a few manual jobs to require much higher educational standards than in the past, (c) the possibility that failures are more certainly and swiftly downgraded than in earlier periods. These factors seem to have a somewhat greater influence over those who leave at 16, rather than at 17 or more.

A simpler explanation which is in accord with other available data is that there is a movement into 'middle class' jobs as age increases.

To avoid the pitfalls of previous analyses we need to be able to define occupational structure so as to link a notion of careers, as patterned changes of work experience, with an adequate concept of occupation. The major problem, then, is to construct an approach which will make clear the relationship between the distribution of occupations in a society, and the processes underlying the distribution of individuals to occupations throughout their working lives. Perhaps a simple analogy will serve to illustrate this distinction. The limitations of any analogy must be borne in mind and certainly this particular one will collapse if pushed too far, but it should serve to clarify some fairly fundamental issues.

The occupational structure, we have argued, is not just a set of occupations between which individuals are distributed, but a system within which they move, frequently with expectations of increasing rewards. That is, the routes along which people move and the distribution of people to the routes and occupations must all be seen as

---

[4] Terminal Education Age. The term is taken from the Census reports and refers to the age of leaving full-time education.

part of the structure. Thus, in our analogy, the occupational structure may be regarded as a railway system of a particular sort. In this system all trains run north from a diversity of points of departure at more or less the same latitude in the south. The stations of the system are occupations, or rather specific jobs, and the further north the job is located, the greater the returns to it and the greater the regard in which it is held. Certain lines are almost isolated from all other lines, but others are interconnected through an extensive system of junctions at various points. The lines run north to different extents. Some run through a very small number of stations set close to one another, or perhaps go nowhere at all, while others run through a large number of stations which may be at some distance from each other.

In studies of occupational stratification there has been a confusion of stations and lines as the positions within the stratification system. For example, Slocum's definition of an occupation is essentially a description of a whole line rather than a single station. As we have seen, it is typical of professional occupations and skilled manual occupations, and they may be seen as relatively isolated lines with limited access from other lines. On the other hand, the distinction of clerical and other lower non-manual occupations as positions in the structure is an identification of actual stations rather than lines. In part, the reason for the discrepancy has been that those positions which have been classed as occupations lie on lines which are extensively interconnected; they are, as it were, the important junctions—significant in their own right and not readily allocated to any particular route. Thus for example, in our analysis of clerical work in the last chapter, clerk, as an occupation, i.e. as a station within the railway system, has persons arriving and leaving under diverse circumstances. Some have reached the end of their journey, some are merely beginning and some lie between these two conditions. Of those who leave, many will share similar incomes and have similar status but be doing very different jobs.

The fact that professions have consistently been identified as occupations rather than sets of occupations is implicit support for the view that the orientation of individuals is to the journey upon which they are engaged rather than the particular station they happen to be on at any time. An occupation, for them, is a set of interlinked positions within a career, though the position is never quite as straightforward as that. There are, within all professions, elite positions which are not within the realm of realistic general expectations, but there has been some tendency in classifications to separate these more senior positions from the other positions which constitute the major part of the occupation. Even within the professions, the highest positions have to be earned after entry. There may be indications from the initial period of training that some members of the profession are more likely than others to reach the highest positions, but there are usually a number of hurdles along the way, and successful careers certainly cannot be predicted at their outset with complete accuracy.

Indeed it would seem sensible to regard all careers as having something of a developmental character, in that expectations are affected by each level of achievement. In many cases outside the professions, it seems unlikely that those entering work with particular qualifications or opportunities to acquire qualifications, will have a clear conception of the whole of their careers. What is likely to be true, however, is that they can judge their experience against groups in definable relationships to themselves. Thus a man with a particular level of qualification will know whether or not he is doing well in comparison with others holding similar qualifications and employed in similar work areas. He is also likely to have some idea of the position of groups he considers superior and groups he considers inferior to himself.

In terms of our railway analogy, the orientation is not to the station upon which an individual finds himself, but to the ticket that he holds for the journey he is taking. In many cases the ticket is not for a unique destination. Rather like a ticket on the London underground, it is potentially for one of several destinations at more or less the same distance from the start of the journey. The characteristic of our system is that the stations for which the ticket is valid are at more or less the same distance north; that is, they provide more or less equivalent returns within a system of occupational stratification.

The components of this general idea have been available in writings on occupational careers for some considerable time. For example, Broom and Smith (1963) introduced the notion of bridging occupations, that is, occupations which allow individuals to transfer from one line to another. This idea obviously incorporates both the conception of lines as occupational situses and greater or lesser difficulty in moving between situses. Sørensen (1970) has discussed the problems of an approach which would compare occupational life histories, and Carr-Hill and Macdonald (1973) have suggested that mobility studies should focus on the similarities between entire occupational trajectories. We would agree with this approach, but available classifications of occupations are not really adequate. To use them would be to distort processes. It would seem that practices in classifying work experience, perhaps as a consequence of their long history, are so well entrenched that the confusion in the classifications between occupations as separate railway lines and the single stations (sometimes serving several lines) has scarcely been discussed. The 'occupational structure' in conventional studies has been the distribution of people to a mixture of lines and stations.

The implications are less serious for studies seeking to compare occupational distributions at different points in time than for studies of inter- and intra-generational mobility. While there would be some difficulty in interpreting the true nature of changes in occupational distributions over time without conceptions of the processes of individual experience of work, at least a similar distribution at two points in time could be interpreted as stability. For mobility studies, however, the implications are far more serious. We have already discussed how certain sorts of occupational change become mobility while others are taken to represent immobility. With tickets for the same length of journey, this implied that those in certain areas do not experience mobility while those in other areas do, despite the fact that their journeys started from similar points and finish at equivalent points. Recruitment to management is a particular case of mobility enforced by the nature of the classification.

In what we have written of the railway system so far, we have not formally defined the tickets which enable the individual to progress to better jobs. What is the basis of advantage? We have already implied, to some extent, that educational attainment may be taken to represent the ticket that an individual holds, that is, his market advantage, but this point must be treated with care. We shall look presently at the difficulty of interpreting qualifications as indicators of real capacity for the production of value, rather than as the marks of conventional distinction within the population, reflecting a social determination of worth rather than an economic determination. For now we would point out that we are not making an assumption that qualifications are valid indicators of productive contribution, merely that within the conventional operation of the system they act as if they were. Also we do not believe that formal educational attainment is the only source of advantage. To a very large extent, tickets, or extensions to tickets, are acquired in work experience. For example, holding one type of job may very well imply progression to higher level jobs, whether or not the occupational achievement is mirrored in educational achievement. It may be that there has been an increasing tendency in recent years towards acquiring formal qualifications, though in certain cases these may best be seen as indicators of occupational success. This is especially true of minor professions, where holding professional qualifications is more likely to reflect the status of the person within the organisation than to be the source of his status. Formal schooling and qualifications, however, are the most accessible indicators of market circumstance and will reward closer examination.

One of the reasons why stations rather than lines are chosen in certain areas of occupational experience is that these are areas from which development is due to qualifications acquired in part-time education after entry to the occupational system; we shall see the consumption of part-time education is rather difficult to predict, and success in terms of acquiring formal qualifications from such education is even more difficult to predict. Though a majority of our White-Collar sample and our General sample have acquired their highest qualifications from part-time study, such study is poorly correlated with the possession of qualifications. Many more attend night school and day-release than ever obtain qualifications. This has led several authors, using forms of correlation analysis, to conclude that part-time study is unimportant as a source of qualifications. This in fact is the opposite of the truth. Though success is uncertain, part-time study for workers in both of our samples is the most important source of qualifications.

The distinction we have drawn between jobs and incumbents allows us to clear up some discrepancies of understanding of the relationship of occupations to stratification, but it should not be overstressed. A fully adequate model would have to recognise that patterns of movement through the system affect, and can change, the nature of the system and that, conversely, changes in the system affect the ability to move or the desirability of movement. An example of the latter point is technical change which undermines conventional skills, moving the jobs associated with them to a more 'southerly' position in the system, cutting off previous promotion routes and making routes into the occupation less attractive. The former point can be illustrated by the peculiar ability of the passengers on a station to move it in a 'northerly' direction by controlling access to it, making sure that only those with more valuable tickets alight. However, whatever the shortcomings of a model built on this distinction, it does provide an approach which clarifies a number of problems concerning the occupational structure and stratification. Further research on this basis may then provide the understanding needed for a more adequate model.

9 Education and Occupation

We now turn to an examination of the relevance for careers of education and qualifications. In particular we shall be looking at the importance of different types and levels of education, and their relationships to subsequent earnings. The fact that education affects incomes is commonplace, but recent empirical studies have purported to demonstrate that the effect is small or even negligible (e.g. Duncan *et al.*, 1968; Jencks, 1973; Psacharopoulos, 1977). We shall show that such arguments are mistaken, and with an adequate conceptualisation of the relation of education to careers, the effect can be seen to be substantial. Our approach will also show that the part-time sector of education, so much neglected in previous research, is in fact of considerable importance in the development of careers.

In arguing the importance of educational experience and qualifications, we are not saying that they measure some sort of individual quality which is rewarded in the level of earnings. Such a view is often assumed, and is contained in what has been called 'human capital' theories, but its validity needs examining both empirically and theoretically. We begin by considering education simply as a potential source of market advantage, and then explore the ways in which such advantage operates.

Here our main source of empirical data is the General sample, for which we have detailed information on educational experience. As we indicated in the Introduction, the sample is drawn from men working in both urban and rural locations in four different areas of the country, centred on Glasgow, Leeds, Leicester and Cambridge. For the present analysis we have been able to use data on 4942 respondents. The sample is highly structured, on the urban/rural divide as mentioned, but above all by occupation. We sampled men in some 150 different occupational categories. Thus our sample cannot be regarded as representative of the working population, and unlike the White-Collar sample, the distribution of respondents on important variables does not resemble the national pattern. There is inevitably an over-representation of less common types of occupation, and one effect of this is that the sample is more highly qualified than the general population. On the other hand, the sample is well suited to arguments about particular types or groups of occupations. Furthermore, though its unrepresentative nature must affect any arguments about general trends, it does not compromise analysis of the structures of educational processes with which we shall be concerned.

As soon as we turn to a direct consideration of the relationship between education and careers, we are faced with a problem of measurement. There has always been a difficulty in arriving at suitable measures of educational attainment in a British context. In American studies the situation has been comparatively simple. There is there an assumption of a formal equivalence of schools, so that the most common practice has been to use grades completed, and/or years of college, as an indicator of educational achievement. Though there are inadequacies inherent in such an assumption, they are somewhat less than those associated with attempts to find a single composite measure in a British context. Duncan (1974) has discussed ways in which such a measure might be developed, but most researchers have chosen to use more than one indicator of educational achievement. Part of the problem is the diversity of schooling within the British Isles.

In Scotland, where part of the General sample was gathered, both the history of schools and the current situation are somewhat different from the rest of Britain. Most importantly, more of each age cohort attended the upper types of schools (senior secondary schools) in the state system, and the examinations taken were different. The Scottish Higher Leaving Certificate was usually taken a year before 'A' Level of the General Certificate of Education in England, and was divided into Higher and Lower levels. More recently, the Scottish Certificate of Education with 'O' Grades taken earlier and Higher Grades taken at the same age as before has been introduced. Obviously, the differences between Scotland and England could, in themselves, be the subject of very extensive enquiry, but for our present purposes we have chosen to combine information on the two countries in such a way as to ignore certain differences. Passes at the Higher level of the SHLC or SCE we have regarded as equivalent of 'A' levels in the GCE Passes at the lower level of the SHLC and 'O' Grades of the SCE we have equated with 'O' levels in the GCE. At post-secondary levels of education we have equated Scottish and English university degrees, despite their different content and the fact that a majority of the former are general rather than honours degrees. Professional qualifications we have also regarded as equivalent.

However, this is only part of the problem for within England alone there is a situation of considerable complexity. Different groups among those currently in full-time employment have had experience of three different types of secondary educational system and each of these types has been internally differentiated. In the pre-war situation only a minority experienced what was defined as secondary education—those attending the intermediate, grammar or private schools; the majority went to senior elementary schools after the age of eleven. Then the post-1944 system introduced secondary education for all, with secondary modern, secondary technical, grammar and private schools. More recently, there have been steady changes towards a system of comprehensive schools and private schools. However, even this diverse picture is a considerable oversimplification; in particular, within the private sector there are major and minor public schools while, since 1944, the elite 'direct grant' grammar schools have bridged the gap between the private and public sectors.

With these problems in mind, we decided that the best measure of educational achievement would be a measure based upon qualifications attained rather than upon the method of obtaining them. Years in full-time or part-time education, taken on their own, were unlikely to be satisfactory measures of education. The authors of the General Household Survey (GHS) for 1974 come to a similar conclusion. They looked at the relationship between school-leaving age and level of qualification and came to the following conclusion. 'If it could be shown that there was a close relationship between age on leaving school (or completing full-time or part-time education) and type of qualification gained, it would in practice be possible to dispense with asking questions about qualifications, and to rely on a question dealing with the completion of education as a proxy for qualification . . . As it is, though this relationship it quite strong . . . it is not strong enough on existing evidence to make it do without detailed information on qualifications.' (OPCS , 1977, p. 151).

However, level of qualification alone does not provide an entirely adequate measure of educational advantage or disadvantage. If we were dealing only with qualifications obtained in post-school education, the situation would be fairly straightforward. From a detailed examination of our General sample, we find that the level of qualification attained in tertiary education is much more important than the method by which it was obtained. Relationships between such qualifications and a variety of other factors are scarcely affected by whether they were obtained in full-time or part-time study or whether those holding them had gone to selective or non-selective schools. However, not everyone is qualified and many receive their highest qualifications at school which introduces complications. For example, among our respondents who had no formal qualifications or only the most minor of qualifications, those who attended grammar or independent schools were at an advantage, in terms of occupation and income, when compared with those who attended non-selective secondary schools. Having gone to the higher type school acts as a qualification in itself. It also appears to enhance the worth of qualifications received at school. Thus, among those who took GCE 'O' level at school, or School Certificate in the case of older respondents, and who subsequently received no higher qualifications, we find a persistent difference between those who attended non-selective state schools and those who attended selective state or private schools. Over the whole age range, the latter have higher mean earnings than the former.

We shall look a little later at the effect of type of school on post-school qualifications, when we shall see that it does have an effect, but that it operates in assigning respondents to different types of qualifications and careers rather than differentiating within types of qualification. In these circumstances level of qualification is not affected as an indicator of advantage from education. In the present case, however, allowance has to be made for type of school as it directly affects advantage within levels of qualification. Thus we have divided the two lowest levels of school qualifications (no qualification/minor qualifications and 'O' levels/School Certificate) by type of school attended. There were insufficient cases of 'A' levels or Higher School Certificates from non-selective schools to determine whether a similar procedure should be followed in that case, and we decided to have only one category of 'A' level.

Table 9.1 shows the highest qualifications of the respondents in the General sample, aged 28 and over, by the method by which they received these qualifications. We have chosen to include only respondents in this age range because inspection of our data suggests that by the age of 28 the process of acquiring qualifications is virtually completed. We have distinguished twelve levels of qualifications, using our judgement to place particular cases in categories defined, most importantly, by well-known qualifications. The success of the procedure can be assessed from subsequent analysis. Information about specific unfamiliar qualifications was gathered from a variety of sources. While we believe that, on the whole, we have arrived at a reasonable categorisation of levels of qualification, we also believe that further

TABLE 9.1 Highest qualifications by method of obtaining them: respondents in the General sample aged 28 and over

	At school	Full-time	Part-time	Mixed full-time and part-time	No qualifi-cations	Total
		In tertiary education			*No*	
Degree including higher degree		420	46	2		468
Major professional association		87	155			242
Minor professional association		15	131			146
Non-graduate teaching diploma		38				38
Higher national diploma and certificate		23	93			116
Ordinary national diploma and certificate		9	68			77
GCE 'A' level etc.	94	3	10			107
GCE 'O' level etc.: higher-schools	258	3	11			272
GCE 'O' level etc.: lower schools	44	4	20			68
City and guilds		9	146	2		157
Non-graduate diploma		25	28			53
Occupationally specific qualifi-cation		41	11			52
Minor or no qualifi-cations: higher schools					414	414
Minor or no qualifi-cations: lower schools					1507	1507
Total	396	677	719	4	1921	3717

distinctions might yield more sensitive results.

We have ordered the categories in terms of their market advantage. Evidence to support the ordering will be presented later, but at this stage it is important to understand that the basis is the economic return to the qualification and not its educational quality (or any measure related to its content). Indeed, any discrepancy between the economic and educational 'worth' of the qualification, however measured, may be instructive in understanding the relationship of education to career processes. The categories are highest qualifications attained, and their ordering takes no account of their value as stepping stones to qualifications bringing in higher returns; for example, the position of GCE 'A' level takes no account of the fact that this is the basic entry qualification for a degree course or that most of those with 'A' levels go on to gain a further qualification. Even if it were desirable, it would be extremely difficult to take account of such latent market advantage, but it is necessary to appreciate this point in the following analysis.

The highest level of qualification in our scheme is a university degree. This category includes higher degrees and other graduate qualifications. Immediately below this level we have placed membership of a major qualifying association, though as we shall see, it really belongs alongside. This is a category which in a more sensitive scale would have to be subdivided. It includes the qualifications for membership of a wide variety of professional associations such as the Institute of Chartered Accountants and the Institution of Mechanical Engineers. Within most of the associations there are levels of membership, but we have not distinguished them here. In a number of cases a degree or a lower level of membership is necessary for entrance to the process of qualifying for a higher level of membership. In these cases, those who had proceeded through the levels of membership would have been coded here, while those with a degree would have been coded to the degree category.

In the analysis of qualifications and income later in this chapter, membership of a major professional association gives slightly higher incomes than degrees over most of the age range, but we excluded self-employed respondents from that analysis, and within professions the self-employed tend to have degrees In general the two groups are probably very close in their ability to command income, and both in certain census data and the General Household Survey they are combined.

Next we placed membership of what we have called minor professional associations. These are less prestigious associations whose examinations are recognised to be at a lower level than the major qualifying associations. Examples among our respondents are the Chartered Insurance Institute, The Institute of Bankers and the Institute of Data Processing, though some might prefer to regard the first as a major association and it was fairly close to the margin in our scheme. Just below these come non-graduate teaching diplomas.

The next category we defined by reference to Higher National Certificates or Higher National Diplomas, placing also in this category qualifications judged to be equivalent. A particular case of an equivalent level of qualification would be the City and Guilds Full Technological

Certificate. However, because of a lack of distinction in our coding, all City and Guilds qualifications were assigned to one category, but we know that few had the higher level of passes. The overwhelming majority have passed the Craft/Ordinary level and that is where we have placed the whole group.

Next come Ordinary National Certificates and Diplomas, followed by 'A' levels of the GCE and Higher School Certificates, then GCE 'O' levels and School Certificates divided by school as outlined earlier. The modest number of respondents with 'O' levels, etc., acquired after secondary schooling have been assigned to the groups with schooling similar to the respondents.

Ordinary level of the City and Guilds comes next, followed by those who attended selective schools but hold no formal qualifications or only the most minor qualifications, and finally those in the equivalent group who attended non-selective schools.

Two other groups are represented in the table, though we have not ranked them in the levels of qualification. These are non-graduate diplomas which cover a wide variety of types and levels of courses (though in so far as there is a typical example it would be Management Studies diplomas) and occupationally specific qualifications which are non-transferable minimum requirements and again cover a wide range. The lowest level of nursing qualification (SEN) would be a good example of these latter.

As we noted earlier, our respondents tend to be more highly qualified than the general working population of males. We can get some measure of the difference by comparing our figures with those of the General Household Survey for 1974 (OPCS, 1977), though a full comparison is not possible because of different interviewing and coding practices. In their category of combined degrees (including higher degrees) and membership of Major Professional Associations, they have six per cent of the economically active male population. In the figures presented in Table 9.1, 19 per cent fall into that category, though if we use the total General sample this falls slightly to 18 per cent because at the younger ages, many of those who will be highly qualified have not yet entered employment. At the other end of the scale, 75 per cent of males aged 16–64 in full-time employment in the GHS have qualifications below the level of City and Guilds ordinary level, while the same is true of only 52 per cent of the General sample aged over 28, and 47 per cent of total sample which is more directly comparable. In this case the fall from 52 to 47 per cent probably reflects the strong trend in recent years towards acquiring qualifications at school.

The White-Collar sample is closer to the national distribution, with 15 per cent who have degrees or major professional qualifications and 47 per cent unqualified. The distribution of qualifications in this sample appears to be quite close to that for the corresponding section of the working population. Accordingly we have used it to check arguments based on the General sample and found consistent results. Although the methods we use are not all independent of the structure of the sample, we are not overly concerned with precise calculations of effects, but rather with general configurations of processes.

Table 9.1 illustrates well one of our central concerns—the division between full-time and part-time education. Leaving aside occupationally specific qualifications where work and study are often difficult to distinguish, we see that full-time education is typical only of degrees and non-graduate teaching diplomas (and some other types of non-graduate diploma). All other qualifications are more likely to be acquired in part-time study. Of all qualified respondents aged 28 and over in the General sample, 40 per cent took their highest qualification in part-time study, 38 per cent in full-time study after leaving school and 22 per cent at secondary school. Because of the bias to higher qualifications, particularly degrees, in the sample, the estimate for part-time study is low compared with the population as a whole. In the White-Collar sample we estimate that a minimum of 52 per cent of the qualified took their highest qualification in part-time study, while among manual workers the figure is probably much higher. Given the importance of this area, both in terms of numbers and of the range of qualifications covered, it is surprising that it has received only cursory treatment in the literature linking education and stratification. Ridge (1974), for example, used a trichotomy ('none' = 1, 'part-time' = 2, 'full-time' = 3) as a measure of 'further education'. It is true that he also includes a measure of qualifications, but this is a simple dichotomy ('none' = 0, 'some' = 1). He was re-analysing the LSE 1949 survey which is the basis of the work on mobility by Glass (1954) and his colleagues, and the data place these restrictions upon him, but the attitude towards tertiary education and qualifications is instructive.

Lee and Hordley (1966) have suggested that part-time education was previously a working class preserve, an alternative route to qualifications, but that it has been progressively appropriated by the middle class. As we shall see, we find some evidence for working class forms of part-time education, though we do not know whether these are being invaded by the middle class, but there are also traditional middle class forms which are important sources of qualifications. In general part-time education is much more important than has been realised.

SECONDARY EDUCATION

Before considering tertiary education in any detail we shall present data on the structure of secondary education. Processes at the later level are affected by those at earlier levels, and we think that the best method of presentation is an incremental model ordered by temporal sequence. Arguments about the effect of family background, for example, upon the consumption of tertiary education cannot be answered without consideration of its effects upon earlier educational experience. In general our object is to examine effects upon educational consumption and educational success, of earlier educational experience and family background (as measured by fathers' occupations at the time respondents left school). We shall rely heavily upon analysis of variance techniques in developing a view of educational processes.

Table 9.2 shows how important is the relationship between type of secondary school attended and whether or not our respondents are likely to have significant qualifications. Only 20 per cent of those who attended non-selective state schools are qualified, while only 24 per cent of those who attended the higher type of school are unqualified. There is obviously, as one would expect, a very high premium upon attending state-selective or independent schools, and an important initial question is the extent to which class background (as measured by fathers'

TABLE 9.2 School-type and significant qualifications of respondents aged 28 and over

| | State selective and independent schools | | Non-selective state schools | | Totals | |
	No.	%	No.	%	No.	%
Possessing significant qualifications	1533	80	461	24	1994	52
No significant qualifications	394	20	1437	76	1831	48
Totals	1927	100	1898	100	3825	100

NOTE
$\phi = 0.55$, $p < 0.001$

occupations) affects the type of school attended. For the purpose of the subsequent analysis, fathers' occupations have been coded to four categories: unskilled manual, skilled manual, clerical and technical, and finally professional and managerial occupations. A more sensitive measure assigning fathers by career rather than by occupations would have been preferred, but the data are not precise enough to allow us to do this with sufficient confidence.

The results of an analysis of variance of type of school by father's occupation are given in Table 9.3. This is a simple 'one-way' analysis, but we shall introduce more complex analyses involving more than two variables as the argument develops. The aim of this sort of analysis is to examine the contributions to the variance of a dependent variable from independent variables, known as *factors*, which are measured in nominal or ordinal categories. The measure of association which is obtained is eta, or in the case of the independent effect after allowing for influences from other factors, beta. As with a product moment correlation, eta is the square root of the ratio of 'explained' to total variance, but in that there need be no assumption of ordering of a factor's categories; it is not strictly comparable. However, in the case of ordered variables such as we are using in the analysis, it may be regarded as measuring the fit to a regression curve through the category means, rather than to a straight line. Provided this is a monotonic function, eta may be regarded as roughly equivalent to a product moment correlation. Where there are two or more independent factors (or interval level independent variables in analysis of covariance), beta is obtained for each by controlling for the other(s). It may be thought of as analogous to a standardised partial regression coefficient—a 'path coefficient'—in regression analysis. We also obtain a multiple eta which is analogous to the multiple correlation of regression analysis in that its square measures the proportion of total variance 'explained' by all the independent variables in combination.

T ABLE 9.3 Type of school attended by father's occupation

	Unskilled manual	Skilled manual	Clerical and technical	Managerial and professional	All	Eta	Signifi- cance
Mean school value	0.30	0.47	0.63	0.83	0.50	0.37	p < 0.001
N	1254	1039	818	539	3650		

In Table 9.3 the dependent variable, type of school, has only two values and is therefore treated as a dummy variable. In the following analyses we use some dependent variables where the measurement is not entirely appropriate, having a limited number of values which are not on strictly equal interval scales. Therefore, compared with the results that would be obtained from more refined measures, the reported coefficients of association are probably a little low, but at no point does this affect the nature of the argument.

The relationship between father's occupation and type of school is highly significant and of a coherent form even if the correlation is only moderately high, with an eta of 0.37.

The next stage of the analysis is to examine the effect of both father's background and type of school upon the length of time spent in school beyond the minimum leaving age. We begin with another analysis of variance, but before presenting the results, a word on the interpretation will be useful. When dealing with two or more factors in an analysis of variance, as in this case, there may be not only direct independent effects—the main effects—from the factors but also *interaction* effects due to the combination of the factors. Such interactions make it difficult to decide how much variance may be attributed to main or to interaction effects. The strategy we have adopted, to minimise the influence of random interaction, is first to extract the main effects and then test for the significance of interaction effects. If the latter are not significant, it is reasonable to limit our interpretation to the significant independent effects.[1]

If, on the other hand, they are significant, then they cannot be ignored, and we must take the analysis further. In either case we obtain category means for each factor which are adjusted to control for other factors, values of beta, and a multiple eta, all of which are based solely on the main effects. When there are significant interactions, these statistics are clearly unsatisfactory and may be crucially affected by the interactions, but they will often give a useful initial guide to interpretation.

From the present analysis of variance we found that father's occupation and the type of school attended had highly significant independent effects upon years spent in school beyond the minimum leaving age. The beta values were 0.27 and 0.53 respectively and the multiple eta was 0.67. The functions were monotonic and in the

---

[1] Because of the large number in the sample, quite small direct and interaction effects will be significant. However, some care in the interpretation of significance levels is called for where we subdivide the sample.

predicted direction, but there was also a highly significant interaction term, which indicated that the relationship of father's occupation to years beyond the minimum was different in the different types of school. Accordingly we looked at the relationship between these variables in the two types of school separately. The results are contained in Table 9.4. In each case there is a highly significant relationship and the function is monotonic, but the level of the relationships varies, (eta is 0.40 in the upper schools, 0.26 in the lower), as does its internal structure. Bearing in mind the anticipated independent effect of type of school, we would expect the mean values to be higher in the higher type of schools, as indeed they are. However, the range is also greater in the higher type of schools, which reflects the interaction effect of school and father's occupation. Father's occupation has a larger effect in the higher than in the lower schools. In fact this is almost entirely due to the large gap between skilled manual fathers and technical and clerical fathers in the higher type schools which is not reproduced in the lower type schools. There the most important division is between respondents with professional or managerial fathers and the rest.

In summary, then, the type of secondary school attended, father's occupation and the relationship between them all had an effect upon the years our respondents stayed on at school beyond the minimum. Father's occupation had a somewhat stronger influence in the higher type of schools, so the advantages of higher class background and higher type of school are increased still further when they occur in combination, which they tend to do.

The next question is the extent to which each of these variables had an

TABLE 9.4 Mean years of schooling beyond the minimum leaving age for type of school by father's occupation

Father's occupation when respondent left school	State selective and independent schools mean	(N)	Non-selective state schools mean	(N)	All mean	(N)
Professional and managerial	2.65	(452)	0.91	(87)	2.37	(539)
Technical and clerical	2.18	(515)	0.35	(303)	1.50	(818)
Skilled manual	1.48	(495)	0.26	(544)	0.84	(1039)
Unskilled manual	1.37	(377)	0.15	(877)	0.52	(1254)
All	1.94	(1839)	0.25	(1811)	1.10	(3650)
Eta	0.40		0.26		0.49	
Significance	$p < 0.001$		$p < 0.001$		$p < 0.001$	

effect upon the level of school qualifications received. Throughout this section school qualifications have been divided into three groups. The first is no qualifications or only the most minor. The second is, for English respondents, 'O' level of the GCE or, for older respondents, School Certificate, and, for Scottish respondents, 'O' Grade of the SCE, or, again for older respondents, passes at the lower level in the SHLC. The third group comprises 'A' levels of the GCE, Higher School Certificates and Scottish Highers. For most purposes we have assigned values of 0, 1 and 2 respectively to these groups.

Once again, we initially conducted an analysis of variance, with the level of school qualification as the dependent variable and each of the prior variables included. All had significant independent effects ($p < 0.001$). The beta values for years at school beyond the minimum, type of school attended and father's occupation at the time respondents left school were 0.72, 0.12 and 0.08 respectively. Each of the functions was monotonic, with the exception that there was virtually no distinction between the two groups of manual fathers. Once again, however, these results cannot be directly interpreted, as there were highly significant interaction terms (which means that the effect of each factor was dependent on the other two), and so we chose to disaggregate the data to examine the nature of these effects in detail.

First we divided the sample by type of school attended and performed an analysis of variance in each type, with qualifications as the dependent variable and years of schooling beyond the minimum and father's occupation as independent variables. In each case there were significant ($p < 0.001$) independent effects. In the higher schools the beta values for years beyond the minimum leaving age and father's occupation were 0.74 and 0.08 respectively. In the lower schools the equivalent values were 0.57 and 0.16. However, both analyses produced significant interactions, and we chose to further disaggregate the date to look at these effects. The results are given in Table 9.5. We have combined the two manual categories of fathers and the two non-manual categories because the numbers of respondents in the lower schools staying for three or more years were very small, and only in such combination did they approach adequacy. In general we can see that in both upper and lower schools the level of qualifications attained increases with years of schooling beyond the minimum, but the increase is more pronounced in the higher type of schools. In addition we may see the distribution of respondents reflects the influences we discussed earlier, in relation to Table 9.4. Very much larger numbers of those in the higher schools stay on than in the lower schools, and in each taken separately, father's

TABLE 9.5 Mean level of school qualifications for categories of father's occupation and type of school and years of schooling beyond the minimum leaving age

| Years beyond minimum | Lower Schools | | | | Higher Schools | | | | All | |
| | Fathers manual | | Fathers non-manual | | Fathers manual | | Fathers non-manual | | | |
	Mean	(N)	Mean	(N)	Mean	(N)	Mean	(N)	Mean	(N)
0	0.01	(1233)	0.03	(276)	0.05	(297)	0.09	(62)	0.02	(1868)
1	0.15	(126)	0.38	(67)	0.59	(209)	0.65	(173)	0.49	(575)
2	0.54	(37)	1.04	(26)	0.93	(164)	1.14	(237)	1.02	(464)
3 and More	0.65	(17)	1.42	(17)	1.73	(198)	1.76	(486)	1.72	(718)
All	0.04	(1413)	0.22	(386)	0.73	(868)	1.30	(958)	0.56	(3625)
Eta	0.49		0.72		0.77		0.70		0.84	
Significance	p<0.001		p<0.001		p<0.001		p<0.001		p<0.001	

occupation is related to staying on but this is more pronounced in the higher schools.

The central point in the table is given visual form in Fig. 9.1. There we have plotted the mean levels of qualifications by years of schooling beyond the minimum for each of the categories of father's occupation in the different types of school. This distinguishes most clearly between respondents with manual fathers who attended non-selective schools and the other three groups. Respondents who attended non-selective schools and had non-manual fathers are not nearly so clearly distinguished from the other two groups. Indeed those who stayed on two years beyond the minimum have rather better mean qualifications than those with manual fathers who attended state selective and independent schools and stayed on for the same length of time, though the numbers in the former category are small. In the higher schools the differences between the groups with manual and non-manual father are relatively small, but all favour the latter group. In general, though the relationships are not all of the same strength, having a non-manual father means that a respondent was more likely to go to a selective or private school, and both of these mean not only that he was more likely to stay on at school, but also that the returns to staying on in terms of qualifications acquired were greater.

One way of looking at the processes involved is to interpret Fig. 9.1 explicitly in terms of the independent direct effects and interaction effects in the analysis of variance. With only direct (i.e. additive) effects we would have four parallel lines with a positive gradient representing a positive direct effect from years beyond the minimum to qualifications. As it is, the slopes of the lines differ, and the differences represent the interaction effects. Since all four lines have positive gradients, it makes sense to think of a direct effect from years of schooling, and this is in keeping with the high betas noted earlier. Not surprisingly, those who stayed longer at school were better qualified regardless of other influences. However, since the four lines almost coincide at no extra years, the differences are essentially due to their slopes, which means the effects are almost all in interaction.

Neither class background nor type of school attended can be thought of as having much influence except indirectly through years of schooling, as noted earlier, and in interaction with each other and with the number of years spent at school. One of the clearest aspects of this is that attending a selective school has the greatest relative advantage for children from manual homes who stay on. The other is the point already mentioned, that background makes most difference for those who stay

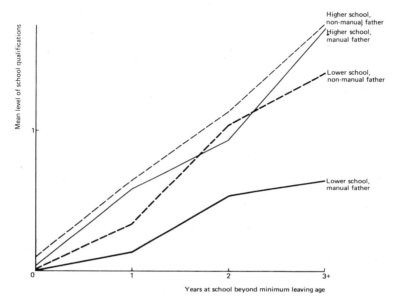

FIG. 9.1 Mean level of school qualifications by years of schooling beyond the minimum, in higher and lower schools for categories of father's occupation

on in non-selective schools; the extra years in such schools lead to relatively little gain in qualifications for those from manual backgrounds, but almost remove the school effect for those from non-manual homes.

TERTIARY EDUCATION

How well does family background and secondary educational experience relate to experience in tertiary education? The simplest answer is rather well. An analysis of variance of the level of highest post-school qualification received by highest school qualification, type of school and father's occupation produces a multiple eta of 0.72. Thus, over half the variance in the level of qualification gained after leaving school is explained by just these three variables of family background and schooling, with all three contributing significantly. There is only one significant interaction effect and that is between father's occupation and highest school qualification. However, this effect is rather complicated and is affected by the method of obtaining higher qualification—whether by part-time or full-time study. Detailed consideration will be given separately, therefore, for qualifications gained by each route, and will be left until after we have looked at the relationship of secondary education and family background to further education in the part-time and full-time systems.

The most important qualifications gained after leaving school are obviously those which raise the individual's levels of qualification above that gained at school. In Table 9.6 we have set out the numbers and proportions of those who took, or failed to take, such qualifications in each of the groupings defined by the method of post-school study, the type of secondary school attended and the level of highest secondary school qualification. In both school types, taking post-school qualifications is strongly associated with the level of school qualifications (gamma = 0.74 for lower schools, 0.62 for higher schools and 0.76 overall). A very large majority (85 per cent in the lower schools and 72 per cent in the higher schools) of those with no significant school qualifications fails to take significant post-school qualifications. Of

TABLE 9.6 Those gaining higher* qualifications from tertiary education by type of secondary school attended and level of qualification gained there

| School | Higher post-school qualification | | | |
qualifications	Full-time	Part-time	None	Total
Higher schools				
Minor or none	37	142	455	634
%	*6*	*22*	*72*	*100*
'O' levels etc.	105	173	256	534
%	*20*	*32*	*48*	*100*
'A' levels etc.	452	84	160	696
%	*65*	*12*	*23*	*100*
Lower schools				
Minor or none	40	223	1522	1785
%	*2*	*12*	*85*	*100*
'O' levels etc.	20	23	44	87
%	*23*	*26*	*51*	*100*
'A' levels etc.	14	5	10	29
%	*48*	*17*	*34*	*100*
Total	668	650	2447	3765
%	*18*	*17*	*65*	*100*

NOTE
* i.e. higher than the level already attained at school.

those with 'O' level or equivalent qualifications from both types of school, about half go on to take higher qualifications in later study. Only those with 'A' levels or equivalent from school have substantial majorities (65 per cent in the lower schools, 77 per cent in the higher schools) who go on to take higher qualification after leaving school.

There is also an independent effect from the type of school attended, as can be seen from the higher proportions in the higher schools who have post-school qualifications within each level of school qualification. Overall, because of the relationship between qualifications gained at school and the type of school attended, there is a substantial association between school and further qualifications (phi = 0.38), but the *independent* effect of school is very much more modest. Furthermore, this effect is almost entirely confined to those with less than 'O' level qualifications from school. At each of the two levels of actual school qualification, the association between type of school and further qualifications is negligible and non-significant, while for those with only minor or no school qualifications the relation is highly significant. Those who left higher schools with no qualifications are more likely to take post-school qualifications than those who left lower schools with no qualifications, though the strength of the relationship is modest (phi = 0.15). This lends support to our decision, reported in discussion of Table 9.1, to divide this category by type of school. Our argument there was based on the market advantage of having attended state-selective or private schools when no qualifications were obtained at school or subsequently. However, we would expect that the sorts of influences which affect market advantage might also affect educational advantage, and we find that this is so among those with no significant qualifications from school, though we should note that this does not appear to be the case among those who left school with 'O' levels.

In Table 9.6 we can also see the relationship of school qualifications to part-time or full-time study as routes to further qualifications. Part-time study includes day-release classes, evening classes, correspondence courses and private study. Full-time is self-explanatory except that sandwich courses, with periods spent in practical experience, have been treated as full-time study. From the table it is obvious that the two types of study are not straightforward alternatives in the sense that they draw equally from the levels of school qualification. Full-time education is the typical route to higher education for those who left schools with 'A' levels or equivalent qualifications. Those in this group who attended the lower schools are almost three times as likely to have gained higher qualifications in full-time as in part-time study; those from the higher schools are more than five times as likely. Furthermore, full-time education is dominated by those with this level of qualification; they form 70 per cent of those who gained their highest qualification by this route.

Respondents with 'O' level qualifications or their equivalent, among those attending either type of school, are more likely to have taken higher qualifications through part-time study, but these groups are not so strongly identified with part-time study as those with 'A' levels etc. are with full-time study. Indeed, in both types of school, taking no higher qualifications in post-school study is more typical of this level of school qualification. In general, part-time study as a route to higher qualifications has more respondents (56 per cent) who had less than 'O' level qualifications on leaving school than the other two groups put together, though this is largely a consequence of the very large number in the former category in lower schools. Among respondents from higher schools, the most common group in part-time education are those with 'O' levels or equivalent.

We have shown earlier that part-time education provides a means to a very wide range of qualifications; and full-time education, despite its close association with high secondary education, is neither unproblematically superior in the sense that it is exclusively associated with higher level qualifications nor straightforwardly prior in the sense that candidates turn to part-time education only when failing to enter, or succeed in, full-time education. Though the mean level of qualification is lower from part-time education, there is a considerable overlap between the two forms; and some high level qualifications, those in accountancy for most of our respondents for example, are taken exclusively in part-time study. With this in mind, we decided that for this relatively brief analysis it was most sensible to consider each type separately. We shall look at full-time further education first (omitting respondents with part-time experience) as if it were an extension of secondary education, then turn to consider part-time education only among the respondents who did not enter full-time education.

FULL-TIME FURTHER EDUCATION

An analysis of variance, with the highest qualification obtained in full-time further education as the dependent variable and highest school qualification, type of school attended and father's occupation as the factors, produced a multiple eta of 0.80. The level of post-school qualification was measured by assigning values from 0 to 8 to the types of qualification set out in Table 9.1, omitting occupationally specific qualifications and non-graduate diplomas. We have not divided the lowest qualifications by type of school as we wish to measure the effect of that variable.

Each of these factors made a significant contribution to the main effects, with highest school qualification having by far the largest effect (beta = 0.71); but there was one significant interaction effect between highest school qualification and father's occupation. The effect from type of school is minimal, and when we control for school qualifications we find that it disappears as a source of effect except in the case of minor or no qualifications (as we found for the simple possession of a higher qualification by either route).

To examine the nature of the interaction of father's occupation and highest school qualification, we conducted separate analyses of highest qualification in full-time study by highest school qualification and type of school for each of the four levels of father's occupation. In three of these four analyses—those for respondents with professional and managerial, clerical and technical and skilled manual fathers—school has no significant effect and there are no significant interaction effects. In the fourth case school has a modest effect (beta = 0.10), and there is an interaction between highest school qualification and type of school, but these are reflections of the relationship between type of school, level of highest school qualification and highest qualification from full-time education we reported above.

The results of the separate analyses are given in Table 9.7. Within each category of father's occupation it presents the mean level of post-school qualification for each level of school qualification after controlling for school type (i.e. what the means would be if school had no effect or were unrelated to school qualifications), and similarly for each school type with control for school qualifications. Values of beta and significance levels give an indication of the importance of the variable in each case. We have simply ignored the interaction effect between school and school qualifications as it is small and does not affect the points illustrated in the table.

Although the independent effects from type of school are slight, they are all in the expected direction, being higher for higher schools. Independent effects from school qualifications are also all in the expected direction and these are very much more substantial. The expected independent effect of father's occupation is represented by increases in the values of a column as one moves across the table from

TABLE 9.7 Mean level of qualifications from full-time further education for father's occupation: independent effects* by school qualifications and type of school

				Father's occupation				
	Unskilled manual		Skilled manual		Technical and clerical		Professional and managerial	
Factors	*Mean*	*(N)*	*Mean*	*(N)*	*Mean*	*(N)*	*Mean*	*(N)*
School qualifications								
Minor or none	0.17	(710)	0.20	(430)	0.35	(272)	0.87	(50)
'O' level etc.	1.94	(41)	2.19	(65)	2.37	(114)	4.55	(83)
'A' level etc.	5.34	(57)	6.59	(91)	6.41	(159)	6.97	(212)
Beta	0.66		0.79		0.72		0.60	
Significance	p 0.001		p 0.001		p 0.001		p 0.001	
School								
Lower	0.50	(604)	1.31	(327)	2.36	(202)	5.15	(48)
Higher	0.97	(204)	1.54	(259)	2.64	(343)	5.53	(297)
Beta	0.10		0.04		0.04		0.04	
Significance	p = 0.001		p = 0.17		p = 0.32		p = 0.45	
All	0.62	(808)	1.41	(586)	2.54	(545)	5.48	(345)
Multiple eta	0.72		0.81		0.74		0.62	

NOTE
* The mean levels of qualifications for each factor are given after control for the other factor.

left to right, where the increases are uniform for all value levels of a column variable. Deviations from this pattern, where values are inconsistently high or low, represent interaction effects, and these are not very great here.

We see that the independent effect of father's occupation is due largely to the advantage of having a professional or managerial father. Taking account of the interaction effects, we see that those with 'O' levels benefit particularly from having such fathers, while an unskilled manual father is a disadvantage for those with 'A' levels or equivalent. In these ways the influence of father's occupation is heightened. The other noticeable interaction shows a small relative advantage to having a skilled manual father for those with 'A' levels, which probably reflects the greater tendency for these sons to progress through mainstream education and so to take degrees rather than minor professional qualifications, but this barely affects the general pattern. It is clear that the influence of father's occupation, and particularly the advantage of having an upper-class father, is not exhausted in secondary education; it has an influence in full-time further education which is independent of educational achievement in secondary education. On the other hand, this is less than the indirect effect through the powerful influence of school attainment.

A final question in dealing with full-time further education in the extent to which it translates into occupational advantage. A full discussion of this would require a more thorough knowledge of the structure of careers than is now available, and we shall have to content ourselves with a somewhat simple analysis of the effect of education upon the first jobs our respondents held and then upon their present jobs, rather than upon their career experiences. First job has the advantage for our analysis of being at the beginning of the career for everyone, whereas present jobs reflect different stages of career development. However, as we have noted in earlier chapters, certain conventional career beginnings are not distinguished very clearly in occupational classifications—clerk as a first occupation, for example, includes those on diverse career paths. Thus first jobs may reflect subsequent high status or may be relatively low level jobs from which the better qualified are likely to be promoted. Consequently the relation between first job and education, to which we now turn, underestimates the influence of education on career beginnings.

An analysis of variance, omitting those with part-time education, with first job as the dependent variable and highest post-school qualifications, school qualifications, type of school and father's occupation as factors produces a very high multiple correlation (multiple eta = 0.82). All main effects are significant, though the effects of type of school and father's background are very modest (eta = 0.08 and 0.09 respectively), and there is also a significant interaction between highest qualification and highest school qualification. However, this is rather difficult to interpret as most of this group have entered employment on the basis of school qualifications, and so we have a mixture of influences through school qualifications and higher qualifications. We believe, therefore, that we can best deal with the first jobs of those with neither part-time nor full-time further education when discussing the first job of those who obtained qualifications part-time. At least both groups enter employment straight from school.

An analysis of variance involving only those who received higher qualifications from full-time study produces no significant interaction terms. There are virtually no direct effects from type of school and father's occupation (beta = 0.04 and 0.00 respectivelly), the main influences coming from the two types of qualification. It is interesting that the greater effect comes from qualifications gained at school (beta = 0.40 for school qualifications, 0.24 for post-school), and this is so not just for the independent effect, but even for the overall association (eta = 0.45 and 0.35 respectively). Also the relation between post-school qualifications and job level is not completely monotonic. These results are partly explicable by particular features of the analysis. Not all those with full-time, post-school education start their courses before entering employment, and in some cases the full-time courses are the culmination of new educational careers begun in part-time study. To the extent that this is so, the first jobs held will be more influenced by school experience than post-school experience. Most of those with their highest qualifications from full-time study who began as manual workers fall into this category, though some, those following certain OND and HND courses, for example, held manual jobs as a condition of the course. The latter point, coupled with the confusions of career beginnings in occupational classifications, helps to explain the non-monotonic nature of the effects from highest post-school qualification.

Table 9.8 comes close to showing the level of job held on first entry to work by the level of qualifications held at that time, and the source of these qualifications. It does not show this exactly, for the reasons we have just outlined. The effect of these discrepancies upon the overall distribution in the table is slight.

Dealing first with those with qualifications from full-time study, we

TABLE 9.8 Level of qualifications at time of completing full-time education by type of first job and where qualifications were obtained (per cent in parentheses)

Qualifications and where obtained	Unskilled manual	Skilled manual	First job Technical and clerical	Professional and managerial	Total
In full-time further education					
'O' Level etc	0	0	6	0	6
	(0)	(0)	(100)	(0)	(100)
'A' Level etc	0	0	2	0	2
	(0)	(0)	(100)	(0)	(100)
O.N.D.	4	1	3	1	9
	(44)	(11)	(33)	(11)	(100)
H.N.D.	5	4	7	10	26
	(19)	(15)	(27)	(38)	(100)
Non-graduate teaching diploma	2	2	10	22	36
	(6)	(6)	(28)	(61)	(100)
Minor professional	0	0	3	12	15
	(0)	(0)	(20)	(80)	(100)
Degree and major professional	19	14	63	396	492
	(4)	(3)	(13)	(80)	(100)
Total full-time	30	21	94	441	586
	(5)	(4)	(16)	(75)	(100)
At school					
Minor or none: lower school	760	639	269	9	1677
	(45)	(38)	(16)	(1)	(100)
Minor or none: higher school	156	207	187	18	568
	(27)	(36)	(33)	(3)	(100)
'O' Level etc.	43	84	276	76	479
	(9)	(18)	(58)	(16)	(100)
'A' Level etc.	22	17	98	108	245
	(9)	(7)	(40)	(44)	(100)
Total school	981	947	830	211	2969
	(33)	(32)	(28)	(7)	(100)
Total	1011	968	924	652	3555
	(28)	(27)	(26)	(18)	(100)

can see that they are heavily concentrated in the highest educational ǀ category and the highest occupational category. Those with degrees or membership of major professional associations form 84 per cent of the total, while 75 per cent began their careers as managers or professionals, and no less than 68 per cent are in both categories. Full-time further education is strongly associated with high level qualifications and high level occupations. Also, in spite of this concentration at the top levels, there is a substantial relationship between the level of qualifications and that of the first job (gamma = 0.58).

The lower half of the table shows the relationship between first job and highest school qualifications for those who left school and started work without further qualifications. Among these men, the levels of their first occupations tend to be much lower, with nearly two-thirds starting in manual work, though the distribution across levels is much more even. The majority left school with only minor qualifications or more often none at all, and most of these (78 per cent) entered manual employment. We have divided the unqualified by the type of school they had attended, and once again we see the disadvantage of having been to the lower type schools. In contrast, those with qualifications at about the standard of GCE 'O'level or above were more likely to enter non-manual jobs. This is particularly so for those with 'A' level or equivalent, who typically started in managerial or professional jobs. Overall there is a clear association between school qualifications and the levels of first jobs (gamma = 0.64).

For a substantial number, entering employment is not the termination of education but the start of part-time study. For those in the lower part of the table, this is the only way to higher qualifications. Thus the occupation entered not only relates to qualifications held at the time but also to those it is hoped to aquire. Accordingly we shall now turn to a consideration of part-time education, looking at the levels of qualification gained and the influences on gaining them.

PART-TIME EDUCATION

In this section, instead of looking at the cumulative effect of family background and secondary education upon tertiary education and then of each upon first jobs, we shall reverse the order at the end of the process and look at the effect of background and secondary education on entry to first jobs and then of each upon higher qualifications. In this way we can examine, though not exactly, the extent to which part-time qualifications are a confirmation of careers rather than the means of creating new career opportunities. As we noted in considering full-time education, the way some initial jobs are classified as parts of careers while others are not, will tend to weaken the relationship between first job and higher qualifications; and the effects that we find can be taken as the minimum influences of career beginnings on subsequent qualifications.

A similar point applies when we look at the effects of secondary schooling and father's occupation upon first jobs. In the section on full-time tertiary education, we argued that we would really wish to place respondents on careers rather than in first jobs. Here this problem is more acute as fewer respondents enter professional and managerial positions directly, and though their careers may be more or less clear both to respondents and to their employers, they are not reflected in the classifications of first jobs. This should be borne in mind when considering the rather lower coefficients we shall find in the analysis for part-time education than we found for full-time education.

As a first stage we conducted an analysis of variance of first job by highest school qualification, type of school attended and father's occupation. The overall relationship is fairly strong (multiple eta $= 0.58$), and all of the main effects are significant. There is one significant two-way interaction, between highest school qualification and father's occupation, and the three-way interaction is also significant. The strongest independent effect is from highest school qualification (beta $= 0.42$), with more modest influences from type of school and father's occupation (with betas of 0.13 and 0.16 respectively).

To examine the nature of the interaction effects, we controlled first for school qualifications, doing an analysis of variance of first job by type of school and father's occupation within each level of school qualification. Among those with any school qualifications, type of school attended has little effect, though such as it is, it is in the right direction. For those with 'O' level or equivalent beta $= 0.09$ ($p = 0.068$), while for those with 'A' levels, etc., beta $= 0.08$ ($p = 0.194$). In neither of these cases is there a significant interaction with father's occupation in the determination of first job. However, among those without school qualifications, the type of school attended has a significant independent effect (beta $= 0.18$, $p < 0.001$), and there is a significant interaction effect with father's occupation. The independent effect is one more indication of the value of having attended a higher type of school when no qualifications have been received. To look at the interaction effect, we divided the unqualified group by type of school and did two separate analyses of variance of first job by father's occupation.

The results are given in Table 9.9 and Fig. 9.2, which also include the effects of father's occupation among those with 'O' levels, etc., and those with 'A' levels, etc. Looking, for the moment, only at the results for the two groups of unqualified respondents, we can see the nature of the interaction effect of school and father's occupation. While both groups show an increase in the mean value of first job for an increase in father's occupation (with a small reversal between skilled manual and clerical and technical fathers for those who attended lower schools), the increase is steeper for those from higher schools. Attending the higher type of schools not only confers an advantage on its own, but serves to increase the effect of father's occupation on first job.

Turning to an examination of Table 9.9 and Fig. 9.2 in general we can see, in the separation of the four groups, the marked effect of the level of

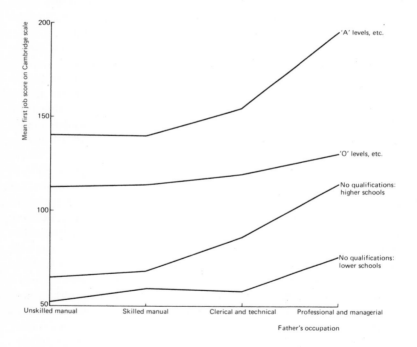

FIG. 9.2 Mean level of first job by father's occupation for different levels of school qualifications (for those with no full-time study)

school qualification (including the type of school at the minium level) upon the level of first job. As a guide to interpretation, 50 is equivalent to

TABLE 9.9 Mean level of first job for highest school qualification by father's occupation (for those who undertook no full-time study)

Father's occupation	Minor or none: lower school		Minor or none: higher school		*School Qualifications* 'O' level etc.		'A' level etc.		All	
	Mean	(N)	Mean	(N)	Mean	(N)	Mean	(N)	Mean	(N)
Unskilled manual	52.4	(810)	65.2	(186)	112.8	(94)	139.9	(37)	62.3	(1127)
Skilled manual	59.7	(484)	68.4	(217)	113.9	(121)	139.6	(48)	73.8	(870)
Technical and clerical	58.0	(247)	86.7	(127)	119.4	(148)	154.9	(79)	91.8	(601)
Professional and managerial	76.0	(52)	113.7	(35)	130.2	(104)	195.2	(79)	137.3	(270)
All	56.2	(1493)	74.3	(565)	119.1	(467)	162.7	(243)	79.0	(2868)
Eta	0.14		0.28		0.10		0.27		0.36	
Significance	$p < 0.001$		$p < 0.001$		$p = 0.217$		$p < 0.001$		$p < 0.001$	

the top end of non-skilled manual occupations on the Cambridge scale, 105 is routine clerical workers, and professional and managerial occupations begin around 200.

The slopes of the lines indicate the effect of father's occupation, with the steepest gradients on the right showing that the advantage accrues primarily to those with professional or managerial fathers. Though it does follow this general pattern, the line for those with 'O' levels is rather flat (and non-significant), showing quite clearly that father's occupation has least effect among those with this level of qualifications. This is the reverse of what we found when looking at the relationship of father's occupation and full-time education, and it may be that the greater than average success in achieving full-time qualifications of middle class sons possessing 'O' levels or equivalent almost exhausts the advantage of a middle class father.

Something like the same process seems to operate in the case of those with no qualifications from the lower schools, where there is also a weak relationship between father and level of first job. We saw earlier that having a middle class father was related both to the likelihood of staying on in the lower schools and particularly to the level of qualifications received for each year beyond the minimum. In this case it may be that the advantage of background has been mainly used up before leaving the secondary system.

The interaction effects of father's occupation and level of qualification (and the three-way interaction which has been illustrated by dividing the school types for the least qualified respondents) can be seen in the somewhat irregular patterns and, more especially, in the increase in the range between the mean values of unskilled manual and professional and managerial fathers as we move from the lowest to the highest school qualifications. In terms of Fig. 9.2 it may be seen in the increasing average slopes of the lines (apart from the one for 'O' levels) as one moves upward from the line for no qualifications at lower type schools. Thus the interaction effect tends to heighten the independent influences from these factors.

When we consider the effects of first job, highest school qualification, type of school and father's occupation upon highest qualification in part-time study, we find that all the main effects are significant, but there are a number of significant interaction effects. The multiple eta is 0.63 and the beta values 0.38, 0.27, 0.05 and 0.07 respectively. There are two-way interactions, significant at the one per cent level, between highest school qualification and both first job and father's occupation and between first job and type of school attended. Though they are significant, the interactions contribute only modestly (even in combination) to the total effects, and as we shall see, some are undoubtedly caused by differences between cells with very few cases, and a clear and unambiguous interpretation is not always possible.

We first divided our respondents by type of school. Among those who attended the higher schools, first job, highest school qualifications and father's occupation all had significant independent effects upon the level of qualifications from part-time study. The multiple eta was 0.60 and the beta values were 0.40, 0.26 and 0.10 respectively. There was only one significant interaction effect—the two-way interaction of first job and highest school qualification. To examine this, we divided the sample by level of highest school qualification and repeated the analysis with first job and father's occupation as the factors. The results are given in Table 9.10. There were no significant interactions between these factors. The independent effects of first job are represented by the consistent rise in mean qualifications from unskilled manual to professional and managerial jobs in each analysis. This is also illustrated in Fig. 9.3 by the positive slopes of the lines. The interaction effect of highest school qualification and first job is quite marked, and more important than the independent effect of the former. It may be seen in the increase in the differences between the mean qualifications of the levels of first job as the level of school qualifications rises, represented in the figure by the divergence of the lines. School qualifications and first job have a cumulative effect, whereby the higher level of the first job, the greater the influence of the highest school qualification (and vice-versa) on the level of qualifications gained from part-time study.

The effects of father's occupation are not so straightforward. Among those with 'A' levels the effect is small and far from significant. For respondents with 'O' levels or equivalent there is an independent effect significant at the one per cent level, and there is one just below this level of significance among respondents with minor or no qualifications. In each case respondents with skilled manual fathers have higher mean qualifications than those with clerical or technical fathers, both before and after controlling for the effects of first jobs. In the case of those with 'O' levels, etc., the sons of clerical and technical fathers have lower mean qualifications than those with unskilled manual fathers. In general this lends support to the view of part-time education, at least at some levels, as a working class route to qualifications, though it should be remembered that the sons of professional and managerial fathers have the highest qualifications from part-time, just as from full-time, education. An initial examination of our data suggests that there may be

TABLE 9.10 Mean level of qualifications from part-time study among respondents who attended state selective or private schools for level of highest school qualifications: independent effects* by first job and father's occupation at time respondent left school

| Factors | School qualifications | | | | | |
| | Minor or none | | 'O' levels etc. | | 'A' levels etc. | |
	Mean	(N)	Mean	(N)	Mean	(N)
First Job						
Unskilled manual	0.33	(153)	0.93	(40)	0.92	(19)
Skilled manual	0.91	(201)	1.58	(49)	2.03	(13)
Clerical and technical	1.22	(183)	2.49	(237)	3.97	(90)
Managerial and professional	2.76	(18)	5.18	(69)	6.83	(102)
Beta	0.24		0.39		0.55	
Significance	p<0.001		p<0.001		p<0.001	
Father's job						
Unskilled manual	0.64	(183)	2.42	(74)	4.52	(34)
Skilled manual	1.10	(212)	2.80	(105)	4.58	(42)
Clerical and technical	0.86	(125)	2.13	(124)	5.23	(72)
Managerial and professional	1.67	(35)	3.54	(92)	5.03	(76)
Beta	0.14		0.16		0.09	
Significance	p = 0.011		p = 0.006		p = 0.450	
All	0.91	(555)	2.69	(395)	4.90	(224)
Multiple eta	0.30		0.43		0.57	

NOTE
* The mean level of qualifications for each factor is given after control for the other factor.

a class division in the type of part-time qualifications acquired, with the middle class more heavily represented in professional, especially minor professional associations, and the working class concentrated in technical education. A more thorough examination of the routes to part-time qualifications than we can present here is likely to be rewarding.

Turning to respondents who attended non-selective state schools, we find that the situation is much less tidy. An analysis of variance of highest qualification by first job, highest school qualification and father's occupation produces a multiple eta of 0.47 and significant independent effects from first job and highest school qualification (betas of 0.37 and 0.18 respectively), but no significant independent effect from father's occupation. However, the two-way interactions of first job and

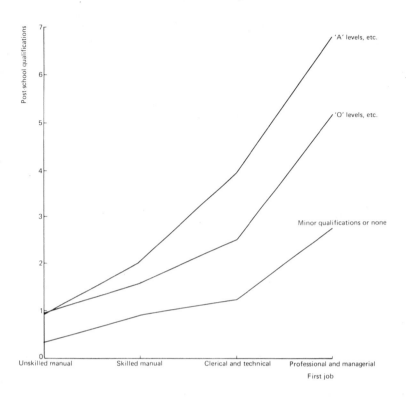

F IG. 9.3 Mean level of post-school qualifications by first jobs for different levels of qualifications from state selective and private schools

highest school qualification and first job and father's occupation are both highly significant and so is the three-way interaction. When we divide respondents by level of school qualification, we find the mean level of higher qualifications increases with the level of school qualification, indicating the direct effect of the latter, and the means are consistently below the corresponding ones for higher type schools, reflecting the independent effect of school type which we noted earlier. However, the number with 'A' levels and equivalent (14) is too small for any useful analysis, and among both those with 'O' levels or equivalent and those with minor or no qualifications, the distributions by level of first job and by father's occupation are very uneven. The number with 'O' level or equivalent qualifications is also very small (62), but the effect of first job on highest qualification is significant at the five per cent level (beta = 0.41). Father's occupation does not influence qualifications among this group (beta = 0.02) and there is no interaction of any size. Within the least qualified group the numbers are much larger (1574), and both independent effects are significant with beta = 0.34 for first jobs and 0.08 for father's occupation. However, their interaction effect is also significant and calls for further investigation.

The results of a final analysis which divided the respondents from non-selective state schools with the minium qualifications by the level of father's occupation, to take account of the interaction with first job, are presented in Table 9.11. The numbers at the highest level of first jobs are too small to be accepted with any confidence, though their extreme nature means that they contribute disproportionately to the measured effects. In general the children of professional and managerial employees have higher qualifications at each of the lowest three levels of first jobs, but there is a fall in their mean between skilled manual and clerical and technical jobs. The other three levels of father's occupation show increasing means with the rise in the level of first job, and an interaction effect is apparent in the divergence of the means between the first and third levels of jobs. This divergence is largely to the advantage of respondents with skilled manual fathers and the disadvantage of those with clerical or technical fathers, whose mean levels of qualifications are consistently below those from skilled backgrounds and in two cases below the mean for unskilled fathers. This lends more weight to the findings above, for respondents from higher schools, that a skilled manual background (and, perhaps, to a lesser extent, an unskilled manual background) is related to success in part-time education. However, it must be borne in mind that father's occupation is related to first jobs in the conventional manner, and first job is the strongest single influence upon part-time qualifications.

PRESENT OCCUPATION

To complete our analysis of the effects of education and family background on occupations, we turn to the relationships with present jobs. This gives some indication of the influences on career development, but as we noted earlier is not entirely satisfactory. Respondents are at different stages in their careers, depending on their ages when they started work, modes of qualification and so on. Taking only respondents over the age of 27 allows some opportunity for movement from first job, thereby avoiding an artefactual relationship between first

Education and Occupation 241

TABLE 9.11 Mean level of qualifications from part-time study among respondents who attended non-selective state schools and left without qualifications, for level of first job by father's occupation

First job	Father's occupation									
	Unskilled manual		Skilled manual		Clerical and technical		Professional and managerial		All	
	Mean	(N)	Mean	(N)	Mean	(N)	Mean	(N)	Mean	(N)
Unskilled manual	0.10	(409)	0.12	(181)	0.08	(106)	0.56	(9)	0.11	(705)
Skilled manual	0.29	(273)	0.44	(219)	0.40	(87)	1.19	(27)	0.41	(606)
Clerical and technical	0.66	(111)	1.04	(78)	.58	(51)	1.07	(15)	0.79	(255)
Professional and managerial	7.50	(4)	4.00	(3)	—	—	0.00	(1)	5.25	(8)
All	0.28	(797)	0.44	(481)	0.30	(244)	1.02	(52)	0.36	(1574)
Eta	0.49		0.32		0.17		0.14		0.34	
Significance	$p < 0.001$		$p < 0.001$		$p = 0.025$		$p = 0.81$		$p < 0.001$	

and present job, but still leaves scope for a wide range of levels of movement. The problem is not simply one of time, however, because of the diverse number of occupational categories used for different careers. For some, including most professions, there is just one career category, while for those who work their way up the hard way, through part-time technical education, there may be several. Thus the influences of education upon careers are inevitably underestimated in this analysis, and in many ways are seen better when we come to look at their effects upon income levels.

There are advantages, however, in taking current job as against first job. Since there has been, on the average, a fair amount of time for careers to develop, there will have been a tendency to move on from misleadingly classified initial occupations; for example, some of those who started as clerks will have had time to progress into management. Thus we may hypothesise that in so far as there are systematic relationships between qualifications from full-time study and career attainment, they will be more visible for present than for first job, in spite of the greater distance · in time. For qualifications from the part-time route, the position is rather different as first job is prior to gaining the qualifications. The qualifications are more occupationally specific so we would expect the relation between present job and these qualifications to be higher than that with full-time qualifications, though this might be modified by the relations involving technical qualifications.

Let us consider first those who gained qualifications from full-time study. An analysis of variance of present job with fathers' occupation and education factors shows there are small independent effects from the type of school and father's occupation (especially professional and managerial against the rest), with betas of 0.09 and 0.08 respectively. However, by this stage the influences of both father's occupation and school are mainly indirect, through the other independent factors or through the interaction effects (which are then lost from the analysis). Accordingly we shall now concentrate our attention on the major independent influences. The main influence is from post-school qualifications, with beta = 0.42 compared with 0.28 from school qualifications. The contributions from the two types of qualification are roughly the reverse of their contributions to first job, and as hypothesised, post-school qualifications have greater effect on the present job.

There is also a two-way interaction effect involving post-school and school qualifications. However, the main reason for this is that the range of qualifications accessible depends on the level of qualifications on leaving school. Thus while this effect does account for a little of the total variance, its form does not alter the general argument.

When we bring in first job as an influence on present job, the independent effect of school qualifications recedes further, as can be seen in Table 9.12. Post-school qualifications and first job have similar

TABLE 9.12 Relationship between present job and first job, post-school and school qualifications; for those with qualifications from full-time and part-time study which are higher than their school qualifications

Influence on present job	Full-time study		Part-time study	
	Eta	*Beta*	*Eta*	*Beta*
First job	0.46	0.36	0.48	0.24
Post-school qualification	0.40	0.27	0.55	0.36
School qualification	0.35	0.08	0.42	0.14
Total	0.55		0.60	
Present job: mean level	239		196	

influences. Which is greater depends on whether we take all with full-time qualifications or restrict the analysis to those with higher qualifications than their school ones. In the latter case we restrict the variance of qualifications and so their relative influence. However, we should note that in all cases the qualifications are dominated by degrees, and the ordering at lower levels is not entirely consistent, probably due to small numbers.

Turning to those who gained their qualifications by the part-time route, the pattern is much the same, with father's occupation and school having only limited independent effects. The main difference is that, as expected, the qualifications gained by part-time study are more closely related to present jobs than those acquired full-time, both in absolute terms and in their independent effect. This is illustrated by the values of eta and beta in Table 9.12 for those who gained higher qualifications after leaving school.

The overall association between first and present job is more or less the same in each case, but because the first job is more of a step on the way to qualifications than a result of them for those who take the part-time route, its independent effect is less. We can also see how school qualifications, being prior in both cases, have substantially reduced independent effects.

The lower mean level of present job for those who gained the qualifications part-time, as shown in Table 9.12, is largely, but not entirely, due to the higher proportion of low level qualifications. An analysis of variance of present job by first job, highest qualifications and their source (full-time, part-time or at school) suggests that the source has a small independent effect (beta = 0.12), with the full-time route having an advantage over the part-time, while the mere fact of undertaking further study by either route in itself leads to a higher job level. However, as we would expect, there are significant interaction effects from the source with both qualifications and first job. Disaggregation would add little to the previous discussion where we considered the full-time and part-time routes separately, and so we have chosen to ignore the source in the next stage of analysis.

In Table 9.13 we present an analysis of present job by first job, highest qualification attained and father's occupation. Here we have brought together all qualifications, regardless of their type, into a single measure as outlined earlier. This also contains the main influence from type of school in the division of those without qualifications or with 'O' level and equivalent qualifications. There is a significant interaction term involving first job and qualification, but its effect is not great and it appears to be due to random fluctuations (the numbers are small in some cells of first job by qualification), so it has been ignored.

The multiple eta is 0.80, accounting for over 60 per cent of the variance. By far the biggest independent effect is from qualifications, (the eta of 0.77 may be compared with a product-moment correlation of 0.73), though in absolute terms the first job is also strongly related to the present one, and father's occupation has a substantial relationship, as may be seen from the values of eta. The order of influence for the different levels of qualification are as expected from our ordering on the basis of income, except for a reversal of HNC and Non-Graduate Teaching Diplomas with Minor Professional qualifications. While this may reflect a discrepancy between occupational level and income for teachers and those who have risen through technical training, it could well be an artefact of the conventional system of occupational classification which *inter alia* assigns minor professionals to clerical jobs when they enter employment. Overall there can be no doubt about the high importance of qualifications in relation to occupational careers.

There is still a small independent advantage to those with professional or managerial fathers. However, the difference between eta and beta shows clearly that, as noted earlier, by this stage the effect of father's occupation is predominantly indirect.

TABLE 9.13 Present job by first job, highest qualification and father's
occupation: association and independent effect

	Present job adjusted mean*	Eta	Beta	(N)
First job				
Unskilled manual	105			(1011)
Skilled manual	115			(964)
Clerical and technical	137	0.69	0.25	(995)
Professional and managerial	167			(630)
Qualifications				
Minor or none: lower school	82			(1491)
Minor or none: higher school	100			(456)
City and guilds	102			(155)
'O' level etc. lower schools	105			(44)
'O' level etc. higher schools	144			(265)
'A' levels	153	0.77	0.56	(118)
ONC and OND	161			(76)
HNC and HND	192			(118)
Non graduate teaching diploma	201			(36)
Minor professional	168			(150)
Degree and major professional	209			(691)
Father's occupation				
Manual, clerical and technical	124			(3074)
Professional and managerial	142	0.39	0.07	(526)
All	127	0.80		(3600)

NOTES
All factors are significant, $p < 0.001$.
* Estimated mean values on the Cambridge scale after control for both of the other factors.

It is difficult to provide a succinct summary of what is, in any case, a very condensed analysis, but perhaps the major point to be made is that the cumulative effect of background and educational experience is more marked than would be obvious from an analysis which ignored the important interaction effects. For example, father's occupation has a continuing effect upon educational success from type of secondary school attended to the level of qualifications obtained in full-time study and on through to present job, but progressively the effects are in complex relationships with the operation of other factors. For the most part, the interaction effects serve to accentuate the value of existing advantages at each stage. Thus, for example, the higher the level of school qualification, the greater the effect of first job upon the level of part-time qualifications.

There are two exceptions to this general rule. The first is the way in which having the good sense to acquire a professional or managerial father can serve to offset some of the worst effects of educational failure at each stage, and the second is that coming from a manual background, particularly with a skilled father, rather than from a clerical or technical background, is a positive advantage for acquiring qualifications in part-time education after all the indirect influences which are more conventional have been taken into account.

Part-time qualifications are well related to first jobs, and to a large extent they are probably indicators of careers rather than the means to careers, in that they are anticipated at entry to the labour market. In certain areas this is so much the case that respondents fail to take, or fail to report, minor professional qualifications which would do little more than confirm occupational status. An example is membership of the Institute of Bankers. Many respondents in senior positions in banking failed to mention any post-school qualifications, though we have reason to believe that some at least were members. To the extent that this sort of under-reporting occurs, the relationship of first job and part-time qualifications will be diminished in our data.

Not all part-time qualifications are merely reflections of occupational careers. Those which would most usually be obtained by workers who first take manual jobs may lead on to specific careers, but they are not typical of the majority of manual workers. It would seem that whereas respondents who subsequently acquire professional qualifications enter careers, those who acquire technical qualifications may have to work to create career opportunities.

Whether qualifications are reflections of careers already started, or criteria of access, it is clear that they are well related to occupational attainment. This may be seen both in the high association of qualifications with present job and in the fact that this association is higher than with first job. However, in understanding the processes involved, we cannot separate the effects of the type and level from where they were attained—or not attained for those without qualifications—and the influence of family background.

10 Education and Incomes

We observed earlier that the confusion of individuals and occupations in terms of market position is probably a consequence of the close relationship, in the public mind, between the nature of the demands of the job tasks in terms of the personal skills of incumbents and the possession of such skills as a consequence of training, among professionals and artisans. For those in other types of job, the popular conception is probably of a much looser relationship between education, as an indicator of general ability, and the demands of job tasks for that ability.

These conceptions contain aspects of what has been called a 'human capital' approach to education. The general theme is of investment in 'human beings', and investment has two aspects which have been summarised by Bowen (1963, pp. 77–8) as:

(1) 'The personal profit orientation' where 'one looks at differences in the net earnings of people with varying amounts of education as evidence of the amount of personal financial gain that can be associated with the attainment of a given level of education', and
(2) 'The national productivity orientation' goes one step further and consists of looking at the education-related income differentials mentioned above as 'partial evidence of the effects of education on the output of the country . . . [It] is based upon the premiss that in a market economy differences in earnings reflect differences in productivity. This orientation is relevant for the question of whether society as a whole is investing the right share of resources in education.'

There are thus two different, but related, forms of cost-benefit analyses which can be undertaken. Attempts can be made to assess the financial costs and benefits of various kinds of educational investment, on the one hand, for the individual, and, on the other, for society in general. The assumption binding these two orientations together is that markets operate in such a way (a) as to give both individuals and societies returns closely related to the nature and extent of labour expended and (b) that the educational system is sensitive to the demands of the market for developing skills. Under these conditions the returns to education are economically determined, and there will be a tendency for individual training and the demand for skills in the market to be in balance. However, this oversimplifies the arguments, as some writers have seen the educational system as a source of new skills which lead to technical development in the productive system and the growth of productive efficiency. What this has in common with the other approaches under the general heading of 'human capital' is an assumption of forces tending to bring into harmony personal educational achievement, the nature of skills required in occupations and the returns to these skills. Insofar as there is a perfect relationship, occupations or, more correctly, occupational careers can stand as efficient indicators of the productive resources of their incumbents, and returns in the market will be based upon the contributions of these resources.

This general approach has been criticised from many sides, but has proved remarkably resilient. We believe this to be due to the claim that its truth would be confirmed by a close association between educational levels and economic returns. Many opponents have, either explicitly or implicitly, accepted this claim and have concentrated their attention upon finding significant discrepancies between education and income. If such discrepancies were found, they would, indeed, undercut 'human capital' arguments (and writers such as Jencks *et al.* (1973), for example, give apparent substance to this approach, though, as we shall see, it is only apparent), but they would also undercut theories which oppose 'human capital' theories. A close relationship between education and income cannot distinguish 'human capital' theories from theories in direct opposition because their critical differences lie at other levels.

For example, within a Marxist account of the operation of capitalism, wages are sensitive to different qualities of labour such that economic returns to skills may be *proportional* to the skill exercised; exploitation consists in the returns not being *commensurate*, in that part of the product of labour has been assigned to 'capital' and appropriated by the capitalist. The relationship of the educational system to the acquisition and to the nature of skills may be far from straightforward, but differences in skills exercised may be associated with differences in education. However, for the most part, the emphasis within this tradition is not upon access to productive positions, but rather upon the relationship between production and distribution, where the more basic flaws of understanding are seen to lie. They believe that human capital theorists misunderstand the operation of the productive system. The social relations of production which determine the use of labour capacity in Marxist theory are seen as an indivisible aspect of experience in capitalist society. To write as if there were general economic relations between the nature of labour and the return to it is, they argue, to misunderstand economic realities. To talk of 'human capital' is to compound the basic misconception of classical economics, that capital is a real factor of production which makes a separate contribution to the value creating process. Only on a misunderstanding of economic problems can capital, *per se*, be seen as contributing to the social product, and there is no way in which labour can be reduced to the category of capital.

Other criticisms have concentrated upon the relationship of education to the productive system, arguing that the population is more or less efficiently placed in the productive system by differentiations made in the educational system, but that such differentiations do not rest upon (or do not entirely rest upon) real differences in skill or productive ability. Qualifications are merely credentials which afford access without reflecting capacities. Such arguments are usually presented without an economic analysis of production and distribution, as if one aspect of the second of Parkin's (1971) two processes of stratification which we quoted in the Introduction (see p. 3), 'the process of recruitment to positions', could be dealt with in isolation from the first, 'the allocation of rewards attaching to positions in society'. In fact this is a view that can be held only in default of a wider consideration of social processes. It is not realistic to believe that rewards will be determined by economic processes uncontaminated by the 'non-productive' distinctions of the educational system. This is not to say that processes of access *and* reward allocation at odds with productive contributions could not be imbedded in a system which was more or less stable in the short term. But the practical processes of the system and their intellectual bases would have to be set out, in much the same way as Marx theorises the contradictions of production and distribution in capitalism. We shall look at the consequences of separating the relations of production from other processes of social reproduction when we come to discuss the work of Wright and Perrone later in the chapter.

There have been attempts to deal with the continuity of social and economic issues. As part of a more extensive debate on the nature of appropriate returns to capital, economists, who have sometimes been termed Neo-Ricardians, have argued that there is no precise economic link between capital, or human capital, advanced and profits obtained (for a discussion of this see, e.g. Berner, 1974). The determination of the rate of profit, they argue, is a social and not an economic process. The market operates upon assumptions that are created in the wider social context, the relative distribution of the total product depends not upon productive contribution, but is rather the outcome of a power struggle which determines what the workers will get. An extreme version of this approach holds that there are no simple and unequivocal procedures by which the product of social labour can be distributed to individuals on the basis of productive capacity in that such capacity is truly social. Reward allocation is not, therefore, a mechanical economic process. Within this view education comes to be not so much the process of increasing productive capacity, personal and social, as one of the processes of class struggle. The advantaged seek to maintain and pass on their positions by establishing rights within the educational system and manipulating links between education and rewards.

Within each of these very different theories a strong relationship between education and income would be expected. Crucial distinctions between the theories lie in other areas. Some of the appropriate data would be cross-national and historical; some would require a detailed examination of educational values and the content of specific qualifications. These lie outside our immediate concerns, but as we are about to examine the link between qualifications and income, we felt it necessary to outline, very briefly, the status of the undertaking and make our own position clear. We are not convinced that the content of education, on the one hand, and the rewards apparently accruing to it, on the other, are brought into balance solely by a strong common bond to productive skills. Education cannot be seen as attributes of individuals imported into the system; it must be seen as an integral part of an encompassing system, in which, however, it is not the sole defining characteristic. At the level of productive relations, understandings are frequently at odds with educational justifications. For example, the attributes of some types of workers which employers most desire, and require, are not reflected in education or experience. As one of the authors (Blackburn and Mann, 1979, p. 280) has previously argued, in the conclusions to a study of non-skilled manual workers, 'little support could be given to the *human capital*, neo-classical view of "worker quality" in the labour market'. What employers most wanted was not intelligence or manual dexterity, but acquiescence, acceptance of subordination. They believed there was a shortage of skill, by which they seemed to mean positive commitment and initiative, but operated on a realistic understanding of the exigencies of reproducing a system which requires routine compliance.

THE ASSOCIATION BETWEEN EDUCATION AND INCOME

Among sociologists in recent years, though not among economists, it has become conventional wisdom that levels of education and levels of income are poorly correlated. Jencks *et al.* (1973), for example, have written, 'Neither family background, cognitive skill, educational attainment, nor occupational status explains much of the variation in men's income'. This work caused a considerable stir when first published, but few of the reviews dealt in any detail with the analysis upon which such assumptions were based. In fact, most of the information on income came from a slight re-working of the data used by Duncan and colleagues (see both Blau and Duncan, 1967, and Duncan, Featherman and Duncan, 1968). Jencks *et al.* used the same basic method of constructing a path model with income as the dependent variable, and they found, as did Duncan, that the residual term was very high. More recently in this country, Psacharopoulos (1977) conducted a similar analysis with data from the General Household Survey for 1974 with similar results. Jencks *et al.* interpret the high residual as meaning that the relationships of the independent variables in the model to the dependent variable, income, are very poor. Duncan *et al.* (1968, pp. 255–6) however, were less concerned with the size of the residual than with examining the relative effects of the different independent variables in the equation. They argue that they are not,

> concerned to move the coefficient of determination much closer toward the asymptote of unity. Instead, we expected to achieve a more thorough understanding of relationships that were already well established, and thus to secure an improved 'explanation' in a sense rather different from that conveyed by the magnitude of the multiple correlation. The final judgement of our success is, of course, to be made by the reader; but we would ask that he takes as his criterion the cogency of the models and the arguments supporting them rather than the purely statistical norm.

It is doubtful if this separation of the relative effects within the model from the adequacy of the model as a whole is valid. For a discussion of this, see Crowder (1974).

A glaring omission from the path model is age as an independent variable. The status of age in a causal model is obviously problematic. It is doubtful if any clear meaning can be given to age as a cause of changes in income, rather than as an indicator associated with processes that affect income. It was probably with such a consideration in mind that Blau and Duncan and Duncan *et al.* sought to overcome the problem of age in their model by separating their sample into four different age bands and conducting identical analyses within each of these different age groupings. The final results presented are a composite of these separate analyses. The main weakness of such a procedure is that it masks processes associated with working life-cycles which affect relationships among the variables in the model. We believe a preferable procedure would be to introduce age as an indicator, though not an entirely adequate indicator, of these processes. The effect of introducing age into the analysis is very considerable.

Although our data in the General sample are not representative of the male working population and in the White-Collar sample are from a limited section of that population, if we treat each set in a way similar to that employed by Duncan *et al.* on their data, then we can produce results for the determination of income which illustrate the problem. We cannot duplicate their model in all respects because we do not have within our data information on the educational levels of our respondents' fathers or number of siblings which they include, but these add little to the variance explained, and in other respects the models are not dissimilar. Where they have taken years of schooling as the measure of education, we have used qualifications, as set out in the last chapter, except that in the White-Collar sample, ONC, 'A' level, etc., and City and Guilds were precoded into one category. As a measure of occupational status, they have used Duncan's Socio-Economic Index, and we have used the Cambridge Scale. In their four age groupings the multiple R^2 of the regression of income on the other variables ranges between 0.13 and 0.22. Over all ages the R^2 is 0.36 in the General sample and 0.27 in the White-Collar sample. Merely by introducing age as a variable in the analyses, these values rise to 0.47 and 0.44 respectively. The effect of age is very considerable.

However, the relationship of age and education to income is not so straightforward. There is an overwhelming interactive effect such that differences in income associated with different levels of education increase with age. It is difficult, therefore, to present these relationships within a path model, and as a first step towards a closer examination of the relationship, we decided to divide each of our two samples by level of qualification and look at how age and income were related within each level separately.

In order that the samples should be comparable we included only those in the General sample who were full-time employees (i.e. excluding self-employed). As our measure of income we chose gross annual income accruing from regular duties in the respondent's major employment. Thus, for example, if the respondent normally worked overtime, earnings from that source were included, but if overtime was exceptional it was excluded. The same applied to bonus payments, etc. Earnings from completely different sources were also excluded.

There were certain difficulties with the White-Collar data that needed to be solved before we could proceed. We believe that because of the way the questionnaire was constructed, in that study we may have under-reported qualifications gained at school. Thus, because we cannot be absolutely confident that they have no qualifications, we have chosen to combine the groups who stayed on beyond the minimum, but report no qualifications, with the expected levels of qualifications for the length of time and type of school. In most cases this meant 'O' level or equivalent.

We knew, in general, the sorts of relationship between age and income to expect. The reports of the US Census contain detailed breakdowns of income by age for different levels of qualification. In this country data of that quality are not available, but there has been some work using rather cruder categories of qualification (see, e.g. Statistics of Education, HMSO, 1971; Blaug, 1970 and more recently the General Household Survey). From these studies we expected earnings for all levels of qualification to rise initially with age, but with a declining rate of increase in every case. At the highest levels of qualification the decline in the rate of increase is slight so that, as we shall see, graduates increase their earnings at an almost continuous rate into their 50s. At the lowest levels of qualifications the decline is much more marked.

For this analysis we did include those under 28 years of age because the principal characteristics of the earnings curves by age of those with lower levels of qualifications—a rapid rise over the first few years in employment followed by a long gradual decline—would be lost if we included only those with completed qualifications. As we shall see, the most important distinctions of income by education are not in the early years of working life. Indeed, in the very early years those with lower qualifications are frequently earning more and, in any event, the spread of incomes is narrow. Thus we do not believe that the results are much distorted by assigning those who were still taking their highest qualifications to lower levels of qualifications, as they will be concentrated in the youngest categories.

In order to examine the nature of the curves in our data we followed a regression procedure. In part we were forced to this by the relatively small numbers in our separate categories. If numbers had been large enough, we might have presented mean incomes of different ages. However, one of the purposes of the analysis was to construct expected values for income, and a procedure of the sort we adopted had obvious advantages. We wished to regress income on some function of age for each level of occupation, allowing the data to dictate the nature of the curves, while at the same time not fitting individual points too closely. The compromise we chose was to set up a regression of the form:

$$\text{income} = a + \sum_{r=1}^{5} b_r \, \text{age}^r$$

and then perform the regression stepwise (i.e. allowing the effect for the most significant power of age before taking account of the next most significant), so that variations to fit random deviations in the data would be minimised.

The results for the General sample are presented in Table 10.1, and graphic representations of six of the curves are presented in Fig. 10.1 to illustrate the general pattern. It can be seen that the curves are of the expected form, though if all twelve were included, the pattern would not be so neat. These data cannot be regarded as providing adequate comparisons of the economic returns associated with different qualifications because they do not take account of education 'careers'. Lower qualifications are frequently held by young men on the way to achieving a higher level, while for others they are the final attainment. Consequently the age distributions of those holding the various qualifications differ quite considerably, and this appears to account for some of the slight untidiness of the results. For these reasons we have not illustrated earnings under age 20, which would be purely notional in some cases, and have taken an upper age limit of 50 since respondents over this age with some of the qualifications are so rare as to make the results unreliable (though the earnings of men with non-graduate teaching diplomas would be underestimated without taking note of respondents over 50). Clearly a notion of the 'income career' of a man with 'A' level or ONC is no more valid than the 'income career of the clerk'. Nevertheless, these data do provide useful estimates of the earnings at different ages of men holding these qualifications, and from these we can confidently conclude that the income advantages of higher levels of qualifications are amplified with increasing age. It would appear that a notional income for all groups at about age 20 would be

TABLE 10.1 Regression equations of income on functions of age for different levels of qualifications

Qualifications	Age	$Age^2/10^2$	$Age^3/10^3$	$Age^4/10^4$	$Age^5/10^5$	Constant	R^2	N
Minor qualifications or none: lower schools	236.4954	−426.2971	0	+3.792058	0	−1554.836	0.86	1389
Minor qualifications or none: higher schools	58.27267	−21.50928	0	0	−0.1351269	+369.1834	.127	350
City and guilds	373.1034	−702.3425	0	+7.06752	0	−3160.897	.185	223
'O' levels etc: lower schools	417.4515	−917.0103	+67.12799	0	0	−3731.806	.504	159
'O' levels etc: higher schools	207.7585	−223.7171	0	+0.3890725	0	−1915.430	.353	311
'A' levels etc.	226.5918	−272.7870	0	+1.811828	0	+2155.244	.392	175
ONC and OND	294.8290	−380.5994	0	0	+0.234538	−2978.568	.290	97
HNC and HND	182.2571	0	−27.91922	0	0	−2071.928	.448	145
Non-graduate teaching diploma	97.35695	0	0	0	−0.2280251	−467.2091	.489	36
Minor professional	138.6235	0	0	0	−0.5815686	−1182.512	.235	145
Major professional	181.6639	0	0	0	−0.5194465	−2154.947	.324	143
Degrees	382.7381	−414.6137	0	0	+0.325048	−4715.77	.480	402

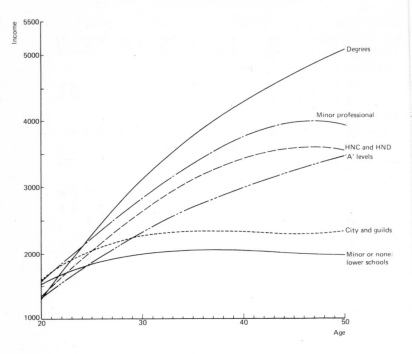

FIG. 10.1 Estimated income by age: examples of different levels of qualifications

very similar and that the patterns of earnings fan out from that point.

We have emphasised the relationship of earnings to age in this analysis, but we also looked at earnings by length of time qualifications had been held. We did this primarily because much play is made in human capital research of variations in earnings by length of service (see, e.g. Mincer, 1976, and Klevmarken, 1972). These variations are held to demonstrate that it is real worth to employers which is being rewarded rather than conventional returns to age. In our data length of time since gaining highest qualifications is less well related to earnings, within each qualification level, than is age. It is tempting, therefore, to present this as evidence for a conventional distribution of incomes, whatever the theory of production, but the issue is rather more complex and the initial argument is, from a human capital standpoint, rather shaky.

All types of employee, even those totally unqualified, increase their earnings with age over the younger ages of employment. In human capital terms, these increases are the returns to experience. This being so, if qualifications are gained after entry to the labour market, we would expect those holding them to receive the minimum returns to such qualifications only if their previous experience is entirely worthless in the work associated with their new qualifications. If this does not hold, they are likely to have earnings closer to the mean for their age within the qualification level.

We have argued that many qualifications gained in part-time education are confirmations of careers rather than the means to careers. We have also argued that certain qualifications which are the means to careers (Higher National Certificate, for example) nonetheless are closely associated with previous experience. In either of these cases, even if the qualifications reflected real productive abilities, we would not anticipate that upon receiving the qualification, individuals of different ages would receive identical salaries at the bottom of the scale. Within human capital arguments, that sort of circumstance would apply only when the qualification enabled a career completely distinct from past experience.

Thus, the fact that age is better related to income than length of time a qualification has been held is not, necessarily, a strong argument against the view that variations in income reflect variations in productive contributions. It may merely mean that there are variations in the time taken to acquire formal qualifications in the structure of standard careers, i.e. careers unified by work experience. It should be remarked, however, that neither finding would confirm that variations in incomes are due directly to variations in skill.

Even if it were true that income differentials were due to skill differentials, this would not confirm human capital arguments as the relationship of earnings and experience has a problematic status in such arguments. What investment is there in experience? In recognising this problem, Mincer (1976, p. 152) argues that the growth of inequality with age can, within a human capital model, 'be explained by the correlation between the stock of human capital at any stage of the life cycle and the volume of subsequent investment. The correlation is understandable, if factors of ability or opportunity which affect individual investment behaviour tend to persist over lengthy periods of a person's life. For example, the absolute growth of dollar earnings with experience is greater at higher schooling levels.'

What this explanation fails to provide is any account of investment in human capital after formal schooling. Even if it were possible to conceive of education as personal investment, there is here no indication of the nature of such investment in work experience. It is by no means clear in the explanation that investment has a place which is distinct from 'ability or opportunity', and that phrase introduces an implicit emphasis upon the differential *exercise* of skills within the system rather than the differential *acquisition* of skills by individuals. 'Opportunity' introduces an unspecified systemic component and lays implicit claim to areas which lie outside human capital analyses.

From the results of the regression analyses, we constructed expected values for income for the two samples. This we did using the regression weights on the age variables for each level of qualification separately. Having obtained expected values, we then returned to the problem of the determination of income. The age and qualification variables were now represented by the expected income variable they had been used to construct. Because of the artificial nature of that variable, we felt it would not be meaningful to include it in a general path analysis model, but its construction had not involved occupation in any way, and we were interested in whether occupation contributed separately to the determination of income. We therefore regressed income firstly on the constructed variable alone, and then secondly on both the constructed variable and occupational level as measured by the Cambridge Scale. The results are in Table 10.2. The first point to note is that combining the effects of education and age in this way explains much more of the

TABLE 10.2 Variance of income explained by combinations of age, qualifications and occupation

Variable in equation	Explained variance (R^2) White-Collar	General
Age and qualifications	0.35	0.41
Age, qualifications and occupation	0.44	0.47
Quage	0.58	0.55
Quage and occupation	0.61	0.58

variance than does treating them as separate variables. In the case of the General sample, the improvement is 14 per cent of the total variance, and of the White-Collar sample 23 per cent. Of course, this largely follows from the method we have adopted, but only because the relationships are real. It will also be seen that the introduction of occupation adds a further three per cent to the variance explained in both samples. It would seem therefore that, at least to some extent, the nature of work determines income independently of qualifications held.

With the constructed variable of expected income, based on qualifications and age, which we shall call 'quage' for convenience, we are able to address ourselves to a number of problems we have raised earlier. We can, for example, examine the relationship between quage and actual income for different groups in our sample, looking for deviations of either higher or lower mean incomes than expected. In this way we can discover if there are variations in returns to qualifications by geographical region, urban or rural location or type of industry. We can also see whether there are occupations, or occupational areas, from which it is an advantage to start a career.

The procedure we used was to regress income on quage for different groups within our data. In the next five figures we present comparisons between sets of regression lines. We have drawn in the 45° lines which would represent an identity of actual and expected income, and we have included with each curve the product moment correlation.

The first set of comparisons is for different regions of the country using the General sample data. We give, in Figs. 10.2 and 10.3, separate comparisons for men working in rural and urban areas, where the urban/rural divide is at population units (towns or contiguous groups of towns) of 15,000 (almost everywhere falling very clearly on one side or the other). We did this because there are different proportions of urban and rural respondents in each region, and as is obvious from a comparison of the two figures, there is a premium on working in an urban location. If we had given merely total figures, they would have confused the urban/rural effects.

From Fig. 10.2 we can see that over most of the range of incomes, rural workers earn less than would be expected on the basis of the income value of their qualifications among the population at large. Because of the differences in slopes, it is difficult to summarise the position for each region. Those around Cambridge are actually estimated to earn about one per cent more than expected at their mean income and only one per cent less at an expected income of £5000. In each of the other three rural areas, estimated earnings are below expected earnings at the level of their mean earnings. Around Glasgow they are five per cent below, around Leicester four per cent and around Leeds three per cent. The percentage gap falls to four per cent for the Scottish group when we consider estimated earnings for expected earnings of £5000. In the other two groups it rises considerably. Around Leeds it is 11 per cent and around Leicester 17 per cent, which amounts to about £850 less than expected.

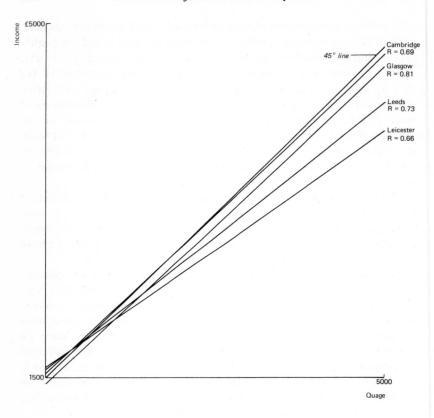

FIG. 10.2 Regression of income on quage: rural areas

The estimated urban earnings are closer between the regions than the rural earnings, though the levels in Cambridge are well above average and those in Leeds seem very low. Among the urban groups, Leeds has the narrowest income distribution and the lowest correlation, and this result should therefore be treated with some caution. We set out to match occupations by region, but only in pairs for most occupations, so that we also allowed for considerable variation between regions. These results must be affected by the non-identical nature of the sub-samples, especially in respect of age and qualifications which are the explanatory variables here, and deviations in expected income by region would be likely to decline if samples were more accurately matched. For the moment our purpose is to indicate general differences and similarities. It seems unlikely that the urban/rural division would disappear as an

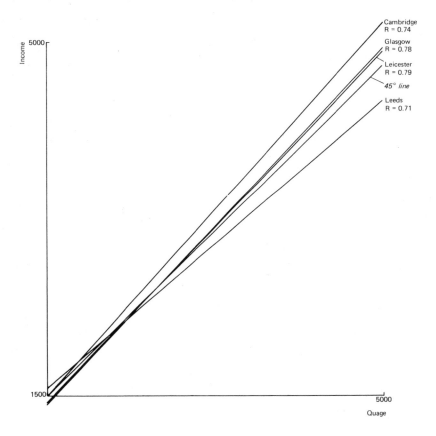

F IG. 10.3 Regression of income on quage: urban areas

influence upon income, but in other respects a more rigorous approach would be likely to improve the consistency of incomes across regions.

Problems of distribution affect all analyses of this sort, but the second set of comparisons involve distinctions where the occupational range is less affected by the groupings chosen. The breakdowns are by three types of employment—insurance, public service and manufacturing industry—within the White-Collar sample. The results of the analysis are in Fig. 10.4 which is in essential respects similar to the previous figures. There we can see that public service and manufacturing industry show almost identical relationships between expected and actual income. Insurance seems to afford lower salaries than expected at lower levels and higher than expected at higher levels, but the differences are slight. It would seem therefore that there are fairly standard returns to different areas of employment.

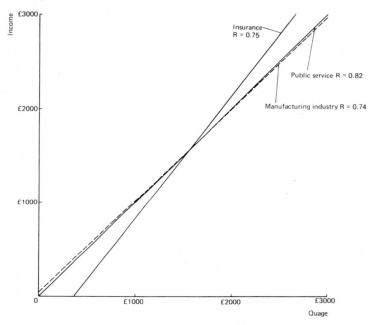

NOTE The *45° line* has been omitted because it is difficult to distinguish between it and the public service line.

FIG. 10.4 Regression of income on quage for different areas of employment

Finally we can address ourselves to a problem we raised earlier—whether there are occupations from which it is an advantage to start one's working life. In particular, are those who start work as clerks disadvantaged in income terms when account is taken of their qualifications, or, in other words, is there a 'status discrepancy', as Lockwood claimed, between education and income? The results of two analyses, one using the White-Collar sample and the other the General sample, are given in Figs 10.5 and 10.6. In this case the results are necessarily affected by the very different age, income and occupation profiles of the different groups. There are specially large differences between those who started in manual work and the other groups. However, the variations are not otherwise very large. Professionals in both samples earn above expectations. Clerks are estimated to earn slightly above expectations in the White-Collar sample and slightly

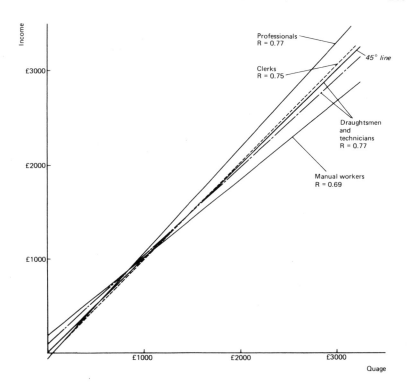

FIG. 10.5 Regression of income on quage for different starting occupations: White-Collar sample

below in the General sample. The reverse is true of draughtsmen and technicians. Given the different nature of the samples, those starting as manual workers have remarkably similar estimates in the two analyses.

There is no support here for a status discrepancy among those starting their career in lower white-collar jobs. They earn about what would be expected on the basis of age and qualifications. An embattled lower white-collar group desperately defending middle-class life-styles on inappropriately low, and falling, incomes is a myth.

EDUCATION AND THE RELATIONS OF PRODUCTION

Although we have stressed the link of education, occupational experience and income, the model we have used up until now has been one

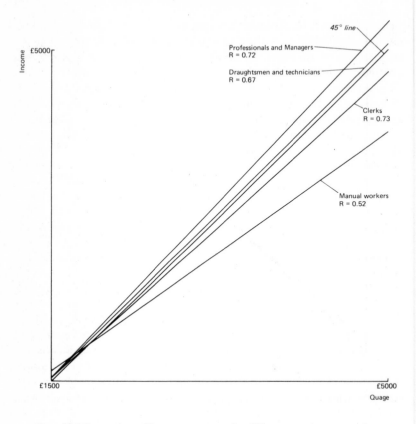

FIG. 10.6 Regression of income on quage for different starting occupations:
General sample

which comes close to the railway analogy outlined in Chapter 8. Quage is
the measure of the distance northward that an individual is expected to
have travelled on the basis of the ticket he holds and the length of time he
has spent on this journey (except that age rather than experience has
been used). Within this model the structure of the system is independent
of the processes of acquiring tickets, and this assumption limits the
usefulness of the model. We have found it heuristically valuable, but the
time has come to move on to a more adequate view of social
relationships. Before doing so, however, the model will bear the weight
of one further observation which has consequences for the ways in which
it must be modified.

Human capital theory places a very strong emphasis upon achievement as a result of personal investment in skill and experience. There should, therefore, be a close relationship between the distribution of education and the distribution of incomes in the long term. Yet the changes in the distribution of education in Britain or the USA since World War II have not been matched by changes in income distribution. Therefore whatever the determinants of income, they cannot be solely personal investments in skill (see, e.g. Sørensen, 1977).

The problem can be understood if we change the railway analogy slightly so that forms of education are not the tickets held, but the currencies with which tickets are bought. A ticket is assumed to guarantee a seat. The currencies will be devalued if there is a rise in the proportion holding them without an equivalent rise in the seats available for journeys, and exchange rates may be modified. Currencies will be revalued upwards if there is a change which produces an excess of seats. That changes in the availability of seats do not match changes in education as the means of purchasing seats means that variations have to be explained in terms other than personal investment.

Separating the system of education from the system of rewards serves to show the limits of human capital theory, but in reality both of these supposed independent systems are parts of the same social whole, and there are limits to the usefulness of their separation. It is not merely that the systems are related, that, for example, qualifications can be used to some extent as economic weapons to change the nature of production and distribution, but that the conceptual distinctions entail forms of analysis which necessarily contain contradictions. In what follows we shall attempt to make such contradictions apparent. Ironically, we shall do this in a critique of an interesting attempt to operationalise and test aspects of a Marxist theory of the relations of production. We say ironically because the Marxist tradition can lay greatest claims to forms of analysis which stress explanatory completeness and unity. However, Wright and Perrone (1977, pp. 36–7), whose work we shall be discussing, make a radical separation between the social relations of production as a system of positions and the characteristics (including education) of individuals assigned to these positions.

They set out to examine class variations in income. By class they do not mean occupational groupings. They write, 'The term "occupation" designates positions within the *technical* division of labour, i.e. an occupation represents a set of activities fulfilling certain technically defined functions. Class, on the other hand, designates positions within the *social* relations of production, i.e. it designates the social relationship between actors.' It is crucially important to their argument that there is some degree of independence between class position and occupation. As they put it, 'A carpenter could easily be a worker, a petty bourgeois producer, a manager or even a small capitalist.'

In the traditional Marxist perspective they distinguish three criteria of the social relations of production: the ownership of the means of production, purchase of labour power of others, and sale of one's own labour power. To this they add one other, the control of the labour power of others. On the basis of these criteria they distinguish four class categories: the capitalists who own the means of production, purchase and control labour power of others; managers who do not own the means of production or purchase the labour power of others, but do control the labour power of others in addition to selling their own labour; workers, who merely sell their own labour power; and the petty bourgeoisie who own the means of production but employ no one. Elsewhere Wright (1976) defines managers as occupying a 'contradictory class location' between the classes of capitalists and workers, and adds two further 'contradictory locations' between the petty bourgeoisie and each of capitalists and workers, but this does not really affect the present argument.

Wright and Perrone (1977, p. 33) stress that the classes (or class categories) constitute positions in the social organisation of production rather than collections of actual individuals, arguing, 'To say that classes constitute positions implies . . . that there are "empty places" in the social structure which are filled by individuals. The analysis of class must be understood primarily as the analysis of such empty places, and only secondarily of the actual individuals who fill the slots.' This division is similar to Parkin's and, as we shall see, raises similar difficulties.

For present purposes we are most concerned with just two of the four classes Wright and Perrone distinguish, managers and workers. What separates these two groups is that while both sell their labour power, only managers control the labour power of others. They are not talking only about managers in the traditional sense, but about anyone who exercises control, e.g. foremen or senior professionals, though in a later paper Wright (1978) uses the ability to hire and fire to distinguish managers. In looking at the issue of class variations in income between the groups, they seek strategies that will show whether or not, in capitalist society, there is a return to the control of others in addition to the return from the sale of labour power. It is not obvious that such a distinction is meaningful, and we shall argue that it is at least misconceived, but for the moment we must present their account. The hypothesis they (1977, p. 37) develop is that class position not only 'has an independent impact on income from occupational position, but also that it affects the extent to which background characteristics themselves can be 'cashed in' in income. In particular, the expectation is that class position will have a strong influence on the extent to which education influences income.' They see the managerial class as not only distinguished from workers by the possession of control but also stratified by the degree of control, and they believe that the higher the level of qualifications, the greater the likely degree of control (also see Wright, 1978, pp. 1371–2).

Thus, in addition to the cost of the reproduction of labour power, there is a further determinant of income due to an interaction of education and class, such that the higher the education, the greater the income advantage to the class who exercise control. They appear to assume that there is also an independent effect from education and to hypothesise one from class, though this latter is not distinguished from a tendency for the management class to earn more which could be due solely to the interaction, while the former may not really be intended.

It is not immediately obvious why background factors are introduced into the argument. They have stressed, after all, that classes are 'positions' in the social organisation of production, and that an analysis of class is not primarily concerned with the way in which individuals come to occupy these positions. Although they use education as an indicator of the degree of control inhering in positions in the managerial class, this cannot be so for the workers. In fact, though they never state it precisely, education comes to stand as a proxy for labour power, and Wright (1978, p. 1371) does make this explicit in the later paper. In looking at the different returns that workers and managers receive in income for their level of qualifications, they believe they are examining the extent to which there is a return to control. When they find that managers have more steeply rising incomes by level of qualification than workers, they believe that that demonstrates the return to control. Of course, some procedure for estimating labour power is necessary for their analysis, because the precise point at issue between them and neo-classical economists is not whether managers earn more (obviously they do), but from whence these earnings accrue. According to neo-classical economists, managers are paid more than workers because their jobs call for greater technical skills and make greater productive contributions. For Wright and Perrone part of the return is to the non-productive control function. If the control component cannot in some way be separated from the basic cost of reproducing labour power, then the theories cannot be distinguished. It may seem strange that they attempt to do this by using education as the indicator for both labour power and control, but as the variations in control are confined to the managerial class, the distinction is not impossible. In matching managers and workers by level of qualifications and looking at the divergence of incomes, they are implicitly assuming that the returns to workers, at each qualification level, are close to the reproduction cost of that _quality_ of labour and that the higher returns of managers show a premium over and above reproduction cost.

The flaw, from their own perspective, is to assume that the labour power that has to be reproduced is located in the education of the individual (in their terms a 'background' factor) and not in the 'position' in the structure that he occupies. At first sight it might seem reasonable to reply that education is used only as an approximation for labour power, indicating the sort of position normally occupied, but then it is only the errors of the indicator which are reflected in the qualifications of people outside such positions.[1] If a graduate is employed as a routine clerk, for example, the cost of his labour power (if this is determined by the cost of reproduction of that labour power) is not the cost of reproducing the skills of a graduate, but the cost of reproducing lower level skills. What has to be reproduced is the system and not the background characteristics of incumbents if, as Wright and Perrone (1977, p. 33) claim, there is a 'logical priority to understanding the empty places into which individuals are sorted.'

It is difficult to locate this logical priority of the productive system. Within traditional Marxist theory what capitalists must pay for the labour power they buy is the cost of reproducing that labour power. The labour power that must be reproduced is not determined _in vacuo_; it is the labour power embodied by the system. There may be some meaning to an abstract cost of the reproduction of forms of labour power, but the quality and quantity of labour power consumed is determined by the system. There will be a tendency for only socially necessary labour to be consumed, i.e. the labour necessary to reproduce the system given the level of development of the forces of production. Given the tendency for all labour to be reduced to simple labour, or even for technological developments to change the demand for skills, there will be, at any time, skilled labour available which will not be employed. No matter how much it cost to produce, it will not be reproduced. The worker with unsaleable skills must sell his simple labour power. The theory does not

---

[1] Exactly the same sort of considerations apply if education is taken as an indicator of control, with the lower class representing the errors.

allow for the systematic reproduction of labour power which has no location in the productive system. In other words the reproduction of labour power is not independent of the consumption of labour power.[2]

It may be helpful to pause and take stock at this point. The basic fallacy of their argument, we have said, is to equate the cost of labour power with characteristics of individuals—their education—independently of positions of the system. This opens the way to the invalid conclusion that the income differences of similarly qualified incumbents of different positions must be due to something other than labour power cost, which Wright and Perrone identify as control. A more consistent Marxist position would be that the income differentials are due to differences in the cost of reproducing labour power associated with positions, while the particular skills of the incumbents need not match the productive requirements of the system.

Given that Wright and Perrone's procedure fails to demonstrate that there is a return to control as such, the question remains to what extent they have shown that there are differentially high returns to those in supervisory positions, whatever the basis of these returns. The answer to this question is not so straightforward as it might appear, as we can illustrate by an analysis of our White-Collar data. We use these data because in the White-Collar study we asked questions which allow us to distinguish supervisors and non-supervisors in much the same way as do Wright and Perrone. They asked, Do you supervise anybody as part of your job?'; we asked, 'Considering a normal working day for you, how many of your subordinates did you see to talk to?', and 'How long did this take?'. Our supervisors or 'managers' may be more restricted than theirs in that there may be a few people with subordinates who do not see any in the course of a normal working day, but for most purposes the questions allow sufficiently similar distinctions to be made. The bases of the samples are very different. Theirs is a random sample of the US population, ours is of male white-collar employees within a 60 mile radius of Cambridge. The closest comparisons are between our sample and their sub-sample of white males. In terms of the theory, which is a

[2] There are modern contributions within the Marxist tradition, such as Baran and Sweezy (1966), which argue that the surplus under monopoly capitalism is so massive that in its disposal precise links between the cost of reproduction of labour power and wages are lost, that the surplus may be used to finance a wide range of non-productive undertakings. But in these circumstances the insulation of the productive system from the processes of allocating individuals to the system is compromised, and a new, and different, form of integration of 'social' and 'economic' factors is necessary.

general one about employees in capitalist societies, the fact that we have no manual workers should not affect the general structure of the results, though to include foremen, who tend to have similar qualifications to the men they supervise, might possibly seem unreasonable. In fact we carried out the analysis twice, with them included and excluded, and got very similar results. In the results presented, they are included.

We followed the same procedure of dividing the sample into workers and managers, and performed simple regressions of income on qualifications separately. The regression slopes are illustrated in Figure 10.7 with the product-moment correlations. Like Wright and Perrone we find an interaction between what they call 'class' and education, but it is less marked; and unlike them we find that there is an independent effect of 'class' which is illustrated by the difference in the constants of the two equations.

Strangely, almost the whole of the difference between 'classes' in their analysis is due to the interaction effect, and insofar as there is an independent effect, it favours the workers. In fact, the intercept terms are negative, indicating negative earning among the lowest qualified groups. Since this cannot be the case in reality, it would seem that in their data the underlying relationship between education and income is not linear, but some form of curve with an increasing gradient. Only in such circumstances could there be negative intercept terms. Their assumption of equal intervals between their educational levels may be regarded as the cause of these results.

One particular consequence we would expect in such circumstances is a steeper slope for the more highly educated class, which is just what they find. However, Wright (1978) repeated the analysis, this time using a larger number of values on the education variable, and specifically considered the question of linearity. The results are reasonably linear, but it appears that different ranges of education were used for the two classes, and the results still show workers earning more than managers at lower levels, which suggests an element of curvilinear effect remains. The two striking changes are that now all earnings are positive and the interaction effect is substantially reduced—both as we would expect from the move to linearity. Without more information it is neither possible to be certain that the direct effect is really negative or non-existent, nor to evaluate the extent of interaction.

Nonetheless, we do find a definite interaction effect in our data. How is it to be explained? We believe that there are two components, one of which (the more important) reflects the way in which movement from non-supervisory positions to supervisory positions is part of *normal*

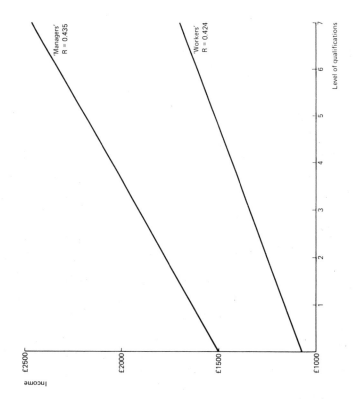

FIG. 10.7 **Regression of income on qualifications of 'managers' and 'workers'**

career development, the other being due to deviations from normal careers. Perhaps this is most easily illustrated by looking at the age distributions of 'managers' and 'workers' among employed professionals. These are given in Table 10.3. We choose professionals because whole careers are gathered under single occupational titles, and the development of careers with age has a relatively straightforward meaning.

From Table 10.3 it is clear that being in a supervisory position is well related to age, the value of gamma being 0.67. Managers and workers

TABLE 10.3 Holding a supervisory position by age, among employed professionals

	Up to 25	26 to 35	Over 35	Total
Professionals in:				
Supervisory positions	15	58	135	208
Non-supervisory positions	47	25	28	100
Total	62	83	163	308

NOTE
gamma = 0.67, p<0.001.

are therefore divided by age, and as we have seen there is a strong interaction of qualifications and age in the determination of income, such that the older the sample, the greater the effect of education on income. If qualification levels were equivalent at every age, this alone would give an interaction effect, but it is accentuated by the tendency for the highly qualified to be in supervisory positions at older ages.

In our data the mean age of managers is 41.6, of workers 35.3. Wright and Perrone report a mean age of 42.3 for managers and 38.2 for workers among white males. That our age gap is larger may be due to our having a White-Collar sample which is better educated in general and therefore likely to have an under-representation of older workers among the lowly qualified, but this does not affect the differential effect on the two classes of the age-qualification interaction.

The construction of our quage variable was an attempt to model the total effects, including interaction, of age and qualifications in the sample as a whole. It also allowed us to discard assumptions of equal intervals on the qualifications measure. If we assume that it provides a model of career development (at least insofar as it is determined by age and qualifications) for the sample as a whole, we can use it to examine the extent to which workers and managers are at different career positions rather than following completely different careers. To do this we first found an average income gap between workers and managers using the procedure suggested by Wright and Perrone. It should be understood that this gap does not represent a direct effect of 'class' on income, but compounds any such effect with the interaction of class and qualifications. There is no unequivocal way to look at the gap between earnings for the two groups, and they chose to examine it halfway between the two mean values of education. This gave a gap of $2436 for white males, where the mean worker income was $6145. By a similar procedure we found a gap of £560 and a mean worker income of £1259, which is roughly comparable. We then took the income levels of workers and managers and sought the levels of quage which were necessary to produce these incomes from separate regressions of income on quage for the two groups. These values of quage represent the expected incomes for the two groups. If the gap between them were as large as between the estimates of actual income, we could conclude that the two samples were not distinguished by different structures of career earnings, but by career positions within a single structure. In fact we find the gap to be £356. In other words nearly two-thirds (66 per cent) of the average income gap is accounted for by different career positions rather than different career structures.

If we return to Table 10.3, in a sense what we have done is, roughly, to account for the dominant trend—the young workers and older managers. The young managers and older workers—the over- and under-achievers in terms of the dominant pattern—represent what remains unexplained, though more precisely the over- and under-achievers should be defined by qualifications and age. It is almost certain that these groups contribute to the interaction effect found by Wright and Perrone. We know that professionals are highly qualified and that their earnings rise steeply with age. Also we know that the variance in earnings for a given level of qualifications similarly increases with age. Therefore, 'success' or 'failure' is closer to a fixed proportion of average earnings than to a constant sum, causing the regression slopes to be pulled apart in the way we find. Across the whole sample a similar situation of 'proportionate' success or failure by level of qualification (rather than age) will have the same effect.

We could not find within our data any type of employment where senior positions did not have a managerial component. For example, among employed professionals there was no route to higher incomes which did not involve supervising others. In these circumstances, decomposing jobs into technical functions associated with labour and control elements associated with capital is virtually impossible. Certainly it cannot be done merely by assuming that the education of non-managers represents the quality of labour power. In any case it is hard to envisage how a major area of employment for well qualified men (i.e. management), where the characteristics of the employees and jobs are generally known ('with respect to authority structures .... education serves as a legitimation for inequalities of power', Wright and Perrone, 1977, p. 52), could consistently give higher returns to education than other areas without attracting the better qualified, i.e. without being incorporated into the structure of standard careers. If it is so incorporated, then to divide managers and workers is to a large extent to divide the successful from the unsuccessful without offering an explanation of success or failure. The effects Wright and Perrone find are then determined by the errors in the relationship of age and education to careers.

Perhaps this is best illustrated by looking at Wright's (1978, p. 1388) explanation of the interaction of race and education in the determination of earnings of male managers. He believed that 'because of restrictions of blacks to lower levels of the authority hierarchy, the hierarchical-promotion mechanism would be blunted among black managers, and thus the returns to education would be less among black than among white managers.' This is in line with his findings. Basically, the argument is that a background factor, race, influences placement in the system which is reflected in rewards. The highest positions are not accessible to blacks, i.e. their careers are truncated, so their education is worth less. Relative success or failure in the authority hierarchy is based upon race. However, when making the manager/worker distinction they are not using prior characteristics, but location within the system; and since the distinction is largely a distinction in terms of career success, it is not very instructive to say that unsuccessful earn less because they are not successful.

This is not meant to imply that we entirely approve of the form of their arguments about race. In both articles Wright and Perrone deal with race and sex as sources of differences in earnings, but they seem to believe that neither is implicated in the social relations of production. Each acts as an influence upon earnings, but neither can be accounted for by a simple structure of wages as reproduction costs of labour value. In fact they seem to believe that these are background factors introduced into the system, just as are age, occupation and education.

Yet the factors operate differentially in the labour market which is, thus, predicated upon a set of social conventions and practices which define it, but which it does not produce. This radical separation of economic and social issues is against the spirit of Marx's analysis, in that he sought to unify social and economic issues in an account of oppression. There is no room in his analysis for pre-theoretical variables which impinge upon his explanations but are not generated within them. He attempts an endogenous account of theory and practice.

We are very much in sympathy with this aim, and we believe that any attempt to produce social explanation which is built upon a distinction between social structure and individual characteristics is built upon a paradox which will ultimately be revealed. If Marxist theory fails to account for the processes which create and maintain the oppression of women or of blacks, then it fails by its own standards. The issues can never be purely empirical. Age, sex, colour, education or family background are only in a trivial sense personal as opposed to social characteristics. Their meanings and significance are social, and they cannot be regarded as having a factual status which is pre-theoretical, in that it can be directly imported into explanations. Meanings are not independent of the relationships of explanation.

EDUCATION, OCCUPATION AND INCOME

In the previous section we showed how clerical employment was neither the basis of class location nor, therefore, of class identification, and we made a distinction between jobs and incumbents. The characteristics of incumbents which we identified were aspects of education, background and previous experience. Though it was useful to regard these as individual characteristics in order to demonstrate the weakness of previous approaches to the relationship of occupations and class, they are in truth aspects of a reproducing social system. In this section we have traced the principal features of the acquisition of qualifications and the relationship between qualifications, occupations and incomes. Though we began with a model which divided the allocation to careers from the rewards accruing to them, we went on to contend that allocative processes cannot be separated from the career structures, and that the incomes of occupational positions must be seen as aspects of such structures, and as such no more independent of the way people are allocated.

We presented an analysis of the continuity of educational and occupational careers. In this we showed not only that arguments attributing low importance to education (e.g. Jencks *et al.*, 1973) are mistaken, but also that the position which recognises an important link of education with occupation but not with income (e.g. Blau and Duncan, 1967) is unsound.

Finally, we demonstrated the necessity of approaching the structuring of social experience as an interrelated totality. The processes of the reproduction of the social system certainly impinge upon individual experience serially, as we have observed with regard to careers and education. However, within an understanding of the system, there is no such underlying temporal order or causal priority; the processes of reproduction are continuously reproducing themselves, and their form is an aspect of the system at each point of time. At any given time the events and experiences occuring in the areas of work and education are equally aspects of the whole society, shaped by the past and shaping the future. To concentrate upon the systematic properties of what are commonly classified as economic issues, and to regard processes which individuals experience before entry to work as *prior* characteristics, is to create a spurious independence between economic and social factors and confuse the true nature of reproductive processes. To attribute the prior characteristics to individuals causes a false division of individual and structure.

11 Conclusion

The central position presented in this monograph is a commitment to understanding social relationships as processes. The necessity of such an approach has, we believe, been amply illustrated in the various sections. We have suggested that issues of stability and change in modern industrial societies have been inadequately understood in much previous research because of rather crude assumptions about the nature of the social processes concerned. As a rough and ready guide to these processes, we can identify three different elements. We do not believe that they are always easy to distinguish in practice, or that for all purposes they represent the most useful theoretical components of social understanding, but they have considerable heuristic value and serve to clarify a number of the issues we raise. The elements are simple reproduction, expanded reproduction and exogenous influences.

By *simple reproduction* we mean processes which, if they were the only sort to occur, would serve to maintain the society in its current state. The regenerative processes of the living organisms are perhaps the simplest analogy. The social processes of reproduction are diverse and complex, but those with which we have been most concerned entail the relationship between the life-cycles of individuals and the occupational structure.

Expanded reproduction we identify with regular social processes, intelligible in terms of current knowledge, which have the practical consequences of transforming social arrangements in consistent directions. The division of simple and expanded reproduction must ultimately be false, but in an initial statement the separation is useful. Expanded reproduction we identify most closely with secular trends in society, in this monograph trends in occupational distributions, but it should be borne in mind that expanded reproduction need not be exclusively associated with smooth and regular processes of change. The practical understandings which govern the development of capitalist society contain contradictions which, it may be expected, will ultimately undermine the system practically and theoretically. In Marx's analysis, for example, the transformation will represent a fundamental break with the past, even though it has arisen from it. It will, none the less, be best understood as the outcome of endogenous processes integral to social development.

The third element, *exogenous change*, looks at first sight rather easier to identify than is, in fact, the case. It refers to unique events which impinge on societies in such a way as to disrupt the standard processes. World War II would appear to be the most important event of this type to impinge upon our immediate concerns in this monograph, but there has been considerable debate about whether war is best understood as an external, disruptive event in the affairs of a society, or a consequence of predictable processes both within and between societies. In either event, for present purposes World War II produced both a range of specific and immediate issues for the form and reproduction of the occupational structure and certain long-term consequences in the development of the productive system.

In most of the issues we have raised in the monograph, all three elements are present, though to differing degrees. To some extent the monograph represents intellectual development from the confused and essentially static assumptions embodied in scales of occupational grading to a fuller understanding of the relationships of the productive process. We have pointed out that though scales of occupational grading see the occupational structure as a set of simple categories across which individuals are distributed, they nevertheless contain diverse, implicit assumptions about the nature of occupational experience. The concepts of professions, covering whole careers, embody a recognition of processes of reproduction. Other specific job titles identify tasks within the productive system, ignoring the structuring of occupational experience through the working lives of those currently employed in the jobs. We have suggested that jobs, rather than careers, are singled out in these cases because of the difficulty in associating these jobs with unique career patterns. The personnel employed in these occupations are at different stages of diverse careers.

A further complication is that, because of the importance of qualifications obtained after entry to the labour market, standard careers are difficult to assign to many individuals at the point of entry to employment. Where full-time education is the typical source of specialist qualifications necessary for entry to a profession, or where there are recognised apprenticeships, professional or manual, which individuals enter directly, then a conception of standard careers is fairly straightforward. There is room for a range of career options and for relative success or failure, but the organisation of all particular tasks under a general occupational title remains intelligible. Where distinctions are made after entry and are relatively difficult to predict on the basis of characteristics at entry, then it is not surprising that task distinctions rather than career distinctions gain ascendancy. However, the confusion implicit in the titles compromises the grading schemes as adequate bases for the understanding of social processes. Studies of mobility or achievement, or background influences upon social experience, are all affected by the nature of the scales. The production of wholly adequate instruments will depend upon much deeper understandings of the processes of the occupational structure.

A clear indication of the dangers contained in a failure to distinguish the elements of social processes occurs in Chapter 7. Though all three elements are at work in the circumstances of managers, we have shown that previous studies have confused simple and expanded reproduction; they have identified different points in the simple reproduction of the occupational structure with expanded reproduction or secular trends. By identifying change with the variations in the characteristics of different age groupings of managers, they have ignored the processes of managerial recruitment, and lent spurious support to an orthodoxy arguing for the progressive bureaucratisation of careers and diminishing opportunities to rise from below. Of course, the structure of managerial employment has been changed both by factors associated with the war and by other processes operating in the post-war era, and, as we have attempted to show, a true understanding will need to take account of each element of structural process. However, the most serious misunderstanding may be seen as the misidentification of stable processes of reproduction as processes of change.

Our extended treatment of the social and economic relations of clerks in Part Two shows how confusion about social processes can be sustained over very long periods and can give rise to extensive bodies of theory and research. Initially the problem is the failure of clerical workers to act in accordance with what is seen as their objective class position. There is an attempt to establish this position without reference to the general processes of reproduction of the occupational structure. The class position of clerks is identified with the conditions of, and returns to, routine clerical work, with no regard to the career experiences of clerical workers. The post-war trend towards the recruitment of manual workers to clerical positions is seen as an aspect of the erosion of clerical advantage. In fact, as we have shown, there is a diversity of objective conditions among those who are currently clerks when they are assigned to standard careers. Furthermore, the sentiments expressed and the alliances formed by different groups of clerical workers are directly in accord with their practical experience. No theories of false consciousness or status discrepancy are necessary to explain their attitudes and behaviour. The same is true of 'affluent' manual workers, whose class position has not become more similar to that of middle class white-collar workers.

In Part Three we presented a model and an analysis of some of the processes of reproduction of the occupational structure. Heuristically we divided occupations, as positions in the economic system, from the processes of 'allocation' to positions which, we argued, can continue throughout working life. In most theories of social class we found a one-sided emphasis upon the reproduction of 'social positions', as if that could be defined separately from the reproduction of allocative processes. Though this is not a feature of Marx's writings, his treatment of the reproduction of labour power is rather rudimentary, and modern Marxists have tended to concentrate upon the relations of production narrowly conceived. We have discussed this at some length in the case of Wright and Perrone, but the problems they raise of the class situation of managers has had very similar treatment by other Marxists. Carchedi (1975, 1977) argues that the middle class is characterised by ambiguities of class situation in that it is involved both in labour and in the control of labour to further capital accumulation. As Crompton and Gubbay (1977, p. 73) put it, following Carchedi:

> Many parts of the management structure will be responsible for this co-ordination in order to ensure completion to tasks stipulated by capital, thereby contributing to the function of the collective worker. On the other hand, insofar as management controls labour in order to further accumulation of capital it carries out the function of global capital.

This is an attempt to identify the economic location of *management*, but we have seen that the vast majority of managers do not spend the whole of their working lives in management. They are recruited from manual work, from non-manual jobs many of which could be clearly consigned to the co-ordination of labour, and from the professions. Even if the economic location of job tasks were stable, the location of those performing the tasks would not be so. On the other hand, as we have seen, the economic returns to groups defined by their qualifications is remarkably similar in areas with very different relationships to the productive system. Qualifications are associated with much the same levels of income in management in manufacturing industry as in government service or in insurance, yet the basis of incomes in the productive system must be different.

There is not a unique allocation to positions in the productive system by type of qualification. Most qualifications will allow entry to a diversity of jobs whose common feature is a broad equivalence of income. Insofar as this is the case, and bearing in mind that many typical careers move individuals and groups across locations in the productive system, strategies to maintain access to highly rewarded positions, in whatever sector of the economy, may make greater economic sense than strategies based upon influencing the rewards to job tasks. This would be true even if the level of rewards were determined purely by the location of job tasks in the productive system.

We do not believe that economic relationships or processes of dominance can be fully understood in a theoretical scheme which divides the operation of the economic system from the social system in general. We noted above how an artificial separation of social and economic considerations has led to mistaken theory based on occupational categories defined in relation to technical demands of the market. Theories based on background characteristics such as education, race or sex regarded as social variables outside the economic system are equally unsound. Men and women, blacks and whites, qualified and unqualified, propertied and proletarians—whatever the divisions we make—they all are part of the social whole. Thus an explanation of structured inequality must fit them all. We do not, of course, mean that the explanation will be precisely the same in relation to each, but the theory must not be at odds with the treatment of any one. For example, if skin colour were purely a personal characteristic, it would not be relevant to systematic inequalities, but in fact the experience of being black (or proletarian or female) is social experience. If dominance is to be understood in terms of the operation of the relations of production, it is not sufficient or even sensible to look elsewhere for an explanation of particular types of dominance. In Marx's analysis the social relations of production are central to the understanding of the society as a whole, and a failure to account for major features of social experience cannot be put right, as some Marxists have believed, by the addition of new explanatory factors. A reconstruction of the central core is necessary.

Too often specifically 'social' explanations or arguments from an 'action' perspective are introduced to fill an explanatory void. The division of circumstance and sentiment rescues explanations which fail because they cannot predict behaviour on the basis of assumed conditions. The 'social' component is usually argued to be central to, and essential for, an adequate explanation, but in truth it is so only by default. If, for example, clerks had behaved like manual workers, Klingender would never have invoked false consciousness. If affluent workers had behaved like the lower middle class, it is unlikely that Goldthorpe and colleagues would introduce explanations based on orientations. These are responses to explanatory failures, but they are weak responses. They do not compete well with other explanations which can produce a new interpretation of circumstance and unite it with sentiment, where conditions and behaviour are in line. We believe that a healthier response to explanatory failure is to look for unrecognised variations of circumstance than to introduce special explanations based upon sentiment.

Within action theory, where the 'social' is identified with human action in that society is formed in and experienced as action, value orientations become divorced from the material circumstances in which they are formed. If individual orientations or action are to be the fundamental categories of explanation, we cannot account for their variation except by reference to the action of others, effectively cutting off the social world from the material circumstances of people's lives. Once this arbitrary limitation on explanation is removed, orientations may be seen as part of the social whole. Certainly they may feature in explanations, but not as orientations which are prior in that they are independent factors in the production of experience, rather than components of experience. Heuristically it may be useful at times to distinguish 'background' factors which influence orientations which in turn influence behaviour, but ultimately the divisions are false; the background includes the changing experience of present circumstances.

From our analysis of occupations and stratification there has emerged an account of a coherent and largely stable structure of inequality, where many features of apparent change are better understood as processes of simple reproduction. In line with our theoretical commitment, outlined in the Introduction, we have been concerned to identify the processes of stability and change in the practical circumstances of social life. We have placed a low emphasis on motives and values as primitive categories of social explanation, seeking rather to locate them within social contexts defined by empirical relationships and practical understandings. This is not a commitment to a positivistic account of society, but to the unity of knowledge of the social and material which is transformed in experience. We hope that our account has contributed to the understanding of this important area, and in so doing has also helped to demonstrate the soundness of the approach.

Bibliography

Acton Society Trust, *Management Succession* (London: The Trust, 1956).

Advisory Council on Scientific Policy, 'The Long-Term Demand for Scientific Manpower' (London: HMSO, 1961).

Allingham, J. D., 'Class Regression: An Aspect of the Social Stratification Process', *American Sociological Review*, 32, 1967.

Bain, G. S., *The Growth of White Collar Unionism* (London: Oxford University Press, 1970).

Bain, G. S. and Price, R., 'Union Growth and Employment Trends in the U.K. 1964–1970', *British Journal of Industrial Relations*, vol. 10, no. 3, 1972.

Baran, P. A. and Sweezy, P. M., *Monopoly Capital* (New York: Monthly Press, 1966).

Bechhofer, F., 'Occupations', in M. Stacey (ed), *Comparability in Social Research* (London: British Sociological Association, Social Science Research Council, 1969).

Bell, D., *The Coming of Post Industrial Society* (New York: Basic Books, 1973).

Benjamin, B., 'Inter-generation differences in occupation', *Population Studies*, 11, 1958.

Berger, P. L. and Luckmann, T., *The Social Construction of Reality* (London: Allen Lane, 1967).

Bernard, J., 'Class Organisation in an Era of Abundance: A New Principal of Class Organisation', *Transactions of the Third World Congress of Sociology*, 3, 1956.

Berner, B., 'Human Capital', Manpower Planning and Economic Theory: Some critical remarks, *Acta Sociologica*, vol. 17, no. 3, 1974.

Blackburn, R. M., *Union Character and Social Class* (London: B. T. Batsford, 1967).

—— 'The Bank Clerks', *New Society*, 1968.

Blackburn, R. M. and M. Mann, *The Working Class in the Labour Market*, (London: Macmillan Press, 1979).

Blackburn, R. M. and K. Prandy, 'White-Collar Unionisation: A Conceptual Framework', *The British Journal of Sociology*, vol. 16, no. 2, 1965.

Blau, P. M. and O. D. Duncan, *The American Occupational Structure* (New York: John Wiley, 1967).

Blaug, M., *An Introduction to the Economics of Education* (Harmondsworth: Penguin, 1970).

Bogardus, E. S., 'A Social Distance Scale', *Sociology and Social Research*, vol. 17, 1933.

Boudon, R., *Mathematical Structures of Social Mobility* (Amsterdam: Elsevier, 1973).

Bowen, W. G., 'Assessing the Economic Contribution of Education' (1963), in M. Blaug (ed), *Economics of Education I*, (Harmondsworth: Penguin, 1968).

Bowen, P. and Shaw, M. P. G., *Attitudes of Industrial Clerks to White-Collar Unionisation*, final report (Social Science Research Council, 1975).

Bowley, A. L., 'Working Class Households in Reading', *Journal of the Royal Statistical Society*, vol. 64, 1912–13.

Braverman, Harry, *Labor and Monopoly Capital: The Degradation of Work in the Twentieth Century* (New York: Monthly Review Press, 1974).

Broom, L., Duncan-Jones, P. Lancaster Jones, F. McDonnell, P., *Occupational Mobility in Australia 1965, 1973: Steps Toward Comparison*, prepared for the Mathematical Social Sciences Board Seminar (Toronto, 1974).

—— *Investigating Social Mobility*, Departmental Monograph no. 1, Dept. of Sociology, Research School of the Social Sciences, Australian National University (Canberra, 1977).

Broom, L. and J. H. Smith, 'Bridging Occupations', *British Journal of Sociology*, vol. 14, no. 4, 1963.

Burns, R. K., 'The Comparative Economic Positions of Manual and White Collar Employees', *The Journal of Business*, vol. 27, 1954.

Carchedi, G., 'On the Economic Identification of the New Middle Class', *Economy and Society*, vol. 4, no. 1, 1975.

—— *On the Economic Identification of Social Classes* (London: Routledge & Kegan Paul, 1977).

Carr-Hill, R. J. and MacDonald K. I., 'Problems in the Analysis of Life Histories', *Sociological Review*, monograph 19, 1973.

Centers, R., *The Psychology of Social Classes* (Princeton: University Press, 1949).

Clark, D. G., *The Industrial Manager: His Background and Career Pattern* (London: Business Publications, 1966).

Clarke, A., *Effects of the Factory System* (1899).

Clements, R. V., *Managers, A Study of Their Careers in Industry* (London: Allen & Unwin, 1958).

Copeman, G. H., *Leaders of British Industry* (London: Business Publications, 1955).

Counts, G. S., 'The Social Status of Occupations: A Problem in Vocational Guidance', *School Review*, vol. 33, 1925.

Coxon, A. P. M. and C. L. Jones, *The Images of Occupational Prestige: A Study in Social Cognition* (London: Macmillan, 1978).

Crompton, R. and Gubbay, J., *Economy and Class Structure* (London: Macmillan, 1977).

Crowder, N. D., 'A Critique of Duncan's Stratification Research', *Sociology*, vol. 8, no. 1, 1974.

Crozier, M., *The World of the Office Worker* (Chicago: University of Chicago Press, 1971).

Dahrendorf, R., *Class and Class Conflict in Industrial Society* (London: Routledge & Kegan Paul, 1959).

Davis, J., 'Testing the Social Attitudes of Children in the Government Schools in Russia', *Am J. Soc.*, vol. 32, no. 6, 1927.

Department of Employment, *Classification of Occupations and Directory of Occupational Titles* (London: HMSO, 1972).

Department of Employment, *Gazette* (London: HMSO, 1949).

Department of Employment, *New Earnings Survey* (London: HMSO, 1970).

Dixon, K., 'Friendship and the Stability of Structural Inequality', mimeo, Simon Fraser University (1976).

Duncan, O. D., 'Reanalysis of the 1949 Survey', in J. M. Ridge (ed), *Mobility in Britain Reconsidered* (Oxford: Clarendon Press, 1974).

—— 'A Socioeconomic index for all occupations', in A. J. Reiss, (et. al) *Occupations and Social Status* (New York: The Free Press, 1961).

—— Reanalysis of the 1949 Survey, in J. M. Ridge (ed), *Mobility in Britain Reconsidered* (London: Oxford University Press, 1973).

Duncan, O. D. and B. Duncan, 'Residential Distribution and Occupational Stratification' in P. Hatt and A. J. Reiss jun., *Cities and Society*, (New York, The Free Press of Glencoe Inc, 1957).

Duncan, O. D., D. L. Featherman and B. Duncan, *Socioeconomic Background and Occupational Achievement: Extentions of a Basic Model*, US Department of Health, Education and Welfare, Washington, D.C. (1968).

Durkheim, E., *The Division of Labour in Society* (London: Macmillan, 1934).

Edwards, A. M., *Socio-Economic Groupings of the Gainfully Employed Workers of the United States*, 1930, Washington, D.C., Government Printing Office (1938).

Featherman, D. L. and R. M. Hauser, 'On the Measurement of Occupations in Social Surveys', *Sociological Methods and Research*, vol. 2, no. 2, 1973.

Garaudy, R., *The Turning Point of Socialism* (London: Fontana, 1970).

General Register Office, *Census 1951, England and Wales: Occupational Tables* (London: HMSO, 1956).

Giddens, A., *The Class Structure of Advanced Societies* (London: Hutchinson, 1973).

—— *New Rules of Sociological Method* (London: Hutchinson, 1976).

Glass, D. V. (ed), *Social Mobility in Britain* (London: Routledge & Kegan Paul, 1954).

Goldstein, S., *Patterns of Mobility 1910–1950* (Philadelphia: University of Pennsylvania Press, 1958).

Goldthorpe, J. H., 'Social Strafication in Industrial Society', in P. Halmos (ed), *The Development of Industrial Societies*, Sociological Review monograph, no. 8 (1964).

Goldthorpe, J. H., and K. Hope, 'Occupational Grading and Occupational Prestige', in K. Hope (ed), 1972.

—— *The Social Grading of Occupations* (Oxford: Clarendon Press, 1974).

Goldthorpe, J. H., D. Lockwood, F. Bechhofer and J. Platt, *The Affluent Worker: Industrial Attitudes and Behaviour* (Cambridge: University Press, 1968).

—— *The Affluent Worker in the Class Structure* (Cambridge: Cambridge University Press, 1969).

Gramsci, A., *The Modern Prince and Other Writings* (London: Lawrence and Wishart, 1957).

Hall, J. and D. C. Jones, 'Social Gradings of Occupations', *British Journal of Sociology*, vol. 1, no. 1, 1950.

Hamilton, R. F., 'The Income Difference Between Skilled and White-Collar Workers', *British Journal of Sociology*, vol. 14, no. 4, 1963.

—— 'The Marginal Middle Class: A Reconsideration', *American Sociological Review*, 31, 1966.

Harcourt, G. C., *Some Cambridge Controversies in the Theory of Capital* (Cambridge: Cambridge University Press, 1972).

Harris, A. I. and P. Clausen, *Labour Mobility in Great Britain* (London: HMSO, 1966).

Hauser, Robert M. and David L. Featherman, 'Trends in the Occupational Mobility of U.S. Men, 1962–1970', *American Sociological Review*, vol. 38, no. 3, 1973.

Hiller, Peter, 'Social Reality & Social Stratification', *The Sociological Review*, vol. 21, no. 1, 1973.

Hobsbawm, E. J., 'The Social Function of the Past: Some Questions', *Past and Present*, vol. 55, 1972.

Hodge, R. W., 'The Status Consistency of Occupational Groups', *American Sociological Review*, 27, 1962.

Hodge, R. W., P. M. Siegal and P. H. Rossi, 'Occupational Prestige in the United States, 1925–63', *American Journal of Sociology*, 70, 1964.

—— 'Occupational Mobility as a Probability Process', *Demography* (1966).

Hoggart, R., *The Uses of Literacy* (London: Chatto & Windus, 1957).

Holmwood, J. M. and Stewart, A., *Science, Society and Human Action* (London: Macmillan, forthcoming).

Hope, K. (ed), *The Analysis of Social Mobility: Methods and Approaches*, Oxford Studies in Social Mobility, Working Papers 1, (Oxford: Oxford University Press, 1972).

Hunt, T. C., 'Occupational Status and Marriage Selection', *American Sociological Review*, 5, 1940.

International Labour Office, *International Standard Classification of Occupations* (Geneva: I.L.O., 1968).

Isaac, P. D. and Poor, D. D. S., 'On the Determination of Appropriate Dimensionality', Unpublished manuscript, Ohio State University, 1972 (referred to in Spence and Graef, 1974).

Jencks, A., *Inequality* (London: Allen Lane, 1973).

Klahr, D., 'A Monte-Carlo investigation of the statistical significance of Kruskal's non-metric scaling procedure', *Psychometrika*, 34, 1969.

Klevmarken, A., *Statistical Methods for the Analysis of Earnings* (Stockholm: Almquist & Wiksell, 1972).

Klingender, F. D., *The Condition of Clerical Labour in Britain* (London: Martin Lawrence, 1935).

Kruskal, J. B., 'Multidimensional scaling by optimizing goodness-of-fit to a non-metric hypothesis', *Psychometrika*, vol. 29, 1964.

—— 'Nonmetric scaling: A numerical method', *Psychometrika*, vol. 29, 1964.

Lane, D., *The End of Inequality?* (London: Penguin, 1971).

Lane, T., *The Union Makes Us Strong* (London: Arrow Books, 1974).

Laumann, E. O., *Prestige and Association in an Urban Community* (New

York: The Bobbs-Merrill Co. Inc, 1966).

—— *Bonds of Pluralism: The Form and Substance of Urban Social Networks* (New York: John Wiley, 1973).

Laumann, E. O. and L. Guttman, 'The Relative associational contiguity of occupations in an urban setting', *American Sociological Review*, vol. 31, 1966.

Lee, D. J., 'Industrial Training and Social Class', *Sociological Review*, vol. 14, no. 3, 1966.

—— 'Class Differentials in Educational Opportunity and Promotion from the Ranks', *Sociology*, vol. 2, no. 3, 1968.

Lee, D. J. and I. Hordley, 'Technical Education—An Alternative Route', *Technical Education*, vol. 8, 1966.

Lenski, G. E., *Power and Privilege: a Theory of Social Stratification* (New York, McGraw-Hill, 1966).

Levison, A., *The Working Class Majority* (New York: Coward, McCann & Geoghegan, 1974).

Lipset, A. M. and R. Bendix, *Social Mobility in Industrial Society* (Berkeley and Los Angeles: University of California Press, 1959).

Little, A. and J. Westergaard, 'The Trend of Class Differentials in Educational Opportunity in England and Wales', *British Journal of Sociology*, vol. 15, no. 4, 1964.

Lockwood, D., *The Blackcoated Worker* (London: Allen & Unwin, 1958).

McDonald, K. I., 'MDSCAL and distance between Socio-economic groups', in K. Hope (ed) (1972).

McGinnis, R., 'A Stochastic Model of Social Mobility' *American Sociological Review*, vol. 33, no. 5, 1968.

McGivering, I. Mathews D., and Scott W. H., *Management in Britain* (Liverpool University Press, Liverpool, 1960).

Mackenzie, G., 'The Economic Dimensions of Embourgeoisement', *British Journal of Sociology*, vol. 18, no. 1, 1967.

—— *The Aristocracy of Labour: The position of Skilled Craftsmen in the American Class Structure* (Cambridge: Cambridge University Press, 1973).

Mallet, S., *La Nouvelle Class Ouvriere* (Paris: Editions du Seuil, 1963).

Mann, M., The Social Cohesion of Liberal Democracy, *Am. Soc. Rev.*, vol. 35, no. 3, 1970.

Marx, K., *Grundrisse* (Harmondsworth: Penguin, 1973).

Marx, K. and Engels, F. *The German Ideology* (London: Lawrence and Wishart, 1970).

Mayer, K. B., *Class and Society* (New York: Random House, 1955).

—— 'Recent Changes in the Class Structure of the United States' *Transactions of the Third World Congress of Sociology*, 3, 1956.

—— 'Diminishing Differentials in the United States', *Kyklos*, 12, 1959.

—— 'The Changing Shape of the American Class Structure', *Social Research*, 30, 1963.

Merrill, F. E., *Society and Culture* (Englewood Cliffs: Prentice Hall, 1961).

Mills, C. Wright, *White Collar* (New York: Oxford University Press, 1956).

Mincer, J., 'Progress in Human Capital Analyses of the Distribution of Earnings', in A. B. Atkinson, *The Personal Distribution of Incomes* (London: Allen & Unwin, 1976).

Ministry of Education, *Statistics of Education, Part I, 1965* (London: HMSO, 1966).

Moorhouse, H., 'Attitudes to Class and Class Relationship in Britain', *Sociology*, vol. 10, no. 3, 1976.

Moser, C. A. and Hall, J. R., 'The Social Grading of Occupations', in Glass, D. V. *Social Mobility in Britain* (London: Routledge & Kegan Paul, 1954).

Mumford, E. and O. Banks, *The Computer and the Clerk* (London: Routledge & Kegan Paul, 1967).

Noble, T., *Modern Britain: Structure and Change* (London: Batsford, 1975).

Office of Population Censuses and Surveys, *Census 1971, Great Britain: Qualified Manpower Tables* (London: HMSO, 1975).

—— *Classification of Occupations* (London: HMSO, 1966).

—— *Classification of Occupations* (London: HMSO, 1970).

Oldman, D. and R. Illsley, 'Measuring the Status of Occupations', *The Sociological Review*, vol. 14, no. 1, 1966.

Palmer, G. L., *Labour Mobility in Six Cities* (New York: Social Science Research Council, 1954).

Parkin, F., *Class Inequality and Political Order* (London: MacGibbon & Kee, 1971).

Parsler, R., 'Some Economic Aspects of Embourgeoisement in Australia', *Sociology*, vol. 4, no. 2, 1970.

Petrie, W. M. Flinders, 'Sequences in Prehistoric Remains,' *Journal of Anthrop. Inst.*, 29, 1899.

Poulantzas, N., *Pouvoir Politique et Classes Sociales* (Paris: Maspero, 1971).

Prandy, K., A. Stewart and R. M. Blackburn, 'Concept and Measures: The Example of Unionateness', *Sociology*, vol. 8, no. 3, 1974.

Prandy, K., Stewart, A. and Blackburn R. M. white-collar work (London: Macmillan, forthcoming).

Psacharopoulos, G., 'Family background, education and achievement: a path model of earnings determinants in the UK and some alternatives', *Brit. J. of Sociol*, vol. 28, no. 3, 1977.

Reiner, R., *The Blue-Coated Worker: A Sociological Study of Police Unionism* (Cambridge, University Press, 1978).

Reiss, A. J. (et al) *Occupations and Social Status* (New York: The Free Press, 1961).

Ridge, J. M. (ed) *Mobility in Britain Reconsidered* (Oxford: Clarendon Press, 1974).

Roskam, E. E., *Metric Analysis of Ordinal Data in Psychology* (Nijmegen: Van-Voorschoten, 1969).

Routh, G., *Occupation and Pay in Great Britain* (Cambridge: Cambridge University Press, 1965).

Runciman, W. G., *Relative Deprivation and Social Justice* (London: Routledge & Kegan Paul, 1966).

Scase, R., *Social Democracy in Capitalist Society: Working Class Policies in Britain and Sweden* (London: Croom Helm, 1977).

Schleindl, H.M.O., *Social Inequality in Australia: Measurement and Theory*, unpublished Ph.D. thesis, Australian National University, Canberra (1975).

Schutz, A. *The Phenomenology of The Social World* (London: Heineman, 1972).

Sherman, C. R., 'Nonmetric Multidimensional Scaling: A Monte Carlo Study of the Basic Parameters', *Psychometrika*, 37, 1972.

Slocum, W. C. *Occupational Careers* (Chicago: Aldine, 1966).

Smith, M., 'An Empirical Scale of Prestige Status of Occupations', *American Sociological Review*, vol. 8, 1943.

Sørensen A. B., *The Occupational Mobility Process: An Analysis of Occupational Covers*, Report 125, Centre for Social Organisation of Schools (John Hopkins University Press, Baltimore, 1970).

—— 'The Structure of Inequality and the Process of Attainment', *Am. Soc. Rev.*, vol. 42, no. 6, 1977.

Sorokin, P. A., *Social and Cultural Mobility* (New York: The Free Press 1964).

Spence, I., *Multidimensional Scaling: An Empirical and Theoretical Investigation*, unpublished Ph.D. thesis, University of Toronto, 1970 (referred to in Spence and Graef, 1974).

Spence, I., and Graef, J., 'The Determination of the Underlying Dimensionality of an Empirically Obtained Matrix of Proximities',

Multivariate Behavioural Research, vol. 8, 1974.

Stanworth, P. and Giddens, A., 'An Economic Elite: A Demographic Profile of Company Chairmen', in Stanworth, P. and Giddens, A. *Elites and Power in British Society* (Cambridge: Cambridge University Press, 1974).

Stenson, H. H. and R. L. Knoll, 'Goodness of Fit for Random Rankings in Kruskal's Non-metric scaling procedure', *Psychological Bulletin*, vol. 71, no. 2, 1969.

Stevenson, T. H. S. *Report of the 1911 Census* (London: HMSO).

Stewart, A. and R. M. Blackburn, 'The Stability of Structural Inequality' *The Sociological Review*, vol. 23, no. 3, 1975.

Stewart, A., K. Prandy and R. M. Blackburn, 'Measuring the Class Structure' *Nature*, 26 Oct. 1973.

Sykes, A. J. M., 'Some Differences in the Attitudes of Clerical & Manual Workers' *Sociological Review*, vol. 13, no. 1, 1965.

Thomas, G., *Labour Mobility in Great Britain 1945–49*, an inquiry carried out for the Ministry of Labour and National Service, mimeographed report 134.

Treiman, D. J., *Occupational Prestige In Comparative Perspective* (New York: Academic Press, 1977).

US Bureau of the Census 'Lifetime Occupational Mobility of Adult Males: March, 1962', *Current Population Reports. Technical Studies*, series P23, no. 11, 12 May 1964.

Wagenaar, W. A., and Padmos, P., 'Quantitative Interpretation of Stress in Kruskal's Multidimensional Scaling Technique', *British Journal of Mathematical and Statistical Psychology*, 24, 1971.

Westergaard, J. and H. Resler, *Class in a Capitalist Society* (London: Heinemann, 1975).

White, H., *Chains of Opportunity: System Models of Mobility in Organisations* (Cambridge: Harvard University Press, 1970).

Wilensky, H. L., 'Orderly Careers and Social Participation: The Impact of Work History on Social Integration in the Middle Mass', *American Sociological Review*, 26, 1961.

Willener, A., *Interprétation de l'Organisation dans l'Industrie* (Paris: Mouton, 1967).

Wright, E. O., 'Class Boundaries in Advanced Capitalist Societies', *New Left Review*, vol. 98, 1976.

—— 'Race Class and Income Inequality', *A. J. S.*, vol. 83, no. 6, 1978.

Wright, E. O. and Perrone, L., 'Marxist Class Categories and Income Inequality', *Am. Soc. Rev.*, vol. 42, no. 1., 1977.

Zweig, F. *The Worker in an Affluent Society* (London: Heinemann, 1961).

Index